P9-DBI-056

Other Books By Amy Sedaris

This Sturdy Book
Belonged To:

25¢

I like you

by Amy Sedaris

HOSPITALITY UNDER THE INFLUENCE

WARNER BOOKS

NEW YORK BOSTON

Warner Books
Hachette Book Group USA
1271 Avenue of the Americas
New York, NY 10020

Visit our Web site at www.HachetteBookGroupUSA.com.

Printed in the United States of America

First Edition: October 2006
10 9 8 7 6 5 4 3 2 1

Design by: Lenny Naar and Jessica Rosenberg

Library of Congress Cataloging-in-Publication Data

Sedaris, Amy.
I like you : hospitality under the influence /
Amy Sedaris. – 1st ed.
p. cm.
"An entertaining book on entertaining from America's most delightfully unconventional hostess, businesswoman Amy Sedaris."–Provided by the publisher
Includes index.
ISBN-13: 978-0-446-57884-4
ISBN-10: 0-446-57884-3
1. Entertaining–Anecdotes. 2. Hospitality–Anecdotes.
3. Recipes. I. Title.
GV1471.S39 2006
793.2–dc22

2006007521

Dedicated to . . .

Mom, Dad, Lisa, David, Gretchen, Tiffany, Paul, Aunt Joyce, Madelyn Rose, Paul Dinello, and Mr. Mushroom

the Table of Contents

Amy

Dear [your name here],

Whether you live in a basement with the income of a ten-year-old girl or on a saffron farm in the south of Spain, the spirit of hospitality is the same. It's the giving of yourself, a present of you to them from me for us.

"Hello, and I like you." This is what you're saying when you invite somebody into your home, without having to hear yourself say it out loud. This colorfully illustrated book (see pictures) is my attempt to share with you something I take very seriously: entertaining in my home, my style. It may not be the proper way, or the most traditional, or even legal, but it works for me. I can't write good, but I can cook even better and I am willing to share with you my sackful of personal jackpot recipes that, because of their proven success, I continue to make, over and over again. I will also show you ways to plan, present, and participate in self-award-winning parties.

Even though the word "entertainment" is commonly used today, to me it sounds charmingly old-fashioned, like courtship or back-alley abortion. I like the traditional idea of entertaining, which for me means lively guests, good food, cocktails, and bubbly conversation. I'd like to bring entertaining back to these essentials. I'm not concerned with proper table settings, seating arrangements, or formal etiquette. Who can have a good time with all those rules? How can you enjoy yourself if you're worried whether you're using the right fork, or wondering whether the pumpkin is the bowl or part of the meal? I'm not trying to discourage you from being creative or encouraging you to neglect the details, but know that the nuts of any good party are the simple basics provided in a warm environment.

I tend to live my life like a deaf person. I communicate with my actions: the way I dress, the way my home is decorated, and the gifts I give all speak for me. I take this to heart when I entertain. My food, my party decorations, the games I create, and the music I play are all personal expressions. This is what will make your party special, sharing a piece of you, a feeling. It's not a competition. You don't have to be the perfect host, just the prettiest.

This is not a joke cookbook. I don't like joke cookbooks because I can't take them seriously. This book is full of real information. Most of the little I know, I learned from my mom, as well as Girl Scouts and Junior Achievements, my second first grade teacher, my family, Aunt Joyce, the backs of boxes, the lady who works at the post office, encyclopedias, the beach, bartending school, grocery stores, airports, waiting on tables, Mrs. Enchandi, nurses, sitcoms, Hugh, listening to the radio, babysitting, rock concerts, summer school, and the House Rabbit Society. I was also fascinated by two local hospitality shows: *At Home with Peggy Mann* and *The Betty Elliot Show*. I wanted to be both those women and now here's my chance, and hopefully, with the help of my book, it will be your chance as well.

Cordially,

Amy Sedaris

Amy Sedaris

amy

Dear [your name here],

It occurred to me that I neglected to acknowledge in my first letter that not everyone is interested in hospitality. There is nothing wrong with not wanting to be a hospitable person and have groups of people in your home touching your personables. Luckily, this sturdy book will also inform you on how to be the perfect guest. From the minute you say "Yes I'll be there," until the moment you say "I'm sorry, I should go," you have an important role in making a party a hit. Remember, one cannot throw a successful party without successful guests.

Cordiallier,

Amy Sedaris

Amy Sedaris

amy

Dear [your name here],

I hate to be a pest, but I was concerned that perhaps in my first two letters I failed to completely convey my passion for entertaining. I go bananas for entertaining! Sometimes though, I feel entertaining is a dying art. My goal is to encourage you, [your name here], to entertain in your home, your style. Having a party is one of the most creative and generous activities that every person can enjoy and indulge in, if you're on the list. Remember, by inviting someone into your home, you're saying "I like you".

Cordialliest,

Amy Sedaris

Amy Sedaris

the Art of HOSPITALITY

What a Party Means to Me

For most people the word "party" conjures up an image that is so intimidating, so overwhelming, so terrifying that they just want to skip the whole thing—it's just too much pressure. A party doesn't necessarily have to be a big extravagant to-do. A party can be as simple as a few people getting together for conversation and snacks. As my guests leave even my most simplest parties, I consistently hear the same thing: "That was the best time I ever had," and it's always me saying it. But I do know in my heart they all feel the same way, probably. I don't even like to use the word "party" because often the word gives people grand expectations. So when you see the word "party" in this book, don't think of pony kegs and loud Southern rock or cigarillos and businesswomen. Don't think of pools and diving for loose change. Don't think about cockfights—even though it's hard not to. Don't think tiki lights and fruity cocktails served in coconut shells on the patio, or a large group of drunken seamen clustered together shouting over each other. Think simplicity. Because if there is one thing I am, it's clinically simple.

Who Am I? Do I Ring a Bell?

When you look in the mirror, what do you see? Well, that's not what most people are saying about you. Before you can give of yourself to others you must know what of yourself you have to give. Every person is special. In all the land there is only one you, possibly two, but seldom more than sixteen. It's a good idea to know your strengths and weaknesses. Are you funny? Are you a good conversationalist? Are you attractive? Are you? Are you a good organizer? Do you have a lot of plates? These are some of the things you should know about yourself before taking on the responsibility of entertaining in your home. Once they've been assessed, it's important to magnify your strengths and ignore your weaknesses. If you have thick ankles, wear pants. If you're boring, pick exciting music to play. If you are a lousy cook, order out. Never overreach to mask your weakness. There is nothing cute or adorable about noticeably reaching beyond your capabilities. Remember, the goal is to entertain, not overtain.

A Self-Realized Person Will . . .

- Be unique in a way that is pleasing to everybody.
- Accentuate the positives—medicate the negatives.
- Have a hairstyle that is flattering to some and offensive to few.
- Have access to money.
- Never cry herself to sleep in front of others.

Learn More About Yourself!

- Make a self-esteem collage using pictures of other people you wish you were.
- Wing it! Quit your job without any financial plan or backup savings.
- Sleep with someone Chinese.
- Spend a lot of time in the bathtub.
- Disguise your voice and call family members posing as a police officer. Suggest that there has been a homicide and then question them about yourself.
- Spend some time at the zoo. Record how the animals react to your presence.
- Write yourself a fan letter.
- Put something small in your anus during lovemaking.
- Fly Air India.

I like you

Planning the Party

Now that we've done some self-discovery (see "Who Am I? Do I Ring a Bell?"), it's time to plan a party and party planning is half the fun of giving a party. The actual party is another half of the fun, and the third half is wiping up and reflecting on the terrific success of your party. But before you start reminiscing about the great party you haven't yet had, let's focus on the great party you're going to have.

This is your party. You are the captain of the ship, the cobbler of the shoes, the Count of Monte Cristo. Even if you have slaves, you still need to tell them what to do. The first step in creating a plan is to know what kind of party you will be having. This is often determined by various factors: What time of year is it? What time of day? Is my dealer in town? Do I have a backup dealer? You also need to consider how much you have to spend. How much space do you have? How much time do you have to prepare? If it's mid-August do you really want the oven on all day? Can you really fit two large ham salads in your refrigerator? A party is also determined by who can come and whether or not you can wrangle someone into doing most of your legwork. Sometimes parties are built around a theme like Barnyard Barbecue, Siesta Fiesta, Casino Nights, Pol Pot Luck, or Puttin' on the Ritz. Of course, your inspiration for having a party can be as simple as desperately wanting companionship.

Once you've decided on the type of party, it's time to consult the party log.

The Party Log

The party log may sound more like something you would leave behind at a party after a big dinner, but it is actually a detailed diary of your past parties—an organized scrapbook containing a collection of snapshots, recipes, hits and misses, menus, guest lists, and souvenir items. Before I insisted to myself that I write a book on hospitality, my version of party logs consisted of random lists written on the back of unopened mail, old notebooks, and the palm of my hand. But, after doing some extensive research for this book, I decided I loved the idea of an official well-organized "party diary." So, I am going to start one along with you.

The reason for a party log is simple: there is nothing more flattering to a guest than for a hostess to remember if he likes capers or raisins, prefers pickles to cucumbers, or has allergies to kelp, figs, or poisonous mushrooms. This is all information that can be recorded in your party log. It's a reference tool that helps you plan the next party (see sample on next page). I also think it's worthwhile to create a party log because it would be a wonderful item for someone to find after you die. I'd buy that at a flea market.

Party Log Sample Page

DATE: June 5th

PLACE: My house

KIND OF PARTY: South of the Border Theme

TIME: 8:00 pm

REASON: Lonely

GUEST LIST: Toby, Jared, Bethany, Warner, Pasquel, Lizzy, Marta, Roby, and myself

DECORATIONS: Hung yellow, black, and red streamers and a donkey piñata. Taped two large googly eyes with a fake mustache on my door.

MUSIC: Played *The Best of Mexico, Vol. 2*

MENU: Appetizer: Cheese ball con carne rolled in pumpkin seeds, served with blue corn tortilla chips

DRINKS AND FOOD: Margaritas, cervezas, Mexican colas, avocado salad, taco buffet, Mexican lasagna, and golden raisin flan.

HITS AND MISSES: Paper plates: bad idea for Mexican food. Cheese ball: big hit. Ran out of toilet paper early, ran out of paper towels later.

GUEST PROFILING: Toby was highly allergic to Mexican food, boiled him some spaghetti. Discovered that Lizzy is a lezzy, left with Bethany. Warner outstayed his visit. Found tooth.

The Guest List

The moment someone says, "Hey, everyone, listen to the words in this song," your party is over. This is why the guest list is the most important aspect to a successful party. It's the people that you specially handpick that make the good times roll.

Whom you invite tells you whom not to invite. If you invite a fox, don't invite a hound—unless you're hunting for trouble. If the party is going to be made up of mostly young pretty girls, then you might want to invite some old men. Nothing makes them feel more alive. If you are having a party for a writer, you might not want to invite only other writers. Writers enjoy talking to all sorts of people who intrigue them, like a doorman, a detective, or an emergency room nurse. If all the guests have the same kind of job, the result can be geeky shoptalk, and that's not a party—that's called a convention. Make sure your guest list isn't always the same—that's a club. If a guest you invite is a shy type, balance that with a show-off, because all show-offs need an audience (we couldn't do it without you).

The Barnacle

A barnacle is that one person in your life you can never get rid of and no one else really likes. They elicit sympathy by attaching themselves to you, making you believe that if it weren't for you, they would have nobody. NOT TRUE. Invite them when it will be just the two of you, or to one of your much bigger blowouts where they will get lost in the crowd. For every barnacle, there is a shipwreck they can attach themselves to—at least for the length of the party. It is not wise to invite them to a dinner for six or less. People might lose their trust in you because you felt obligated to invite a barnacle, and that puts your party's good reputation on the line. You should never invite a guest solely because you feel obligated; that's no way to cast a party.

Possible Guest Combinations to Avoid

- [x] Astrologer & astronomer
- [ ] Fraternity brother & anyone else
- [ ] Psychologist & psychiatrist
- [ ] Movie star & a scene-stealer
- [ ] The newly divorced couple
- [ ] Director & out-of-work actor
- [ ] A girl, her boyfriend, & his secret girlfriend
- [ ] Serial killer & a drunken teenager

Invitations

The last time I sent a handwritten dinner invitation, I was in junior high and my mom let me invite eight friends over because that was the length of the table. We got to eat in the basement because that would feel special, and I made rock cornish hens, brown rice, frenched beans, and lemon tarts. The point of the story is this: I usually do my invitations by phone so I get a response quicker. But the even pointier point of the story is: whether you send a formal invitation, a written invitation, or make a phone call, invitations need to include specific information. Be crystal clear about the time, place, and location of the party. Include enough information so that you don't raise any questions. If you do your invitations over the phone, don't call the same day of the party unless you call everyone the same day. No one wants to be the last thing on your mind. But don't be discouraged from having last-minute parties. They can be fun because of the spontaneity, such as, "Ruth made it back from Alaska and caught a smoked salmon. Join us at eight."

Leave enough information so that people don't have to call back. Don't make your messages vague: "So hopefully I'll see you a couple of weeks from yesterday!" This is eyebrow-knitting. What if they get the message a week later, or are out of the country? "Late in the afternoon . . . " could mean morning to some people, especially hospital workers, and does "late in the afternoon" mean a late lunch or an early dinner? Whereas, "Friday, May 13th, 6:00 pm" isn't confusing. Don't ask, "What are you doing on the 18th?" It's none of your beeswax. This sort of question puts people on the spot. Don't use a speakerphone under any circumstances. Let your guests know if the party is a special occasion or involves a theme. If the people you are inviting have never been to your house, make sure to include simple directions. If it's complicated, include a map. If there's a gate, include the code. Inform them about parking, construction, or gay day parades. An invitation is the first impression your guest will have of the party, so keep it light, congenial, and of course, informative.

The following are examples of written invitations:

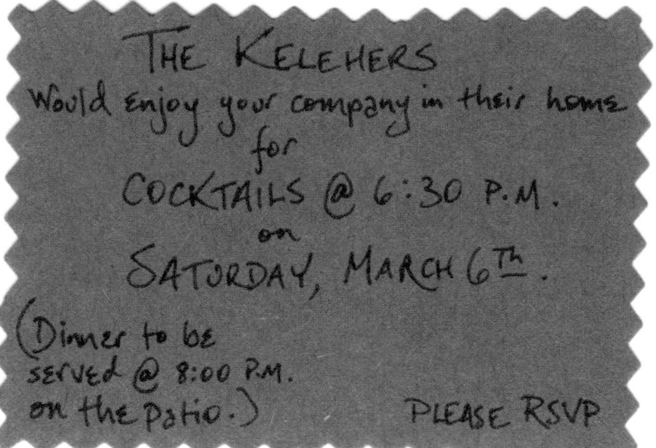
THE KELEHERS
Would enjoy your company in their home
for
COCKTAILS @ 6:30 P.M.
on
SATURDAY, MARCH 6TH.
(Dinner to be
served @ 8:00 P.M.
on the patio.)
PLEASE RSVP

This invitation tells me exactly what to expect. I have no questions. I think I'll wear white jeans.

We are having a barbecue
on Saturday the 4th of
Julune and would Love for
you to Come. The charcoal
will be glowing by two!
Bring one of your children.

This well composed invitation is bristling with information, but be careful to not ask your guest to make too many decisions. Be specific about what kind of children you want at the party so that they can easily narrow it down. Julune?

It's Betty's 1st AA
anniversary, bring joke
gift. Wear low heels
because we will be
celebrating on a golf
course

Excellent! I never thought Betty would stick with the program this long. Go Betty! When is it?

WE'D APPRECIATE IF YOU
AND GUS COME OVER FOR
DINNER NEXT THURSDAY THE 31ST.
FATHER DOMBALAS AND HIS
DAUGHTER STAVROULA WILL BE
HERE FROM TARBORO AND,
THEY LOVE PING PONG SO I'M
HOPING THE SHNOOKS CAN
COME TO DINNER IN THE
EVENING.

Hmm? Good invitation, but what time is dinner and do I bring my paddle?

Please come to our
yard party at our neighbor's
house out in the country on
Sunday the 18th. They're out
of town, so be discreet. It's
easy to get here from there,
expect about an hour to sixty
minutes travel. You can take
the five train, which leaves
at 4:07, or you can take
the Morehead bus which
leaves at 5:08. Or you can
rent a car but don't forget
the time change. Bring a
prepared ice cream dessert.

This invitation would make a good dustpan.

Always RSVP. I'm what you call a shamagrammer. Because I'm a night owl, I call people back late at night when I know they are not in the office and leave my message on an answering machine. I only like to talk on the phone when I want to.

The most important thing to remember when putting together an invitation is, sometimes the less you write, the more you mean!

Guest Etiquette

So you've been invited to a party. Now what? Accepting an invitation is riddled with responsibilities. Chances are if you've been invited to a party, your hostess has chosen you for a reason, either for your good company or, in my case, to exploit you.

If you receive an invitation, respond immediately. Don't teeter-totter. It's insulting to your hostess. They'll think you're lazy or just waiting for something better to come along. How do you expect someone to plan a menu when they don't know how many people they are cooking for? Commit or decline. If you cannot come to the party, do not cancel at the last minute or give a message to a child to inform the host. And don't bother explaining why you can't attend because anything after "because" is bullshit.

Never bring along a guest without asking. Of course, a good hostess will be prepared for this inconvenience and will not make this situation embarrassing even though she is burning up inside and you most certainly will be crossed off any future guest list. Don't call last minute to see if you can bring a girlfriend. I said yes to this once, had to run out my door on New Year's Eve, caught the butcher just before he closed and the girl never showed up. I was frazzled and stuck with an extra steak.

ANYTHING AFTER BECAUSE IS BULLSHIT!

If you want to bring something to the party, ask the hostess what kind of wine she is serving and bring a bottle of that. Don't offer to help the hostess in a way that will slow her down. If someone calls and says, "So for your party, I was thinking I would love to learn how to boil something. Why don't I try to bake . . . " I cut them off. Your party is not the place for others' culinary experiments. Save that for the bedroom. I do not like it when someone brings an unexpected dish unless of course the theme of the party is potluck (see "Grieving," page 122). One Greek Easter, I was preparing a traditional menu and a guest showed up with unexpected parents and a three-story chocolate cake: TURTLE WINS RACE, HEADLINE NEWS, GUEST BRINGS PARENTS, THEN WHAT? I would never have served this dessert with my menu and now it took up valuable counter space, which is always scarce. This guest then proceeded to cut into the cake while I was still serving seconds of my Spanakopita. Not to mention, with her parents in the mix, there go the four-letter words, nunchucks, and throwing stars. She and her family took up the whole length of the couch so my real guests and I spent the entire party in my hallway-size kitchen.

Don't ever come early unless asked. Those last fifteen minutes before a party are vital and for me the most enjoyable. I just love that time to myself. No one wants to be rushed when making a last-minute roux, putting on eyebrows, or waiting for that double-whammy you just swallowed to kick in.

As a guest arriving at the party, don't enter saying "I hate Florida" or "I hate my life, I'm so depressed I almost killed myself last night." Yeah well, you didn't. Don't set a negative tone walking through the door. Don't go into long involved stories with the hostess while other people are still coming in or insist on dominating her time. The host has a job to do and you're not the only guest. Don't ask for an outlet to plug a light box into to show slides

of some historic ruins or sundowns or rocks. Don't bring a light box. I had another party where a guest brought over a short film she had made and insisted that we watch it right then and there on the spot. It stopped the party dead. I had to jump-start it all over again. Remember, television ruins a party, unless of course that's your theme (see "Price Chompers," page 167), as does turning the music down unexpectedly or having the music too loud, which then dominates the room.

A guest shouldn't bring over anything that isn't assembled, like raw vegetables with spinach dip served in a bread bowl (a favorite among the lesbians), because this requires valuable counter space, a cutting board, and a knife. Don't show up with a raw chicken breast and some mushroom caps, or anything that needs to be put in the oven for a long time, or needs room in the freezer. I like it when someone brings over something practical that they know I'll use, like butter. Butter is expensive and has many uses. I like when a guest shows up with confectioners' sugar, lightbulbs, or a roll of those heavy blue gas station paper towels. A classy bottle of water is always nice. A roll of quarters, peppercorns, or carrot tops for my rabbit will make me happy.

Next time you're about to pick up flowers, think. When reaching for those last minute "these will make me look good" dyed carnations, baby's breath, and sunflowers, what are you really saying to your hostess? How much thought and effort does a grocery bouquet require? It's like dropping unwanted change into a tip cup. No regard. They may seem like a charming idea, but truly can cause more aggravation than joy, actually slowing down a hostess. She has to stop what she is doing, react to the flowers, cut them down, find a vase, fill it with water, which could be difficult because the sink could already be occupied with lettuce or a colander of clams. So if you bring flowers, bring them already in something. Bringing flowers can be risky, because often they don't go with the decorations that the host has already displayed. Maybe the party has a southwestern theme and the hostess has sprinkled cacti about the room, but now you've got blossoms fighting for attention. Don't you dare show up with bamboo! You might as well show up with a turtle. If you must bring a plant, it better be of the five-fingered variety. Flowers are good delivered the day after a party as a thank-you. Now that's class! But for parties of eight or more, showing up with flowers can cause a lot of anxiety.

If you are asked to bring something, bring it and show up on time. If you are asked to bring alcohol, don't call up on Sunday at 6:00 pm and ask what liquor stores are open. It's like asking someone what they want for Christmas on Christmas Eve. If you neglect to pick up the item you agreed to bring, you may as well not show up. You're better off lying and saying you were mutilated in a closing subway door (see "Grieving," page 122).

At the party, notice if there

are ashtrays visible. If not, don't smoke in the house. I don't smoke but I don't mind if people smoke in my apartment. I just hope that they are courteous enough not to smoke while someone else is smoking so the room doesn't fill up with smoke. Don't take advantage and make it a great American puff-out night. As far as ashtrays go, make sure that you don't use them for anything other than stamping out butts. No one wants to stare at your chewed up gum or peach pit or wadded up beverage napkin. Don't be "polite" and empty the ashtrays. There might be a roach or a tooth or something the hostess doesn't want thrown out.

Don't overstay your welcome, know when it's time to go. It's always a good idea, especially if you want to be invited to another party, to call the next day and reiterate what a great time you had or send off a quick note, or even better, a quick check. Nothing makes the hostesses happier than a glowing review.

Now that you've learned all the rules of guest etiquette, relax and have fun, but remember: NO BAMBOO, TURTLES, OR SUNFLOWERS!

More Party Don'ts

- Never try to out dress the hostess unless you are the guest of honor, or a transvestite.
- As far as bathroom etiquette goes: number 1, no number 2.
- Don't bring your dog.
- Don't go through the medicine chest, steal toilet paper, or leave with someone else's coat, shoes, or buttons.

The Menu

As I said earlier, half the fun of having a party is planning the party, and all of that half belongs to meal planning. Other than massaging my rabbit or frosting cupcakes, there is nothing I would rather do than plan a menu for a party. Growing up in Raleigh, my favorite part of the local Sunday paper was a section called The Mini Page, which was devoted to children. Included among the word scrambles and picture jumbles was the following week's lunch menu for the public schools. They would use

words like "carrot coins" and "pickle spears." All of the lunch menus would end with "cookie, milk" as in, "Baked chicken, rice with gravy, green beans, cookie, milk." I became obsessed with what foods were chosen to go together, and appreciated their combinations. I remember thinking menu planning would be a fun job to have.

My mother was a really good meal planner. The first thing she thought about after waking up and yelling at my father was, "What will we be having for dinner?" There was always something defrosting on the counter or upside down in a shallow pan of hot water. I used to love watching the old soap operas like *Secret Storm* or *The Edge of Night* because regardless of what drama was going on the wife had a roast in the oven and it was always about the roast, no matter what the crisis was.

A well-planned menu is important because it ties the whole party together. The most impressive trick is organizing the menu so that everything is ready on time and what is supposed to be served hot is hot. You will find that if you can

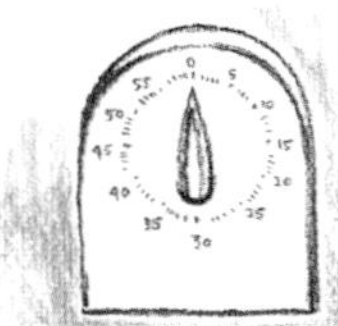

achieve this, your guests will be impressed. Trust me they will notice. If you have successfully preplanned, you will just have to add finishing touches by the time your guests arrive, like a quickly heated sauce or warmed up vegetable. I like to use Revere ware for this purpose. I find that brand is like a camper's tool: it will heat anything up in an instant. I also like to use it for popcorn (see page 194). Try to avoid using the broiler when people are on the way over because it smokes up the room and can cause the smoke alarm to go off, unless that's what you want. I dismantled mine (it kept going off during my grease fires).

Before planning a menu it's a good idea to consult the party log to remind yourself of your guests' likes, dislikes, and dietary restrictions and to avoid repeating a menu. I wouldn't call a guest to ask if they eat meat because it would ruin the surprise of what I was serving and to me this is like calling someone for their address because you want to send them a card. Why bother sending it? Now they know it's coming.

Always plan a menu with your guests' special needs in mind. Are they dieters? If you are serving a dish with sauces, glazes, and/or dressings, you might want to serve those on the side, but do it for everyone. You don't want your dieting guests to feel uncomfortable. Be careful about topping a dessert with alcohol. The last thing you want to do is knock a guest off the wagon with a tiramisu or bourbon balls. If you are entertaining someone with the misfortune of bad skin, stray from serving cranberry muffins or pizza or any other food that might mimic their face. You wouldn't want to embarrass them. Always make eye contact with these guests, for they are very sensitive and have low self-esteem. To get them out of their shell, give them a chore; build up their confidence a bit. This will distract them from thinking about themselves and how bad their skin is compared to other complexions in the room.

The menu often depends on the number of guests. If it's dinner for two I probably wouldn't want more than three things on a plate, two if they are dieting. I have to

be careful that I don't make too much, unless my purpose was to send the individual home with leftovers (see "Gypsy," page 163). Dinner for four means I need to be prepared for surprises. If it's Friday night and I want a fish dinner (see "T.G.I.F.," page 41) and my guests are first-timers, virgins to my party log, I should keep a chop or two in the refrigerator in case someone doesn't eat fish. I can always freeze the chop and eat it later when I am just cooking for one (see "Cooking for One," page 192). With six or more guests, plan on do-ahead dishes. Make a dessert the night before or half-bake a dish and finish cooking it the day of the party.

Eight guests means batten down the hatches, hike up the britches, and pull the table from the wall because now you've got a shindig. For this many guests, I serve cafeteria style, doling it out in the kitchen. For ten to fourteen, unless you already own a battleship-size table, you can rent one along with chairs or go buffet. A buffet means that your guests will probably be standing or using their laps. Serve food that can be broken up with a fork, as knives are awkward. I would steer clear of stews and chili. Things are bound to spill and this can also be a hazard. I once saw a girl on stilts slip on an olive.

It's important to make it clear to guests that dinner will be served at a specific time. If I invite people over at 8, it means dinner will begin at 8. The food is ready to go on the table at 8. I do this for three reasons:

1: I don't have to consider many appetizers or worry about multiple predinner cocktails.

2: People won't eat and run because as they finish dinner, the party is just beginning.

3: Nobody wants to arrive and see the hostess putting a raw turkey in the oven. Don't assume you are that interesting to hang out with. Not to mention that you will be trussed up in the kitchen the whole time and that's rude.

If you can't avoid spending large amounts of time in the kitchen during the beginning of a party, ask a friend to play cocktologist and pass out peanuts. I don't normally serve appetizers, but if I do have something out it is usually one of my famous Lil' Smoky Cheese Balls (see "My Success Story," page 180). Cheese balls are good if you are on a budget, because one can serve a cheese ball while entertaining friends on Monday, spend Tuesday perking up the ball, and then serve it to a different group of friends on Wednesday. They'll never know the difference. To freshen up a cheese ball, merely reshape the ball back into its original form, being careful to cover the gouge marks, and then roll it through the remaining nut shake to mask the renovation. Decorate with a poke or party pick.

As you are discovering, planning a menu is dictated by many things, such as the number of guests, the season, the party theme or gimmick, the time of day, the size of your space, the amount of time you have, and the budget. But even with these considerations there are some general rules you can follow to help you assemble a successful menu that will guarantee repeat business.

Mixing a Menu by Color

As I said, I tend to live my life like a deaf person. I like to plan a menu visually. I try to mix a variety of colors on my plate. If the main dish is the color of a Band-Aid, I would contrast it with beets, tomatoes, peas, carrot coins, or a darker leaf, like spinach. You wouldn't want to serve a white fish with white rice and pearl onions on a white plate with a creamy coleslaw, and rice pudding unless you were dining with the Imperial Wizard of the Ku Klux Klan (see "Blind Date," page 47). Think of little ways to add color, like paprika on deviled eggs, chives on baked potatoes, a lemon wedge next to fish, parsley on fettuccini alfredo or nutmeg on top of a cream sauce. A red onion and pumpernickel croutons will jazz up any salad. Adding color is an easy way to help a meal come alive.

Menus by Texture

If the texture of the food you are serving is creamy, flatter it with crispy. Crunchy will always punch up soggy. And nothing complements chewy more than crusty. Prickly next to scaly? Not a good idea. And, as a general rule, never have bumpy and lumpy on the same plate.

Menus by Theme

I often plan the menu by theme. That way I have boundaries and boundaries are good because they narrow down our choices. Sometimes I'll have Country Kitchen Southern Night where I'll make barbecue ribs, sweet potatoes, Southern Green Beans (see page 239), and corny bread. Or I'll have Je M'appèlle French Night, which might include French onion soup, French, fries, French bread, and an endive salad with French dressing (see page 257). It's not a good idea to mix and match different cultural foods unless of course the theme is Patches.

Menus by Flavor

You never want one flavor to dominate the whole menu. Think twice before you serve a tomato soup with a tomato salad followed by spaghetti marinara, and Bloody Marys for cocktails. That's a lot of acid to drop in one night. It's also not a good idea to have too many strong flavors competing, like serving chicken teriyaki with meatballs and barbecue baked beans followed by a hazelnut mousse.

Menus by Decoration

Julia Child said never put anything inedible on a plate. I think that was sound advice. Try carving radishes or carrots into cheerful shapes, or if you are like me and don't possess any whittling skills, you can always melt Life Savers on a cookie sheet and make stained glass windows. Of course, you might have a tough time coming up with a meal that is complemented by an artificially flavored candy. You can also decorate a meal just by changing the shape of your food. If you usually make a meat loaf in a rectangular pan, use a ring pan and make it a Meat Loaf Wreath (see page 171). Make a roll cake instead of a sheet cake. If you are making something with a crust, cut out shapes with cookie cutters and place them on top. For example: tomahawks for a Powwow Birthday or bats and an owl on pumpkin pie for a Fall Festivity (see page 168).

Shopping

Once you have your menu plan, it's time to go shopping. I find the quote, "hungry people make poor shoppers" to be quite accurate. That is why for me it's a hot creamy meal, a generous wedge of pound cake, grab the tote, and it's off to the store!

Shopping is so entertaining to me because you can tell so much about people by what they buy. When I was a cashier at Winn-Dixie people would walk up with such telling combinations as a small bottle of vanilla and a frozen dinner. Sometimes the items leave more of a mystery, like lentils and panty hose (see "Eye Burrito," page 267). I loved it on that old family TV show *The Waltons*, when the mother announced that she was going to make a birthday cake, and would go to Ike's store and ask for a vanilla bean, a sack of flour, and a yard of nails. I couldn't fathom how she was going to hammer out that cake.

Don't do the bulk of your shopping the day of the party. You never know what a store might be out of, and then you will be forced to either rush to another store or alter your menu plan. When I worked in a grocery store, I loved nothing more than watching last-minute shoppers panic. Sometimes even now, I'll pop into a grocery store on a holiday just for my own amusement. Thank you, lady trying to buy a turkey on Thanksgiving. And thank you, sir scrambling to find hamburger buns on the 4th of July and settling for waffles. Much appreciated. Enjoy your burgers, and pass the maple syrup please.

It's wise to make a list before you go shopping. I like to make a list but I never look at it until after I've left the store and then I test myself to see if I have forgotten something. Another thing I like to do is never ask where an item is: I would rather look for it than hear them say they don't have it. I like that feeling of hope. I don't use coupons because I don't want to bother the cashier, but it would probably be a good idea to do so because coupons equal money.

Growing up, I went grocery shopping with my father every Friday night. I learned a lot of tricks, like if you reach far back enough into the shelf, you might be fortunate to find a can that hasn't been marked up because sometimes clerks are too lazy to reach all the way back and change them. If you have a guinea pig, hamster, or rabbit, you can get discarded greens from the produce department for free. If you have a dog, the butcher often has bones he's not using.

I wish products still came with presents. I remember buying syrup and there would be a roll of Scotch tape with it, or a smoked drinking glass with laundry detergent, or dog food would have a pair of knee-highs. I still haven't

figured that one out. Tape and syrup makes sense to me because they're both sticky, but dog food and knee-highs? Is it because that's the point of view of the dog? I also like to see where castaway items end up, when people change their minds at the last minute and drop the item they are holding wherever it's convenient. Once I saw a chicken resting in the spice section. Nobody's going to buy that chicken now or the spices it was resting on (see Contamination).

I once read that illiterate people shop by the pictures on the package. They might think that a powdered sugar box with a picture of brownies on it promises they'll find brownies inside, or a can of Crisco contains fried chicken or a whole piece of cherry pie.

Also I noticed in some stores that accept food stamps that they lock certain items up, like vanilla and baby formula, so that you have to find a manager with a key to get it for you. When buying vanilla, always make sure the bottles are full. Twice I've gotten home and found the vanilla bottles were empty, bone dry. If you know someone who owns a restaurant, you could ask them to order a bottle of vanilla for you because they get it wholesale and it's so expensive. A great gift idea for bakers.

Be able to get the most out of what you buy. If I have a choice between something packaged in a box or a bag, I'll pick the boxed item because I can use the empty box later to put cookies in, transport three cupcakes, or bury a turtle. I also buy Land O Lakes butter because I can get a card out of it.

If you have the opportunity to go to specialty shops (cheese, green grocer, fish monger, bakery, etc.), do so. Often the selection is better, the merchant is more knowledgeable, and the food is fresher. Don't forget the American farmer. Farmers' markets are where food is at its freshest. Going to a farmers' market is worth it for the atmosphere alone—great accents and people watching. I don't know how fruits and vegetables are supposed to feel when you buy them, but I do know that someone does. If you need to know, look it up or ask somebody who does. I don't. Although, I do know two things: the heavier the orange, the more the juice, and a Vidalia onion can be eaten like an apple. It says so on the box.

Shop Talk

- Don't buy fish on Sunday.
- If you do not work 9 to 5, go shopping 9 to 5. The same applies to laundry, be considerate.
- When ordering in a deli, announce loudly how many items you'll be ordering so customers behind you know what to expect and won't be irritated. The same applies in chocolate shops.
- Government checks are issued on the 1st and the 15th, which means crowds of families on these dates. Keep that in mind.
- Don't shop from someone else's food cart.
- Buy organic lemons, if for no other reason than because the puckered tips make great nipples to stuff in your bra.
- Notice in local health food stores how unhealthy the people tend to look.
- And notice in heliolithic stores that when you throw out "thanks" they hear that and respond sincerely, so if you say "thank you," mean it.
- Cashiers will notice patterns like ice cream at midnight three days in a row. The same is true for liquor. Rotate your stores.
- If you genuinely see something you can compliment your cashier on, do it. It'll make their day. Conversely, if you want to destroy their day, ask to see the manager.
- Remember, grocery store butchers always tuck the fat.

TCB-ING IT!

I love that time before a party when your mind kicks into high gear, like a lightning bolt, and you realize the party is quickly approaching and you still have everything to do and you're still in bed. This is when I'm at my best. Racing against the clock gives me an adrenaline rush that even my dealer can't provide. This manic energy carries through to the party and often ignites my guests. I call this my TCB (Taking Care of Business) time. It's important to roll with this feeling, whether it strikes you a week or a minute before the party. You will find that during this period you will have your most productive moments, allowing valuable breathing room when the actual party arrives.

When I get struck with this force, I usually start with cleaning the house, because not only does cleaning have to be done before a party, it is a mindless chore that gives my imagination the chance to run wild and it's in these moments that I come up with the same old ideas that will make my party original. For some people, this mindless activity might be a walk or painting a door or rocking back and forth at a rapid pace but, regardless, letting your imagination loose is the best part of busy work.

I always feel grateful to have a sink full of dirty dishes when I'm mad at somebody. It gives me something to do with my hands, which allows me the freedom to imagine all the horrific ways they might catch fire or be set up for a false drug bust that will imprison them forever.

I also use this energy to inspire my decorations. I like decorations that are simple and inexpensive. If it's Calabash Seafood Night, maybe I'll put a conch shell in a beach hat and use clamshells for ashtrays. If it's South of the Border Night, I'll get out my tablecloth with donkeys and napping peasants and place a sombrero with a chip-filled brim in the center of the table (see picture, page 255). I might make flowers out of tissue paper (see page 283), or cut them out of paper plates and pin them to my curtains and walls or iron leaves between pieces of wax paper and hang them in my windows (see page 190). Gift wrap the framed artwork on your walls and rehang them—what's nicer than a wall of presents to look at? For me, a handmade decoration that expresses the theme of the party cannot be beat. Occasionally, when some of my more crafty friends are invited they will contribute to the party decorations during the party. It makes for a fun party activity. I'm also a sucker for anything with "googly" eyes, those shakable eyes that are often attached to puppet skulls or doll heads. I've always said that when I die, I want to be displayed in an open casket with googly eyes replacing my own.

Also during this time I decide what I'm going to wear. I like to think of my outfits more like costumes. Once I step into the role of being a hostess, I want to feel transformed. The perfect outfit will help set the party tone and immediately puts your company in a festive mood. You might want to try on your outfit before the party to make sure it still fits. Your guests should be noticing the rolls on the table, not the rolls on your back. I love aprons. I feel naked without one on. Often, an apron can pull a whole outfit together and hide some of the trouble spots. Not all clothes are appropriate for entertaining. You wouldn't want to wear a bikini when panfrying pork chops any more than you would want to wear wizard sleeves or anything that's flammable when you are serving food on fire, like shish kebabs or cherries jubilee.

No WIZARD SLEEVES

During my TCB time, I might marinate ribs or pre-roll silverware in a napkin if I'm serving buffet style. I never set the table with valuable silver because with the type of friends I have, I can't keep it in the house. I might also prepare a do-ahead dish or clean the rabbit hay box to reduce that ever-present goat smell. I always start making ice in advance and then tub it. I think it's cheating to go out and buy a bag unless it's specialty ice, such as crushed, shaved, or chipped. Nothing depresses me more than an empty ice cube tray. The point is to take advantage of the energy burst you get from the excitement of soon hosting a party.

The Day of the Party

I never dread the day of the party, I'm eager: I can't wait for my company to arrive. Rarely do I have the jitters, because, like a good Girl Scout (which I was until the day they forced me out), I am prepared. I've done all my TCB-ing and now I have an entire day to attend to small details and light chores, while still allowing me some time for myself. I take my time bathing, check for lumps, and dress leisurely.

The more you've TCB-ed it, the better prepared you'll be for the unexpected surprises or disasters that are bound to happen the day of the party. Once I had a refrigerator break down on Thanksgiving Day. Luckily I lived in Chicago and it was cold enough to set everything on the porch. Another time I had a surprise attack visit from a plumber saying he needed to remove my toilet in order to look for leaks an hour before my guests were to arrive. Then there was the time I planned a party around a Virginia smoked ham from North Carolina and it never showed up. It still hasn't. I had to run out, and all I could find last minute was a honey-glazed ham, which threw everything else off, especially my side dishes. Sometimes you're the cause of your own mishap. One Easter I put a deboned leg of lamb in the oven and forgot to turn it on; I was too dressed up to notice. I suppose I cared more about how I looked than how I cooked. When I returned to check on it, the oven was stone cold and inside rested a sagging, uncooked leg of lamb.

When a major setback occurs, don't snap your bean. Make a joke out of the situation, turn it around. Take a snapshot of the rump roast you just dropped and send everyone a copy the next day. Your relaxed attitude will put everyone at ease. During a crisis, it may be a good time to ask a friend to play deputy hostess. While you spend time mopping up the gravy or smothering the grease fire, your newly appointed second-in-command can temporarily attend to the needs of guests, such as refreshing their drinks or clearing their empty plates.

Lighting should flatter your guests. Think mood lighting. Use it to create a magical illusion where your guests look appetizing to one another but it's not so dark that your guests appear as vague shadowy figures. You've worked hard to create a colorful menu, let them see it. Think warm gentle tones where the result will be "Lady, can I get you a drink?" instead of "Lady, can I get you a cab?"

DRINK

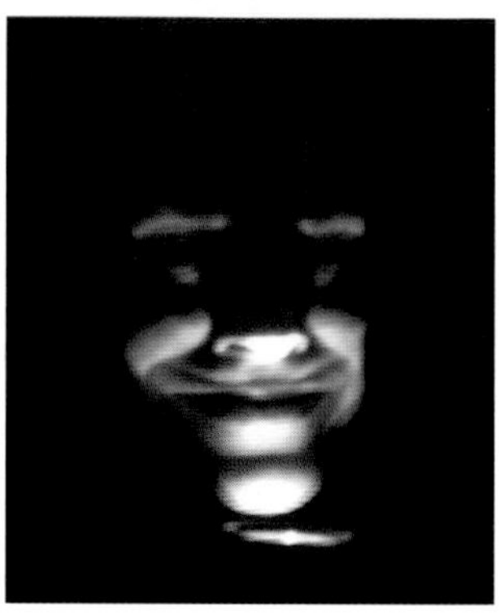

CAB

Candles cast a pleasant glow, but don't overdo it; you're not hosting a sacrifice (see "Blind Date," page 47). If you use scented candles, make sure they complement the aroma of the food. If you must use overhead lighting, it's a bright idea to have a dimmer.

Your music is just as important as your lighting. I often use it to create an atmosphere that will enhance the mood, not dominate it. You don't want the room to feel dead any more than you want it to feel like a roller disco.

Make your music selections before the party. The last thing people want to hear as they settle onto your couch with a drink and an appetizer is, "What does everybody want to listen to?" Actually that is the second-to-last thing people want to hear at a party. The first is, "All right, everybody take off your shoes and sit on the floor, we're going Japanese!"

If you're going to have flowers, then have flowers. Don't just have one bunch stuck in a glass on a shelf. And remember not all flowers smell as good inside as they do outside. You will also want to consider the color and style of the flowers you choose. They should complement your theme and decorations. Fill the room with cherry blossoms for a Spring Soiree, carnations for grieving (see page 122), and tulips jammed in clogs when entertaining the Dutch.

If you are serving cocktails and need some extra room for a blender or beverages use your ironing board and cover it with a nice tablecloth. I always keep a package of T-shirts handy in case someone is burning up and needs to shed a layer. I have prescription allergy medicine at the ready for those guests who discover they are allergic to lobster claws or stone crab. I keep a box of Nat Sherman colored party cigarettes in my freezer for those people who just want "one" (see picture, page 130).

The day of the party is also the time when I go around the house organizing my sale items. I may have failed to mention earlier, but I like to make money from my party guests (see "Money Jar," below).

The Money Jar (Entertaining for Profit)

As I mentioned earlier (see "The Day of the Party," page 31), I like to make money at my parties. It all started with my Funny Face Club. I would pencil draw smiley faces on pieces of notebook paper with "25 cents" written in the corner and go door to door trying to sell them. I also collected Coke bottles, set up Kool-Aid stands, sang country songs at the airport, and got rid of people's pumpkins all for the price of 25 cents. Still, to this day, there is virtually no situation that comes up that I don't see as a ripe opportunity to make 25 cents. And there is nothing riper than a party. You've got a large group of people, they're liquored up, they are in a giving mood, and they are confined to your home. Cha-ching. Trust me, this involves a lot less legwork than trying to sell pencil drawings of smiley faces door to door. I've come a long way from dragging rotting jack-o'-lanterns into the middle of the street. Today, in order to make 25 cents, my methods are much more refined. They include indoor garage sales, exploiting my rabbit, or selling commercial barbecue sauce repackaged with my face on the label.

It is simple to set up an indoor garage sale. Create a display table and make a sign that reads, "Everything Must Go, 25 Cents" and you've got yourself a garage sale. I also place an enamel cup on the table with a smaller "25 Cents" sign on it so customers have a place to drop a quarter in. I usually customize the "for sale" items on my table to fit my guests' personalities. Products could include anything from half bottles of fancy lotion, pharmaceutical goods, handmade items, movies, dish detergent, pot holders, matches, lighters, toothbrushes, motel toiletries, used batteries, shells, postcards, tea bags, and any kind of makeshift container for aspirin or vitamins. For those guests who use the excuse "I really can't buy anything, because I'm traveling tomorrow and I don't want any of this stuff in my bag," I offer my cupcakes. If, after being confronted with a cupcake, they use the excuse "I'm hypoglycemic," then I get angry. Don't put anything on the table that is not for sale, it's annoying.

For larger items, I place a box outside my door. This is usually filled with such bargains as fans, buckets, pillows, vases, frames, pans, handbags, and hospitality books. I personally man the box because it's more about the transaction than the quarter. I try to keep the line moving by putting a limit on browsing, and I'm careful not to be too chatty with each customer.

I have three simple rules for shoppers.

RULE 1: It has to be a quarter, can't be three nickels and a dime or two dimes and a nickel. They are not worth the money they are worth.

RULE 2: You breakey, you boughty.

RULE 3: You boughty, you takey.

The point is to get the stuff out of my house.

Another great way to make money is the instant camera. A must-have for all parties. You can have your picture taken with my rabbit for 25 cents, couples 25 cents apiece. I make souvenir booklets using construction paper, fold them in half, insert the snapshot on the inside jacket and personalize the outside. And then of course, I'll laminate a baby picture or other personal item from your wallet or customize a lighter by wrapping sticky shelf paper around it. First one's free (see "Personalized Lighters," page 288).

Ding Dong, Guests Arriving

When I was a waitress, I learned that the most important position in a restaurant is the host. It's the host's job to welcome the guests, and it is often the first thing the guests see. I like to think of my front door as my greeter. For other people it might be their butler or a bush. I try to make my door inviting. I try to have it speak for me since I have a limited vocabulary. I want my door to set the tone and give the arriving guest a glimpse into the festivities. For an Autumn Harvest, I'll put a squirrel surrounded by cutouts of acorns or leaves with my friends' names on them. Or maybe for April Showers I'll make umbrella shapes and rain clouds using cotton balls and string. Sometimes I'll take the eviction notice off my neighbor's apartment door and slap it on my own (also a good item to have when invited to someone else's home). Even when there is no specific holiday, I have a special knocker and a hand-painted apartment number. Let your door represent you.

Once your door swings open, your party has started. This is where your hospitality will shine. Greet each guest with genuine enthusiasm. Give them your full attention. If you are excited, they will be excited. Allow your guests to soak up the environment you have created. There is no need to point things out. They don't need to be made aware of how much work you've done right away; you've got plenty of time to tell them. And don't show it in your appearance either. You must look radiant; no one wants to open the door to a tired, anxious, overworked raccoon-eyed hostess. It should appear as though you've used witchcraft. The party should seem effortless.

If your guests bring a little something-something, make a mental note or discreetly write it down so you can acknowledge it when they are leaving. Let's say Lily brought over ice cream and I just realized that she has a wandering eye. Now I can associate her wandering eye with the ice cream she brought. I will remember that Lily brought ice cream because I got "the scoop" on her eye. Simple. If J.D. brought mushrooms and he has a toadstool shaped mole sprouting from the side of his nose, make a mental note. This way, if you send off a thank-you card you can be specific. Everyone likes to receive a little feedback on gifts, especially if they put a lot of time and thought into them.

A thank-you card should feel personal, not like a form letter, unless that's the joke. I recently received a thank-you letter that read, "I loved all my anniversary gifts, every single one. Thank you so much. They all mean so much to me as do you. Thank you so much." This letter is as vague as my memory of his party.

Try and provide a place where people can put their coats once they've arrived. If your place is small, hang them on the shower rod in the bathroom. But be aware of pickpocketers (see "Blind Date," page 47). If you toss garments on the bed or in another room, provide a small mirror because girls and certain types of men like to take a quick look-see after they've taken off their coats.

When introducing people, try to avoid saying something that could be embarrassing like: "This is Barbara, she can't have children," or "Matt's on mood stabilizers," or "Lenny just got fired. He was the promotions manager at Nowells." Also try and avoid introducing people by

Blueberry Pie

categorizing them, such as "He's a dancer at Wag Tails," or "She's in the outdoor musical *The Lost Colony,*" or "He's the guy who found the girl in the well." Give your guests an opportunity to share what they wish to share.

Once everyone has arrived, the first fifteen minutes are the most important. This often will set the tone for the whole party. You must use constant owl-like behavior in order to monitor how the party is shaping up and intervene when necessary. Occasionally a party will need a bit of initial poking and prodding. If the energy seems low, work the room. Engage as many people as you can. Bring guests together that you think might enjoy talking to each other. "Alice, you remember Ilene, she was at Riker's the same time you were." Keep the cocktails flowing. Make sure everybody has a fresh beverage and pour heavy. Change the music or the lighting if you feel it will pump up the energy.

If your preplanning is successful, you won't be stuck in the kitchen. Use this time to work the room and enjoy the party yourself. Mingle. It is as important for you to have a good time as it is for your guests. Offer everyone a drink, but don't ask in a way that assumes that they drink alcohol, such as "Name your poison," or "How 'bout a cocktail?" This might be awkward for guests who don't drink or alcoholics who are in the program. They hear it in a different way. No one wants to tempt an alcoholic: you don't want that on your shoulders (see "Alcoholics," page 86). Create your own special drink that can be served with or without alcohol. That way nobody will know who is or who isn't drinking. It's more discreet, like medication.

At the Party

As the party hits full swing, it often doesn't matter what you've preplanned, you have to be in the moment and open for whatever may come your way. If the guests are not ready for a sit-down buffet because they're having a good time, let the party go on. Don't try to control every moment.

During the party you'll want to tidy up as if you were a ghost. Be discreet when emptying ashtrays and clearing glasses and plates. It makes the guests uncomfortable otherwise. Continually check on the bathroom in case there has been a "toilet accident." (You know who you are, Alice!) Don't be a pusher with the food or drink, that's annoying: "One more glass of wine won't hurt you," or "Come on, I've seen bigger asses than yours, have a piece of cake," or "Just taste it, trust me the eyes are the best part." If you are offering someone a second or third drink, never say, "Can I get you another gimlet?" Just offer to get them a gimlet and don't remind them that they already had a few. This appears judgmental. However, if it's clear that they have had too much, it's better to cut them off rather than to pretend it's not happening and then allow them to stay over and wet your bed (see "Blind Date," page 47).

Don't make guests uncomfortable by putting them on the spot insisting they tell a particular story or joke or sing a song or say something in a different language. They might not be in the mood. They might not be up for making some sound effects or ready to show their surgery scars. Don't exploit them, although I do.

Oftentimes during a party people tend to cluster together in one clump. In order to get them to circulate, I'll put a cheese ball in the bedroom to lure some of the guests in an attempt to de-clump them.

If you see someone boring someone else, just be grateful it's not you. If you see someone hogging the conversation, create an opening and try to include someone else. Have something ready in your apron pocket to talk about. My line is, "Yes, paella is very traditional to the Spaniards." Or "Wasn't that British territory?" If you see a shy person, ask them some questions like, "Why are you so shy? Tell everyone, we're all listening."

Saying Good-bye

As a friend's mother once said about a tree her late husband had planted with tenderness that now stood leafless and brittle: "Daddy's tree! Chop it down and drag it to the curb." Thus is the healthy attitude at the end of a party. When it's over, it's over. Pack 'em up and get 'em out. There is no point in dragging out the end, regardless of how successful the beginning and the middle have been. The end of a party is no time for sentiment. You'll have plenty of time to reminisce later. For now, it's time to say good-bye.

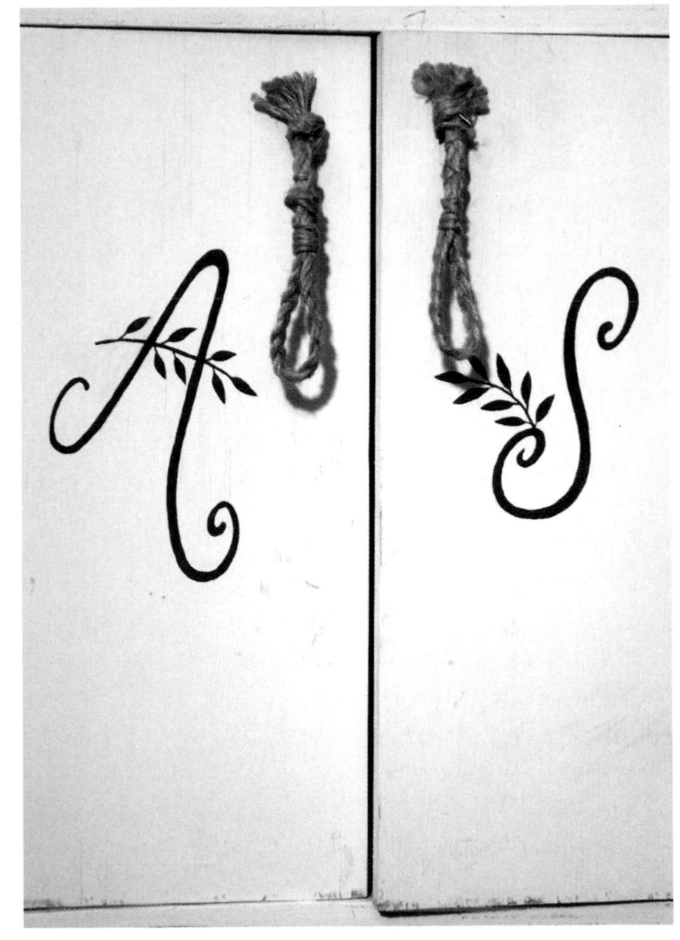

When the time for farewells comes, don't say your good-byes in the hallway or on the street, the neighbors might be sleeping. Say them once and make them quick. You don't want to encourage lingerers, stragglers, or carnies. Sometimes I walk them to the elevator to make sure they have left the building and I double-check the stairwell to make sure they are gone. I don't want them standing outside my door listening to me talking about how they ruined my party. If they brought over a dish, I like to return it that night. If you made money off them, make sure they've paid, and make doubly sure they leave with their on-spot souvenir.

Don't start cleaning up while your guests are leaving, save it for later. I actually love nothing more than doing my dishes after a party because it gives me time to reflect. Time to think of the highlights, the lowlifes, the hits and misses, and the person who fell asleep in my bed. If you have the energy, you can make an entry in your party log, count your quarters, or reform your cheese ball for tomorrow night's party. On the off chance that you have children, don't clean up at all. As children, my brother and sisters and I loved waking up early and playing cocktail party with the leftover debris. As you can tell, those were my first steps in hospitality.

Hospitality in Action

Fried Fish Fillets

I invited four businessmen over for dinner on a Friday night after their workday. I wasn't quite sure what to expect, because I don't usually associate with businessmen on a personal level. I've never held a white-collar job. Apparently, most white-collar jobs require some sort of schooling, and to me, the only thing more dull than a white-collar job is schooling. That is not to say that I do not respect people who work nine to five, Monday through Friday. I appreciate their dedication to regimen. But for me, I tend to work around my random spurts of energy.

The theme for the party was nautical, because growing up we always had fish on Friday. For my door decoration, I put up a tissue-paper lobster that had a small sign attached to it that said: "Pinch Me, It's T.G.I.F." I used a tablecloth printed with ships' wheels and anchors. My dinner napkins had a sailing theme and I made a matching apron to match. For my centerpiece, I displayed a conch shell in a beach hat. I used clamshells to hold peanuts and I put sand in the ashtrays. I also placed a tip jar on the table, but they all stiffed me. Everyone knows seamen and businessmen don't tip.

Because my knowledge of boats and shipping is limited, I included pirate references. I even considered wearing an eye patch, but limiting my vision while frying flounder felt unnecessarily risky, so instead I wore a hook hand.

I also thought it would be fun to introduce my white-collar guests to the world of blue collar. I fashioned a small corner of my kitchen into a break room, thinking that if my businessmen needed to get away from the party for a moment they would have somewhere to go. I put a large crab ashtray (indicating cancer) on a stool so they would have a designated smoking area. On the wall I hung a time clock so each of my guests could punch in and punch out to "play blue collar."

My menu was simple. It included Captain Stack's Fried Flounder or Broiled Seaman's Red Snapper, Skipper's Dock Romaine Salad, and Neptune's Hush Puppies, with a "Pier" Pressure Choice of baked potato, French fries, or rice, and a monkey dish of Coleslaw of the Dunes served on the side. I also made my Captain's Mouthwatering Bite-size Blue Ball Cheese Balls. Blue Balls are bite-size cheese balls made out of blue cheese. For dessert, I made it to the bakery and bought a Beachcomber's Lemon Meringue Pie. I also readied my liquor cabinet, because from what I learned watching old soap operas, your average businessman likes to unwind.

Around six o'clock they arrived, just in time for happy hour. I made a runner out of plywood so when they walked into the room, their feet would make the same sound you might hear walking down a wooden dock on your way to a boathouse fish shanty. After a quick "Ahoy!" I escorted them into the living room and offered them a drink, which they eagerly accepted. Initially, the party seemed stiff, mostly standing around and small chatter on such mind-numbing subjects as "the Teasdale Account," and "the Neeves' Memo." From the kitchen I heard the topic change to dimples and rushed in thinking I could finally contribute to the conversation only to find out they were talking about some new golf ball. I quickly excused myself, but soon came rushing back when I heard the words "pan head" only to find they were still talking about a golf ball. After five Salty Dogs, my businessmateys began to loosen up. Coats were shed, ties were loosened, and from what I could make out from the kitchen, suggestive comments were tossed off in my direction. I rushed in a third time, and to my surprise discovered the saucy banter was aimed at my next-door neighbor and delivered from my window. Well, shiver me timbers.

By the time I served the fish, the party had already set sail with a clear but uncharted course for inebriation. The evening was beginning to flounder. I tried to avoid getting crabby, and realized I needed to do something quick before the tide completely turned. I cheerfully suggested a party game—Charades—but from their mostly mumbled responses ("Show us your tits") it was clear not only that they were not keen on guessing the titles to movies by acting them out, but that I had a full mutiny on my hands. My only recourse was to run this shipwreck aground. So, thinking fast, I sent them on a treasure hunt toward my neighbor's booty. They bought that hook, line, and sinker and set sail, all men overboard.

Possible Origins of the term "Monkey Dish"

- A small dish no bigger than a monkey's paw.
- A small dish that would serve monkey.
- Originally a dish made from a monkey's skull.

Menu

Captain's Mouthwatering Bite-size Blue Ball Cheese Balls

Skipper's Dock Romaine Salad

Captain Stack's Fried Flounder with Shelly's Tartar Sauce, or Broiled Seaman's Red Snapper

Neptune's Hush Puppies (see page 237)

Pier Pressure Choice

Baked Potato All the Way, French Fries, or Rice

Coleslaw of the Dunes (see page 259)

Salty Dog on the Rocks

Beachcomber's Lemon Meringue Pie 
(recipe not included, buy one)

Sandy's Coffee

CAPTAIN STACK'S FRIED FLOUNDER

1/2 teaspoon of salt

1/2 teaspoon of pepper

1/3 cup cornmeal or breadcrumbs

4 pieces of flounder fillet

Vegetable oil

Leave fillets wet. Dredge fish in salt, pepper, and cornmeal or breadcrumbs. Deep fry in oil at 375°F until golden brown.

BROILED SEAMAN'S RED SNAPPER

3 pounds of red snapper fillets

½ cup olive oil

Juice of 1 lemon

1½ teaspoons oregano

3 garlic cloves

Sprinkle salt and pepper on fillets, to taste, and place them under broiler. Set aside one tablespoon olive oil. Mix the lemon, oregano, and the rest of the olive oil together and pour over the snapper. Broil until it is tender. While the fish is broiling, dice the garlic and fry it in the tablespoon of oil. When the fish is about to be served, top with the garlic mixture.

CAPTAIN'S MOUTHWATERING BITE-SIZE BLUE BALL CHEESE BALLS

1 cup of grated Cheddar cheese

4 ounces of cream cheese

2 ounces of crumbled blue cheese

2 tablespoons of butter

1 tablespoon of chopped green onions (optional)

1/2 teaspoon of Worcestershire sauce

1 tablespoon of white wine or milk

1/4 cup of chopped walnuts

Ritz crackers

Bring all cheeses to room temperature. Beat with mixer. Add butter, onions (optional), Worcestershire sauce, and milk or wine, and continue beating. Chill overnight. Shape mixture into tumor-size balls. Roll in chopped nuts. Let stand 15 minutes. Spread on a Ritz.

SALTY DOG ON THE ROCKS

1½ ounces vodka

4 ounces grapefruit juice

Mix and pour over ice in a glass rimmed with sea salt.

SKIPPER'S DOCK ROMAINE SALAD

3 heads of romaine lettuce chopped (cold)

Croutons (as many as you wish)

6 tablespoons of garlic oil

Salt and pepper

1 tablespoon of Worcestershire sauce

1/4 cup of olive oil

3/4 cup of vegetable oil

6 tablespoons of grated Romano cheese

1 egg

Juice of 3 lemons

Arrange the romaine lettuce, croutons, garlic oil, salt and pepper, Worcestershire sauce, olive oil, vegetable oil, and cheese in a bowl. Break egg over the salad and pour lemon juice on top of the egg. Toss the salad from the bottom.

SHELLY'S TARTAR SAUCE

1 tablespoon of dill pickles

1 tablespoon of sour pickles

1 tablespoon of chives

1/2 tablespoon of chopped green olives (optional)

1 tablespoon of parsley

1/2 cup of mayonnaise

Chop the pickles, chives, olives, and parsley into fine pieces. Wring these ingredients in a cloth to get all the liquid out. Combine with the mayonnaise. Mix it up. Courtesy of Jennifer McCullen.

Two Fishhook Incidents:

1. My friend's mother saw her cat swallow a fishhook in the shed. Rather than see the cat suffer, she shot it in the back of the head with a gun.
2. My sister had a fishhook hanging in her shower. She slipped and the hook went through her lip. The only good thing is that it plumped up her thin lips for a while.

Optional Menu Suggestion

Steak with Red Wine Butter Sauce

Julius Caesar Salad (see page 258)

Gloria's Peas and Onions

Baked Potato All the Way

Cousin Kathy's Cheesecake (see page 233)

Coffee

A great tool to use for steak night is a stovetop grill, which fits snuggly over two burners. I can fit up to eight slipper-size steaks on it or two porterhouse steaks. What I like about using the grill is that it makes you feel like a line cook, especially when all your guests request steaks at different temperatures. I find that I can judge people by the temperature of their steak. I serve my steaks with a red wine butter sauce and a steak temperature poke.

Buy steaks that include a bone. Bones are good items to sell at the end of the night to dog owners. $

RED WINE STEAK BUTTER SAUCE

My mother got this recipe out of a *Playboy* magazine. She made it whenever we had a roast beef or steaks. Usually it was made late, so I always saw a small saucepan in the freezer chilling to speed along the hardening of the butter.

Remove skin of 3 shallots, chop fine, toss in a small saucepan with 2 tablespoons of butter, simmer until tanned. Add 1/2 cup dry red wine. Continue cooking until the wine is reduced to 1/4 cup. Place saucepan in the refrigerator to cool off. Mix one stick of soft butter into the mixture and blend well. Spoon on roast beast or steaks.

GLORIA'S PEAS AND ONIONS

3 sweet (white) Vidalia onions

1/2 cup of olive oil

4 cans of Green Giant peas

Slice onions thinly and sauté in oil on medium to low heat, stirring with a wooden spoon. Onions should be stirred frequently, as to NOT BROWN at all. Cook until pearlized. Drain canned peas and add to cooked onions. Fold in gently and keep on warm until serving. Serves 8. Courtesy of Dino Deguiceis.

BAKED POTATO ALL THE WAY

Scrub your potatoes and stab several times with a fork. Put them in an oven at 400 degrees F for 1 hour. Remove from the oven and make a slit down the middle lengthwise. Press the 2 ends a little towards each other until the insides come out of the slit. Top with butter, sour cream, diced chives, salt, and freshly cracked pepper.

Chicken of the Taverns

Blind Date

I LIKE YOU

I LIKE YOU

I like having a first date in my home. I feel more comfortable when I can control the evening. The goal is to impress him, and this is easier for me when he is on my turf. I can put my skills to work: I can cast a spell. I don't like a lot of small talk, so I allow my home and homemaking abilities to speak for me. I'm guessing a stranger can get a pretty good idea as to who I am by observing the medical wax model of a canker sore I have hanging on a wall, or my antique correction shoe displayed on a bookshelf, or the fact that my place is organized primarily to accommodate my rabbit (see "And Rabbits," page 179). First dates often have an air of illusion swirling around them. Because typically on a first date, people don't know much about each other so they tend to reinvent themselves for the occasion as well as project onto the other what qualities they desire most in a mate. Many times, it's not until well after you've said "I do" that the fantasy fades and it becomes up to your lawyer to help you settle the custody for the leather Dale Earnhardt jacket.

Many first dates take place in restaurants, but restaurants make me anxious. Waiting in line for a table, the lighting, figuring out the menu, and the general hubbub always make me wish I was at home, cooking. I like working in restaurants, not dining in them. I especially enjoyed waiting on couples that were having a first date. What a treat to observe the two sitting there, soaking in that awkward silence, then fumbling for something interesting to say, and all the half smiles and clumsy nodding, without having to experience that nervous knot in my stomach. That is great entertainment.

Having a first date at home allows you plenty of busy work. When things get uncomfortable, one can always torch the Baked Alaska, or malletize the meat. It's also a great opportunity to show off your abilities. Imagine having a first date with someone from Argentina. You need to think: How can I make this magical? You want him to like the food, like your home, and like you. Maybe, to make him feel more relaxed and at home, you could impress him by preparing authentic foods from his homeland. But if you are not familiar with Argentinean cuisine, you are actually showing him what you don't know. It's not a good idea to use the event of a first date to make something you have never made before. If you are set on trying something new, rehearse it first on somebody you would never date, like your ex-husband or former fiancé. To relieve yourself of much pressure and stress for the evening, you could always decide to take a first date to a part of the world you're more familiar with, and in my case I would take him to Greece. It's the only authentic ethnic food I have a handle on, so I like to assume everybody is Greek, whether they are Argentinean, Spanish, or French.

If there are two things I know for sure, it's that animals love snacks and boys eat a lot. So, when I'm cooking for two, I cook for four. This way I'm covered, and if there are leftovers, I can send him home with a package that will remind him of me the next morning.

Of course, having a first date in your home can be risky. If it's not going well, you're stuck. I once agreed to have a first date over for dinner and then found out I had to work that day. I pressed my pantsuit, got my apartment spic-and-span, and decided on a meal that I felt confident I could prepare in an hour: a porterhouse steak, mashed potatoes, salad, and watermelon wedges for dessert. I also planned on serving sangria, because I had a pile of fruit that was beginning to turn. I put out some unshelled walnuts in a bowl to complement the sangria.

When I got home from work, I immediately boiled water for the potatoes, turned on the broiler, and threw my steak in. I only had an hour, but because I had preplanned well, I knew I would make it just under the deadline. Unfortunately, my date showed up fifteen minutes early, empty-handed, and with a friend that wasn't invited. They had stopped for a slice of pizza on the way over, so they said they didn't want to eat "until all that cheese settled." My date then turned on the television so he could catch the last few minutes of the Hornets game. He and his buddy drank multiple glasses of sangria, ate fistfuls of caramels, and emptied my nut bowl as those few minutes dragged on for more than an hour and a half. By the time dinner was on the table the sangria was gone, the potatoes were cold, the salad was limp, and my steak was not only exhausted, it was humiliated. When we got around to dessert, he insisted on carving the watermelon, but dropped it on the floor. Too drunk to hail a cab, he sent his friend home, fell asleep on my bed, and woke up in his own vomit. We dated for two years.

To achieve this look see page 273.

Blind Date Conversational Suggestions

Don't ask hard questions or questions that involve a lot of thinking, such as:

- Does the sun make noise?
- Do you tip a cobbler?
- How do you teach hope?
- When can we see each other again?

Don't Assume Things

- Where did you go to high school? (Maybe he didn't.)
- What does your father do? (Maybe his was murdered.)
- Who did you vote for? (Don't assume he's allowed to.)
- What do you think of my hospitality book? (Don't assume he can read.)

Other Don'ts

- Don't tell everything about yourself, save it for your gynecologist.
- Don't cry.
- If you are drunk, don't call him after he leaves.
- Don't dress too young.
- Don't act too self-sufficient, you'll drive him away.
- Don't answer the door in a wedding dress and veil, he might not think you're joking.
- Be ready when your date arrives; don't pick that time to hop in the shower.
- Don't be a jabber jaw. You learn more by listening than by talking. (However, if your date is a poor storyteller, it's best to sit there silent.)

Remember . . .

- Shower perks you up.
- Bath relaxes you.
- Digestion starts in the mouth.

How to Remove Vomit Stains

Get off as much as you can, soak stain in detergent (enzyme), and run it through some warm water. When you put it in the washing machine, use some bleach. Or just toss it, chances are you've stained it before.

Menu

Stabrous's Tzatziki Sauce with Pita Scoops
Tula's Country-Style Greek Salad (see page 82)
Chicken of the Taverns (see page 202)
Mixed Greek Olives
Panos Manousakis's Galataboureko (Milk Pie)

STABROUS'S TZATZIKI SAUCE WITH PITA SCOOPS

- 1 cucumber
- 1 crushed garlic clove (at least)
- 1 cup plain Greek yogurt*
- 2 teaspoons lemon juice
- 1 teaspoon of dill or mint (optional)

Peel cucumber, quarter lengthwise, and remove seeds. Slice thinly and place in a shallow bowl with coarse salt. Weigh down with plate. Refrigerate for an hour or more. Ring out liquid by handfuls then ring it out in a dish towel.

Mix cucumber and crushed garlic into yogurt. Add lemon juice and dill or mint. Salt to taste. Serve with bread or pita scoops or with a salad.

*If you can't find Greek yogurt, you can place regular plain yogurt in a coffee filter over a bowl, and drain it in the refrigerator overnight.

PANOS MANOUSAKIS'S GALATABOUREKO (MILK PIE)

- ¼ cup of butter plus 1 stick of butter, melted
- 4 cups of milk
- ¾ cup of sugar
- ¾ cup of fine semolina
- Grated rind of half a lemon
- 1 cinnamon stick
- Pinch of salt
- 2 teaspoons of pure vanilla extract
- 5 eggs, lightly beaten
- 1 pound box of phyllo dough
- Syrup (recipe follows)

Mix the ¼ cup butter, milk, sugar, semolina, lemon rind, cinnamon stick, and salt in a heavy saucepan and heat until thick, stirring constantly. Let it bubble over low heat for 3–5 minutes. Remove from heat and remove the cinnamon stick. Cover mixture with a piece of buttered waxed paper to prevent skin from forming. When cool, blend in the vanilla and eggs.

Butter a 13 x 9 x 3-inch oven dish. Place 6 sheets of phyllo in the dish, brushing each sheet with the melted butter. Pour in the custard and top with remaining sheets (about 8), again brushing each sheet with the melted butter. Brush the top with remaining butter and score through top 3 sheets of phyllo, making 3-inch squares. Using a sharp knife, trim the edges and bake in oven at 350 degrees for 45 minutes until golden brown. Let cool. Make syrup and pour over the pie. Let pie cool before serving.

SYRUP FOR GALATABOUREKO:

1 cup of sugar

1 cup of water

1 cinnamon stick

1/2 tablespoon of lemon juice

Put all the ingredients into a saucepan and stir until the sugar dissolves.

Bring the mixture to a boil (should be on stove for about 10 minutes).

Strain the syrup and when it is lukewarm pour it over the pie.

If you're the one leaving:

- Pack an overnight bag, you don't want to be seen walking the beltline in a Greek dress the next morning.

- Don't leave a piece of jewelry at his house so you can go back and get it later; he may be with his real girlfriend.

If he's the one staying:

- Pack the medicine chest: Trojans.

> $ Start a money jar together, matching what he has in his wallet, and then continue this on every date. If you choose to stop seeing each other, you'll have a jar full of money that you can spend on a Grieving Kit (see page 123) for yourself. It's similar to divorce money.

If you end up spending a lot of time in bed together with nothing to do, quiz each other on all the states capitals, then move on to learning 10 new vocabulary words a night. Good times.

Frigid, incontinent, impudent, Clydesdale, vaginitis, homosexual, ennui, ampersand, charcuterie, abstinence.

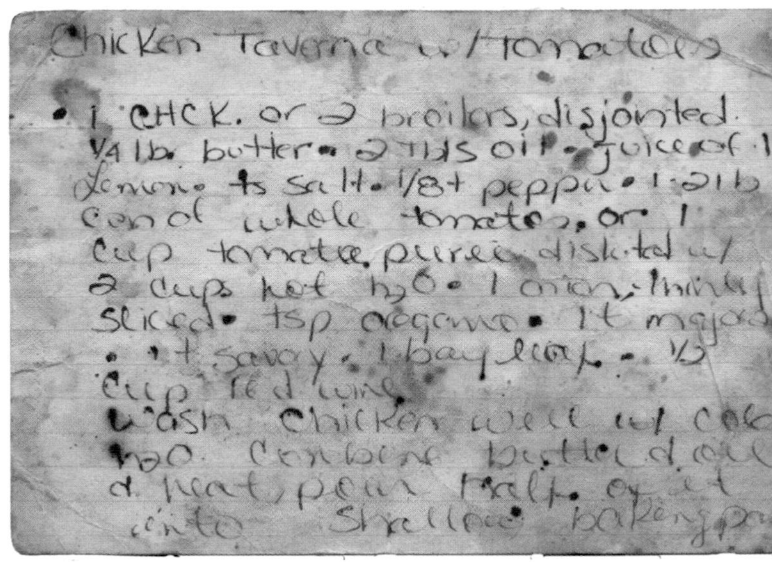

Chicken Taverna w/ Tomatoes

• 1 CHCK. or 2 broilers, disjointed. 1/4 lb. butter • 2 TBS oil • juice of 1 lemon • ts salt • 1/8 t pepper • 1-2 lb can of whole tomatoes, or 1 cup tomato puree diluted w/ 2 cups hot H2O • 1 onion, thinly sliced • tsp oregano • 1t marjoram • 1t savory, 1 bay leaf • 1/2 cup red wine. Wash chicken well w/ cold H2O. Combine butter, oil & heat, pour half of it into shallow baking pan

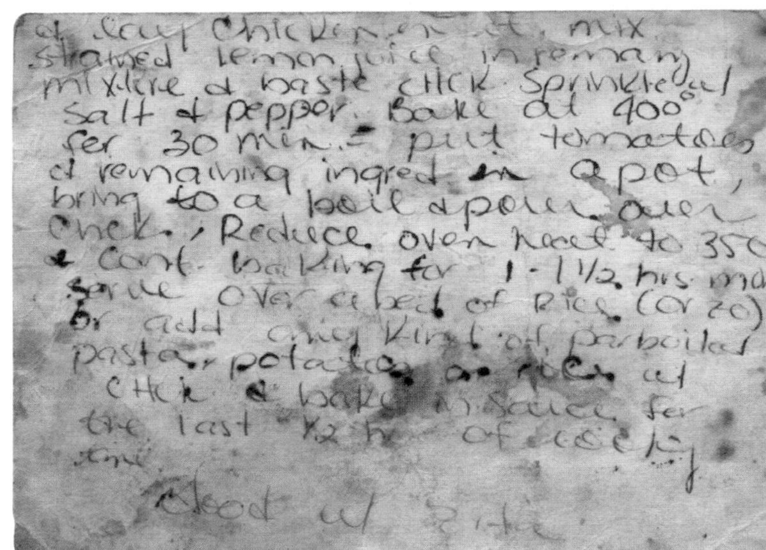

& lay chicken on it. mix strained lemon juice in remaining mixture & baste chick. Sprinkle w/ salt & pepper. Bake at 400° for 30 min. – put tomatoes & remaining ingred in a pot, bring to a boil & pour over chick., Reduce oven heat to 350 & cont. baking for 1-1 1/2 hrs more. Serve over a bed of Rice (or zo) or add any kind of parboiled pasta, potatoes or rice at chick & bake in sauce for the last 1/2 hr of cooking time.

Good w/ pita

Gift Idea for Ex If You Are Still on Speaking Terms

If you have a lot photographs of your ex and feel bad about cutting them up and throwing them away, take the pictures and make a self-esteem collage with them and give it to the person on their next birthday disguised as a card. If it's a good picture of them they would want it back anyway.

✈ Guys don't like skimpy meals, salads, lamb chops with handles, hot fruit.

✱ Guys like meat, extra portions, pies, gravy, toothpicks, and pussy.

Extra, Extra

In Greece, umbilical cords are saved from baby boys and frozen (see What Not to Put in Your Refrigerator). When someone gets pregnant, fresh bread is baked using the cord and fed to the pregnant woman in hopes that she will have a baby boy, because girls don't count.

Optional Menu
Telly Savalas Chicken
Roasted Potatoes in Their Jackets
Hercules Creamed Rice
Coffee

HERCULES CREAMED RICE (PUDDING)

1 cup of water

1/2 cup of short grain rice

4 cups of milk

1/4 teaspoon of salt

2 egg yolks

2 teaspoons of corn flour

3 tablespoons of sugar

1 teaspoon of pure vanilla extract

Ground nutmeg or cinnamon

Using a heavy saucepan, boil the water, stir in rice and cook until water is gone.

Add milk and salt and bring to a boil, stirring occasionally. Cook uncovered for about 20 minutes.

In a separate bowl, blend egg yolks with corn flour and add a little cold milk.

Mix in 1/2 cup of the hot creamed rice, then return to pan contents, stirring over heat, until it thickens. Add the vanilla, and some sugar to taste. Pour into individual bowls. Sprinkle a little nutmeg or cinnamon on top.

You can eat this warm or cold.

TELLY SAVALAS CHICKEN

2 small whole chickens

1/2 cup fresh lemon juice

Oregano

Salt and pepper

Season the cavity of the chicken with lemon juice, oregano, salt, and pepper.

Rub skin with oil. Sprinkle with more seasonings and lemon juice to coat evenly. Broil the chicken 3–5 minutes on each side, turning three to five times until brown and crusty on all sides. Set chicken aside.

About an hour before serving, preheat oven to 325 degrees F. Bake chicken 45–60 minutes.

When done baking, skim the fat from the pan juices, then spoon drippings over chicken. Sprinkle with lemon juice. Garnish with lemon slices and parsley.

ROASTED POTATOES IN THEIR JACKETS*

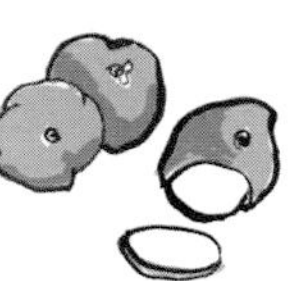

Use as many small red or creamer potatoes as you wish

Olive oil

Sea salt

Put olive oil in a roasting pan and add plenty of coarse sea salt. Add potatoes (whole) and bake at 400 degrees F for 45 minutes. Shake the pan once in a while so the salt will coat the potatoes. You can add any herbs you want to. These are good served at room temperature, or cold the next day.

*Pictured on page 48.

Pork Medallions

a Rich Uncle comes to Visit

Entertainingly speaking, nothing is more taxing than having an unexpected guest drop by, or an out-of-town guest looking for a place to stay (see "The Unexpected Guest," page 59), but occasionally there can be a circumstance where you are actually motivated to be hospitable to this type of special needs person. The circumstance sometimes comes in the form of a rich uncle. One might wonder why some guests are more important to impress than others. Well, officially all guests should be treated the same. But let's say a rich uncle does come to visit—this might be a perfect opportunity to see just how much you can class up your act. Make a game of it. Make it your goal to impress your rich uncle to the point where his heart is so filled with unbridled gratitude that he will kick up his heels or perhaps bump up your take of his fortune when he adjusts his will.

Even if by most standards you live modestly, there are plenty of simple touches you can do that will make even the most jaded rich uncle think twice about your inheritance.

One afternoon, I was graced by a surprise visit from my rich uncle. Not having seen him in years, I initially mistook him for a confused old dandy, so I showered him with insults and was gearing up for a door slam when he informed me that he was my rich uncle from upstate. I turned on a dime and immediately ushered him in, making light of the many colorful quips I had made earlier such as, "Why don't you try the train station, that's where all the old fags go to prey on young boys." I think this turned out to be a pretty good icebreaker. After I took his cane, along with his cap and cape, he informed me that he had some banking business in town and had hoped to stay the night. I couldn't have been more enthused! I quickly made him comfortable on the couch, offered him a cocktail, and told him I had a few preparations to make. I tossed on my old apron—the one with all the holes in it—because it is comfortable. I joked with my rich uncle that even if I did have the money to buy a new apron I might decide to keep this old tattered one anyway, just for sentimental reasons. In the bedroom, I rotated the mattress so it felt brand new and firm. I provided a rack for his suitcase and cleared the closet for a place to hang his cape. I made sure there was an extra blanket. I set a collection of short stories that I put together myself (see page 57) on a small table next to the bed. I also placed a good reading lamp, an alarm clock, and a tea bell (see page 162) on the table. After refreshing my rich uncle's cocktail, I told him I had a few more preparations to make in the bedroom. When he suggested that he sleep on the couch, I insisted he sleep in the bedroom. I apologized for not having a bigger apartment, and added that because rents are so expensive in the city, this working girl will just have to make do. I smiled and headed back into the bedroom with a number of items to place by the bed: a bowl of plastic fruit, fresh water, a bottle of aspirin, hand cream, a writing tablet, a pen, paper, envelopes, and stamps. Since my room doesn't have a window, I put up a picture of a window and then added drapes. After he fell asleep, I sprinkled a trail of glitter from the window to his bed so when he awoke he could imagine a fairy had come to visit him while he was sleeping. I also gathered some bricks and stones from the basement that I could heat in the oven and place around his pillow to keep his head warm (see picture of "Potato Stone," page 56). I placed a pair of his underpants on the radiator so they would be nice and

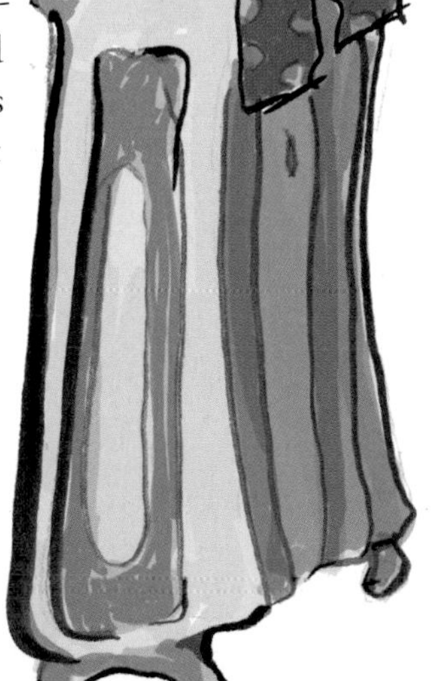

toasty after his morning bath. I quickly grabbed an old pair of pantyhose and fashioned a bath sachet (see page 267) and I filled the other leg with a bag of lima beans to make an "eye burrito," which I put in the freezer until well chilled for him to place on his eyes or neck as a soothing compress (see page 267). As I planned the menu for dinner, my Rich Uncle commented on the broom straw I had just placed through my earring holes. I mentioned that this was a good way to keep the holes from closing until I could scrape up enough money to buy some store-bought earrings or, if that proved too difficult, I could collect some returnable bottles, and with the change, purchase some string that I could use to replace the straw.

The next morning, after my rich uncle left, I was quite surprised to find, in the donation can I had absentmindedly left by the side of his bed, a check made out to me. A good host provides warmth and comfort without expecting anything in return, but occasionally our sincere and honorable actions are rewarded, though not always in the amount that we had hoped and are certain a rich uncle can afford.

Menu

Silver Bullet Smoky Martini
Pork Medallions
Golden Yukon Potato Wedges French Fried in Olive Oil
Carrot Coins
Rich Chocolate Cake
Coffee or Tea

Breakfast Menu

Silver Dollar Pancakes
Coffee or Tea

SILVER BULLET SMOKY MARTINI

½ ounce gin

¼ ounce dry vermouth

float 1½ ounces Scotch

Serve straight up in a chilled martini glass. Garnish with a lemon zest or olive.

PORK MEDALLIONS

2 pork tenderloins, rubbed with garlic, salt, and pepper

Heat ovenproof skillet with enough olive oil to coat the bottom, plus 1 tablespoon of butter. Sear (brown) on all sides. Finish in a 350 degree F oven, 20–25 minutes. Remove, allow to relax. Slice the pork into medallions at thicker ends.

How to Remove Wine Stains

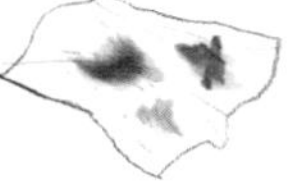

You don't. Boil your garment in a pot of hot chopped beets and water.

CARROT COINS

Slice carrots so they look like coins. Sauté with butter, salt, and pepper.

GOLDEN YUKON POTATO WEDGES FRENCH FRIED IN OLIVE OIL

6 medium/large Yukon gold potatoes, olive oil (or olive pomace or sunflower oil), salt, pepper, and parsley

Wash potatoes well. Wrap them individually in aluminum foil and bake at 400 degrees F, for 30–35 minutes (¾ of the way through). Remove from oven and allow to cool. Cut in ½ lengthwise and again into wedges (steak cut). Using a deep pan, fill it ⅔ full with oil. Heat to 350 degrees F. Drop wedges into the oil in small batches, and fry until golden brown (they will rise to the top). Remove to paper towel and season with salt and pepper immediately. Garnish with chopped parsley leaves.

SILVER DOLLAR PANCAKES

2 cups flour	2 eggs
1 teaspoon baking soda	2 cups buttermilk
¼ teaspoon salt	1 tablespoon butter, melted
2 tablespoons sugar	1 cup banana, mashed, optional

Mix dry ingredients together. Beat eggs and buttermilk together, and add dry ingredients. Beat until smooth and add butter. Pour into pitcher. Heat and grease griddle. Pour batter into 2" rounds. Brown and flip when air bubbles form in the batter.

How To:

Measure felt around book leaving 3 or 4 inches on each side to fold under and 1/4 inch extra on top and bottom edges. Cut. Fold sides and stitch on top and bottom to create pocket. Stitch to center front of book cover. Trim and decorate with appliqués and embroidery. Fill with your favorite short stories. Excellent.

RICH CHOCOLATE CAKE

You will need:

Water, cocoa, buttermilk, unsalted butter, sugar, eggs, vanilla, flour, baking soda, baking powder, salt

I use this recipe for chocolate cupcakes as well.

In a bowl combine: ¾ cup of boiling water, ¾ cup of cocoa, 1 cup buttermilk and mix together until smooth and then set aside. In a mixer, beat 1½ sticks unsalted butter and 1¾ cups sugar until fluffy. Add 4 eggs, beating after you add each one. Add 2 teaspoons vanilla, 2½ cups flour, 1½ teaspoons of baking soda, ½ teaspoon baking powder, and 1 teaspoon salt, and combine this mixture with the chocolate mixture. Pour into a sheet pan or a cupcake pan or two 9-inch cake pans. Bake for about 25 minutes.

FROSTING:

Rich chocolate whipped cream:

6 tablespoons of cocoa, 1 cup of sugar, 2 cups of whipping cream, ¼ teaspoon of salt

Stir well and chill for an hour or two. Then whip in chilled bowl using chilled beaters.

First-Class Suggestions Fit for a King

Put the cake plates in the freezer to serve dessert or salad on.

Chill your beer mugs and martini glasses; nothing is better than a frosty mug or glass.

Heat your dinner plates in the oven, or if you have a dishwasher, run them through the dry cycle. (The dishwasher is also a good place to steam fish, by putting it in foil and having the dishwasher steam it for you.)

See how to make this fake cake on page 279.

the Unexpected Guest

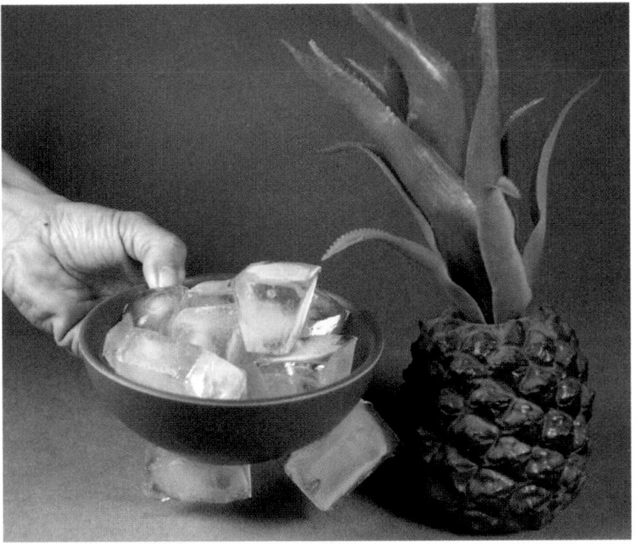

Unfortunately, not all unexpected guests are rich uncles, but fortunately, I have a doorman so I can pretend I am not at home. I seldom answer my phone anyway because I can't hear it; the volume is turned down. Either way, I am prepared. But if my defenses fail and the unexpected guest does slip through, I accept the inconvenience and act as hospitable as possible. I make a point never to apologize for being caught unprepared, for they're the ones who busted in on me.

The unexpected guest comes in many forms, sizes, and shapes. It could be a fair-weather friend, a former teacher, a police officer, or a priest. You could get a call from someone at the bus station looking to kill a couple of hours or they could "just happen to be in the lobby" or neighborhood. Maybe they grew up in your home before you lived there and want to reminisce. Perhaps it's a Girl Scout selling cookies or an escaped convict on the run. Maybe Social Services has dropped by and it's important to play a gracious host while concealing what they are so desperate to find. Whatever the situation, this is where your hospitality is put to the test.

Because I live in a small apartment, I can't stock a lot of food due to a lack of space, not to mention cockroaches, mice, and the occasional rat. But I do try to be prepared the best I can when unexpected guests arrive by having a few basic things in the refrigerator that I can whip into something for drive-bys or munchies. Canned goods are a safe bet. I always have a couple of jars of stuffed grape leaves or a can of peanuts. I have spaghetti, butter, and of course, lots of greens (because that's all my rabbit eats), things that can be thrown together in 15 minutes (see "15-Minute Meals in 20 Minutes," page 196), as well as plenty of cupcakes and cheese balls, because of my business. Growing up, my neighbors always had a frozen cake in their coffin-like freezer in the basement for an unexpected guest, because it thaws out fast. I also know someone who kept pineapple flavored ice cubes somewhere in the house to add to a drink to make it special.

An unexpected guest means you have to be quick on your feet and adapt to any situation. If someone brings their two-year-old to my home I have to immediately hide my reaction and quickly think about what might be at their eye level, like knives, lighters, or candles.

If the unexpected guest is pressuring you to allow them to crash on your futon for the night, be prepared to pull out one of those excuses you've been saving in your back pocket, like, "I'd love for you to stay, but they're fumigating for rats," or "I found a spider sack."

Feel free to turn the tables on an unexpected guest. If you are a single girl, an old person, or someone who is injured, sick, or obese, take advantage of having an extra set of hands. Have them put a shelf up, set clocks back, remove a mouse from a mousetrap, rotate a mattress, or snake a drain. If you're the unexpected guest doing the visiting, be considerate and appear with something heavy that is a pain in the ass to haul up six flights of stairs, such as fireplace logs, kitty litter, charcoal, bottled water, or birdseed.

I find my timer to be a great tool when it comes to unexpected visitors because it keeps track of the time so you don't have to. I bring one with me when I drop in on people.

5406 Nut Meat Beige 5406

1812 Dries Darker Beige 1812

727 Beigier Beige 727

690 Stale Beige 690

224 Thin Gravy Beige 224

1020 Barely Beige 1020

40 Lighter Than The One Above This One 40

Unfortunately, the one thing you can expect with most unexpected guests is that they are not expected anywhere. So when the unexpected guest doesn't know when to leave, expect to educate them. I recently had a gay friend drop by unannounced. This is always a high-alert situation. If you don't act quickly he may become a permanent fixture. You can always lie. Make up a story, such as: "Don't mind me. The doctors said the best thing for my yeast infection was to expose my vagina to the air."

OR

"Oh, I'm so glad you're here. You can help me pick out the best photos of my vagina from these contact sheets."

OR

"You can't stay. It's March Madness" (or whatever month Madness it is when they drop in). This is a sports-related reference and will work well on all but the jockiest gay men.

OR

"If you stay, you can help me babysit the babies in the back room—I'll go get them."

Homosexuals are easy to fool because they have such great imaginations. Try to avoid allowing him to get high or drunk. This will really cloud his sense of time. If he does insist on drinking, this is your chance to empty your stash of weird liquors. Gay men will drink anything alcoholic because most of them feel a great need to escape, but pour heavy because he's not leaving until those bottles are empty. Never ask for advice, such as his opinion on beige versus tan. He will go on for hours. As a last recourse, yawn a lot, especially when he's speaking. Hopefully he'll get tired of hearing you say, "I'm sorry, what was that?"

Kourambiethes

Cold Cuts Anytime

As an unexpected guest, you present quite a challenge to your gracious host, but nothing nearly as crippling as the out-of-town guest. When the unexpected guest hijacks a host's valuable time it's only for hours, while an out-of-town guest can be around for days, even weeks. So, if you are an out-of-town guest, be classy and find somewhere else to stay. If you're not classy or you're a family member, here are a few suggestions on how to be a tolerable out-of-town guest:

- Make it clear to your host exactly how long you will be staying. This allows them to see a light at the end of the tunnel.
- Never arrive uninvited, like an earthquake, with a lame excuse. Nobody likes a shocker.
- Try to be in good spirits. You've already burdened your host with your stay, don't add insult to injury by expressing your disappointment about not getting better tickets to *No, No, Nanette* or *The Drowsy Chaperone* on off Broadway.
- Don't arrive saying you have chiggers, scabies, ringworm, or lice. Keep your parasites to yourself.
- Make sure you have a game plan for your trip so your host doesn't have to also play events coordinator. The last thing your host wants to hear from you is, "So, what's shakin' for today?"
- Bring two books to read or one to write.
- Don't bring a gift like flavored coffee or a personalized mug unless you know for sure that's what your host is into or even worse, don't show up empty-handed. If you don't know your host's tastes, bring a little something like a bottle of wine or stamps. Then, be a good detective while you're there. Scope something out that would be more appropriate for her, like a new pair of dish washing gloves, coffee filters, a romance novel, a carton of cigarettes or, better yet, how about replacing that bottle of Tia Maria you emptied? You can always send them a gift after you've left, along with your thank-you check.

- Don't show up with a pet you need to bury.
- Pack lightly when visiting. Nothing will scare a host more than matching luggage and a hatbox.
- Never put down your host's town or compare it to where you are from.
- Keep your belongings together and not scattered about. This applies double in the bathroom. Bring a dopp kit.
- If you are sleeping on the couch, fold your bedding and put it away before you get up and don't oversleep.
- Don't make extra work for your host. Clean up after yourself. If you drop change on the floor or see packing peanuts, pick them up.
- Don't expect to be waited on.
- Don't steal anything and stay out of the medicine chest.
- Be respectful of furniture and other belongings. Don't put your luggage on the table afraid that the rabbit might chew on the identification tag, or sit on the couch and pour iodine on an open sore.
- If you break something, replace it. I once had a friend over who broke a dinner plate and he was gay enough to realize that the plate he broke was a Russell Wright. The next day I received eight of them.
- If you take a nap, leave your clothes on. Don't get naked and get under the covers. Naps involve clothing.
- Don't invite other people over, answer the phone or the door, or adjust the temperature. Don't turn on the TV or hi-fi without asking.
- Don't give your host's number out so you can receive personal calls, especially if it's a drug connection. Always pay for any calls that you make.
- When given choices, make a decision. Breast or thigh? Can or bottle? Parcheesi or Chinese checkers? Grand Central Station or JFK? Pick one.
- Let your host know of any dietary restrictions. Are you fatally allergic to root vegetables or only eating purple foods this month?
- Offer to help with household chores such as setting the table, raking leaves, washing windows, painting baseboards, or digging a grave.
- If you do smoke cigarettes or marijuana, or you drink a lot of beer, then bring it with you. Don't suck the hostess dry and then just leave. I went to a wedding on a boat once, and my date was a smoker and didn't even bring any cigarettes. He mooched off other people all night long on a four-hour boat ride. He should have bought three packs just so people could mooch off him.
- Don't flirt with the boyfriend or husband.
- Don't leave anything behind—nothing's worse than your host having to mail your forgotten golf umbrella.

- Don't dye your hair while you're there.
- My mother always said "Don't bother other people." I think that's good advice.

Other Preparations for an Out-of -Town Guest

Regardless of the situation an out-of-town guest presents, it's important to rise to the occasion and be the best host that you can be. Here are a few ways to make your out-of-towner's stay as painless and pleasant as possible.

- Offer them a ride to the airport.
- Ask if your guest needs anything, like an iron, hangers, or a razor. Always have spares.
- Never, under any circumstances, leave a guest alone in your apartment, especially if you have something to hide. They will find it because they are looking for it.
- Take into consideration how they traveled to get to you. Are they jet-lagged, fresh off a boat, or cramped from an eighteen-hour bus ride?
- Always act interested in their small-town stories even if you aren't. Don't assume that your stories are any more interesting than theirs.
- You should let your guest know ahead of time if you've planned a certain activity (see example below), so they have enough time to psych themselves up or to pack the proper tranquilizer if it's something they loathe to do.

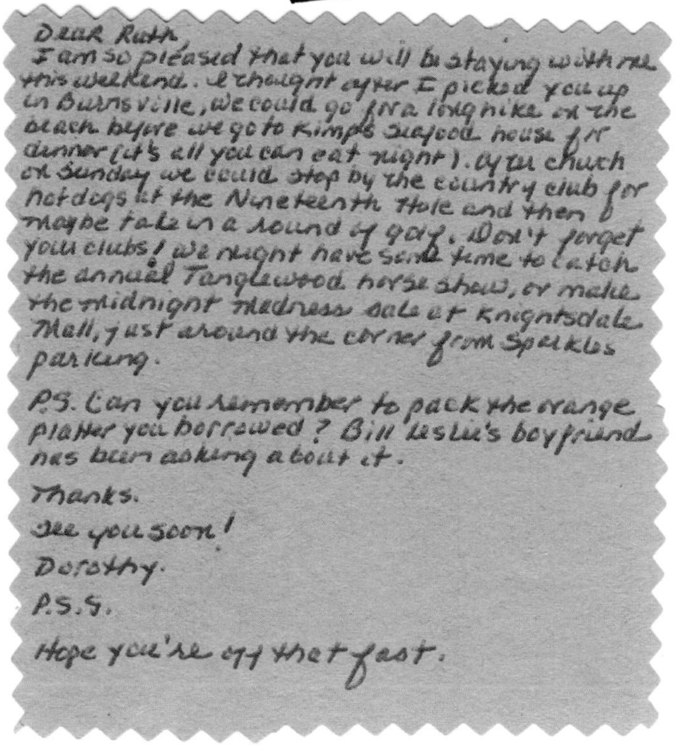

Dear Ruth,
I am so pleased that you will be staying with me this weekend. I thought after I picked you up in Burnsville, we could go for a long hike on the beach before we go to Kimp's Seafood House for dinner (it's all you can eat night). After church on Sunday we could stop by the country club for hot dogs at the Nineteenth Hole and then maybe take in a round of golf. Don't forget your clubs! We might have some time to catch the annual Tanglewood horse show, or make the Midnight Madness sale at Knightsdale Mall, just around the corner from Sparkles parking.

P.S. Can you remember to pack the orange platter you borrowed? Bill Leslie's boyfriend has been asking about it.

Thanks.

See you soon!

Dorothy.

P.S.S.

Hope you're off that fast.

This invitation tells Ruth exactly what to pack.

- Don't plan every minute of your guest's stay. They might have planned their own trip or simply not want a plan at all.
- If you want to splurge, show them one of your money jars and tell them, "This is what we have to blow" or better yet, ask them to contribute to it before they leave.
- If you know what your guest likes, stock a few of their favorite food items or drinks. And if this particular guest comes to visit often, consider having something monogrammed for them, such as towels or a branding iron for steaks. Triple initials, Jocelyn Ellen Wortis.
- Plan a menu that will provide you with multiple meals such as a ham, turkey, or a meat loaf or plenty of cold cuts. This way your guest can make himself sandwiches or a late-night snack. Do-ahead dishes are great for weekend stays.
- Have some busy work you can do together while sitting around catching up, like frosting cupcakes, snapping beans, shucking corn, squeezing limes, or shelling walnuts. Good mindless things make it easy to carry on a conversation. Avoid counting change, reading, playing solitaire, or listening to music with headphones. These activities don't leave you open for conversation.
- If you have a lot of errands to run, invite your guest along; it's a good time to talk and it's a great way for them to sightsee.
- A good trick is to fill your medicine cabinet with marbles. Nothing announces a nosey guest better than an avalanche of marbles hitting a porcelain sink. Plus you'll know which guest is a junkie whore or gutter hype, and you'll know what else to hide. Count your stash or remove the labels from your prescription bottles.

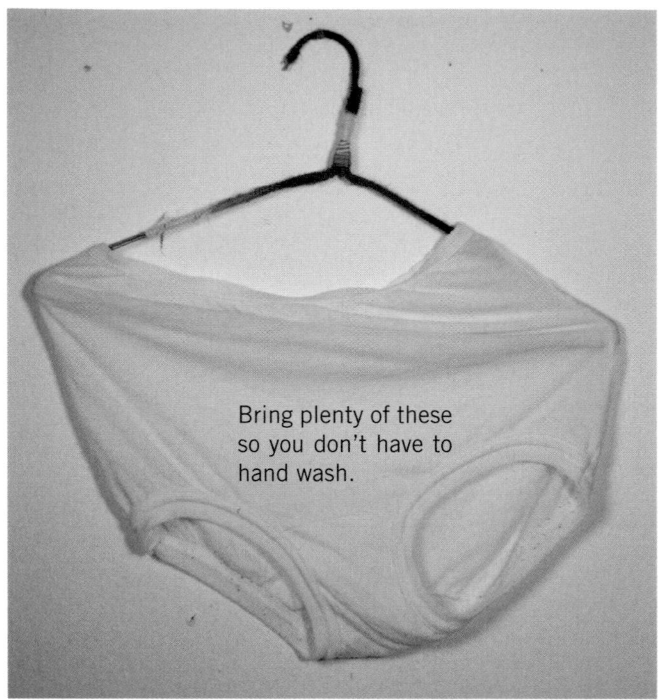

Bring plenty of these so you don't have to hand wash.

Gift Suggestions for a Hostess from an Out-of-Town Guest

Books

Flowers or plants, depending on yard

Tree identification tags (see picture, page 293)

Ashtray

Hairbrush

Umbrella

Stationery for guest room

Personalized matches

Expensive candle

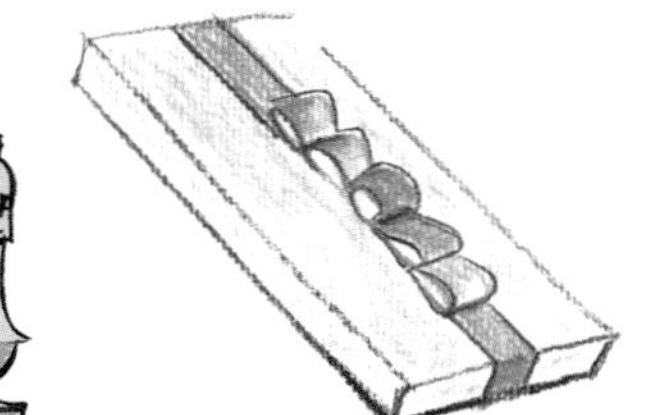

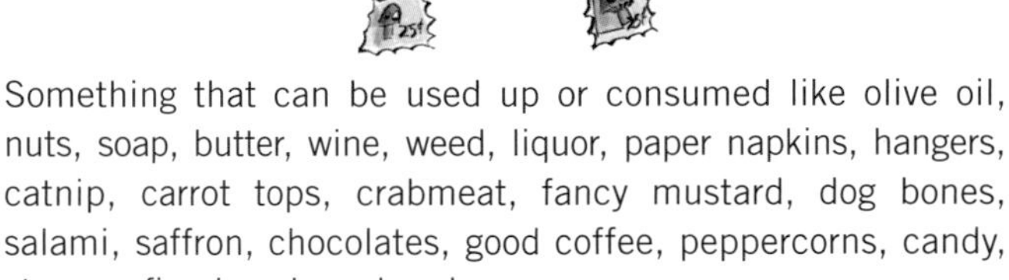

Something that can be used up or consumed like olive oil, nuts, soap, butter, wine, weed, liquor, paper napkins, hangers, catnip, carrot tops, crabmeat, fancy mustard, dog bones, salami, saffron, chocolates, good coffee, peppercorns, candy, stamps, fireplace logs, hand cream.

Breakfast for Sleepy Hollow Heads

There is an old saying that goes, "Eat breakfast like a king, lunch like a citizen, and dinner like a beggar." I don't live by that, but I like repeating it. For me I prefer, "Eat breakfast like a peasant on a hunger strike, lunch like a serf with gastroenteritis, and dinner like a jester who has just raided the pantry when the king's away." In other words, I don't eat breakfast. Lunch weighs me down and dinner never ends (see "Munchies," page 96). Of course, this lifestyle probably explains my problem areas. Although I don't eat breakfast, I do sometimes contribute to the breakfast table on special occasions. I like to make coffee cake. Coffee cake is also an appropriate dish to give to a person when they have lost someone special, or when you want to bring a tasty treat to a morning meeting. I make this cake every Christmas morning. The recipe is based on a recipe from an old Sunset cookbook my mother had that I can't find.

CINNAMON SOUR CREAM COFFEE CAKE

You will be placing this cake in a cold oven, then setting the oven to 350 degrees and baking for 55 minutes. You will need 9-inch greased tube pan.

Beat until light and fluffy:

2 sticks of unsalted butter

1¼ cups of sugar

2 eggs

Blend in:

1 cup of sour cream

2 cups of sifted flour

½ teaspoon of baking soda

1½ teaspoons of baking powder

Add into butter mixture.

Add: 2 teaspoons of pure vanilla extract

Blend well.

Spoon half the mixture into the tube pan (this batter will be thick), sprinkle half the nut mixture (below) over the batter. Then spoon the rest of the thick batter on top of that and top with remaining nut mixture.

For the nut mixture, I use a small, hand, nut grinder: Grind 1 cup of finely chopped walnut meats and mix with 1¼ teaspoons of cinnamon and 2 tablespoons of sugar.

Coffee Cake

Carrot and Potato Bracelet instructions on page 281.

I LIKE
YOU

Strawberry Shortcake

LUMBERJAC

No one appreciates a hot, hearty lunch quite like a lumberjack. These brawny, bearded men definitely know how to work up an appetite. What with their logrolling, vertical chopping, and sawing, it's no wonder they grab for seconds. Most of the lumberjacks I know have a simple palate. They tend to like their whole meal on one plate or in a single bowl, which is why I'll be making stew. Lumberjacks are no nonsense. I never serve appetizers to my lumberjacks. They don't like cocktails and they don't like cordials. They're not big on nuts. Perhaps it's all the squirrels they come in contact with on the job, or it could be unshelled nuts are just not worth a lumberjack's effort. Lumberjacks have a one-track mind. Like a brown bear fresh from hibernation, they can become confused and easily agitated when not fed quickly. It's important not to dillydally in the presence of a lumberjack. The last thing a lumberjack wants to hear on a lunch break is, "Why don't you relax while I prepare you some lunch." A lumberjack is a working man and his time is limited.

It's fine to serve a lumberjack food on plastic dishware and you should always permit them to use bread as a utensil. As a general rule allow a lumberjack to dine alone. Treat them like fireworks: "light fuse and back away." Serve them large portions quickly, and then swiftly retreat to a "safe place" until the gorging has ended.

Don't question a lumberjack and never look one in the eye. Be polite when suggesting they remove their cleats, but be prepared if they don't. I always have a clear path to the table, and another to the bathroom. Feeding lumberjacks can be very rewarding when you take care to follow all the necessary precautions.

Lumberjack Prayer

Bless us O Lord for logs we chop,

Logs we roll and trees we drop,

We swing our ax until we stop,

For rolls with butter and pork of chop,

We'll chow until the forest beckons,

A hearty stew of potatoes and bacons,

Oh O Lord, one thing we reckons,

Enough with the chatter, how 'bout seconds?

by Sven Halvorson

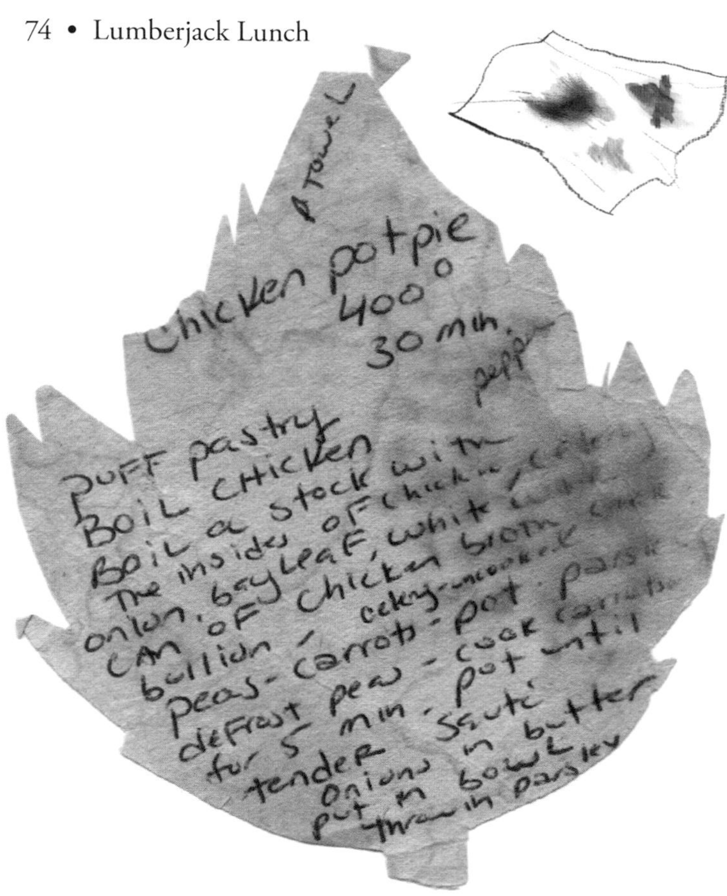

Mud Stain Removal

Make sure that the mud stain on the rug has dried. Vacuum the dirt off. Take some laundry soap and work it into the stain. This should work. If not just turn the rug over and deny it ever happened.

Gift Ideas for Lumberjacks

LUMBER JACK

- Underpants
- Harmonica and neck supporter
- Ax guard
- Socks
- Insect repellent
- Sandwich meat
- Guide on poisonous plants
- Tweezers for splinters
- Tea tree oil shampoo
- Book of haunted stories
- White jeans
- Wood grain lighter (see "Personalized Lighters," page 288)
- Toilet paper caddy
- Sit-upon
- Compass
- Buck knife
- Paper cutter

Menu

Crosscut Stump Stew

Stack of White Bread

Lumberjack's Vanishing Oatmeal Raisin Cookies
(see page 231)

CROSSCUT STUMP STEW

Preheat oven to 350 degrees F. Serves one lumberjack, or six people.

- 2 pounds of stewing beef, (cut into 2-inch cubes)
- 3 tablespoons of olive oil
- 1 medium onion, chopped
- 2 garlic cloves, crushed
- 1 cup tomato puree
- 1/2 cup of red wine
- 2 tablespoons of wine vinegar
- 1 bay leaf
- 1 3-inch cinnamon stick
- 4 whole cloves
- Sugar
- Salt and pepper
- 1 1/2 pounds of small pearl onions

Brown your cubed beef on all sides in a pan of hot oil and then transfer to a casserole dish. Add onion and garlic to the pan. Add more oil or butter if you need to, fry until the onion is soft. Add tomato puree, wine, and vinegar and stir. Pour this over the meat cubes in the casserole dish, and add the bay leaf, cinnamon, cloves, sugar, and salt and pepper.

Cover and cook in oven for 1 hour, or cook on stove, slowly. While beef is cooking, boil a pan of water. Remove roots and tops of pearl onions. Crosscut (score) the root end and place in a bowl. Cover in boiling water for 2 minutes, then drain off water. The skins will slip off easily. Add the onions to stew and continue to simmer on low until the meat and onions are tender and the sauce is thick. (About 1 1/2 hours or longer.)

Optional Menu

Chip Chop Chicken Pot Pie (see page 205)

Stack of White Bread

Bailiwick Gingersnaps (see page 231)

HOW TO MAKE A SIT-UPON —

This is really big in Brownies. A sit-upon is seating for outdoor events like sing-alongs and native american melodramas. Also protection from the cold linoleum floor of the school lunchroom where brownie meetings often occur.

YOU CAN USE A VYNLE BACKED TABLE CLOTH OR ANY PIECE OF NAUGAHIDE THAT MAY BE LAYING AROUND IF YOU USE A STORE BOUGHT TABLE CLOTH. THE NORMAL SIZE IT COMES IN IS 54"x90" —THESE DON'T COST TOO MUCH AND YOU CAN MAKE AROUND 9 SIT-UPONS. YOU DO THE MATH!

- TO MAKE A BASIC SITUPON CUT THE VYNLE, NAUGAHIDE, WHAT HAVE YOU, INTO 15"x30" RECTANGLE USING PINKING SHEARS IF YOU HAVE THEM.

USE A HOLE PUNCH TO PUNCH HOLES ABOUT EVERY INCH ALL THE WAY AROUND 1/2" FROM THE SIDE.

- IF YOU ARE DEALING WITH SMALL CHILDREN YOU MAY HAVE TO PUNCH HOLES FOR THEM

- AFTER FOLDING THE VYNLE OR WHATEVER. IN HALF YOU SHOULD STUFF IT WITH A 13"x13" PIECE OF OLD CARPET PADDING OR OTHER THIN FOAM OR IF YOU REALLY HAVE NOTHING THEN FOLDED NEWSPAPERS

- USING YARN OR STRING WRAPPED WITH A PIECE OF TAPE (ANY) ON ONE END, TO ACT AS A SEWING NEEDLE YOU CAN SEW ALL THE WAY AROUND USING A STRAIGHT OR OVERLAY STITCH - THEN TIE OFF THE YARN OR STRING AND VOILA

- TIP YOU CAN DECORATE YOUR SIT UPON WITH NAIL POLISH, SPRAY PAINT OR MODEL CAR ENAMEL PAINTS.
- AND USE PIRATE IMAGRY.

Lemon Chess Tarts

Out to Brunch

I don't like brunch. Brunch is a combination of breakfast and lunch. I could never date somebody who was into brunch, that's a deal breaker. I don't like the ceremony attached to brunch. Brunch requires me to gather in the early afternoon or late morning with other people so we can talk while we eat a big meal and then when it's over, what? I'm stuffed, I'm talked out, I'm tired and lazy as if all my bones left my body and it's not even one o'clock in the afternoon. I like looking forward to dinner, and a lunchtime breakfast burrito or a heaping helping of huevos rancheros robs me of that. People who normally like to drink during the day love brunch because they can drink and not hide it. With brunch, they don't have to be embarrassed about being soused in the middle of the afternoon.

The last time I hosted a brunch was New Year's Day a number of years ago. I only agreed to have it because it was a request. I didn't call it brunch because I don't like the term.

Because brunches at home tend to be buffet style, it's a great opportunity to be brave and serve a dish you have never made before. That way, you can mix it amongst the more common dishes and take note of its reception. When using a large table to display your brunch buffet, it's fun to go crazy with the food decorations, like butter molds and radish carvings or create pickle fans and celery curls. Brunch is also a good time to serve exotic teas. Because brunch is a daytime activity, people feel comfortable bringing their children. My brunch was no exception. Fortunately I was able to turn this unfortunate facet of brunch into a money-making opportunity because, after all, who doesn't want a photo of their child taken on the first day of the year, especially when it costs only peanuts?

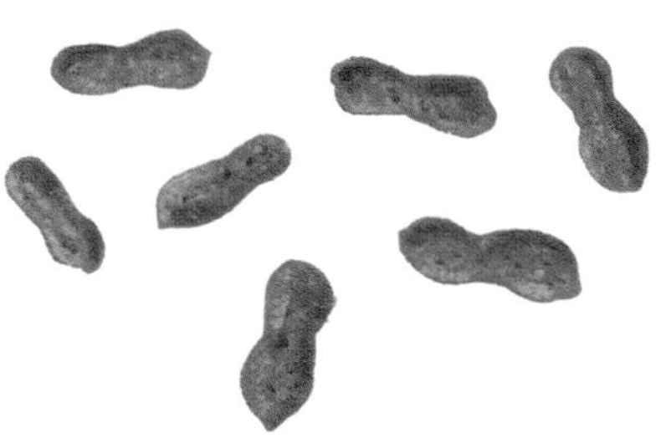

HOT ICED TEA

4 boiling cups of water

4 standard tea bags (sometimes I'll add 3 bags black tea, then make the 4th peppermint or lemon)

Let it steep. Remove bags and let it sit awhile on its own before putting it in the refrigerator. Pour over ice with a lemon wheel. If tea becomes cloudy that's OK.

Greek Beans

The following is the menu I served for brunch. In creating it, I had to take into account that it would be served on New Year's Day and I had plans New Year's Eve, which meant I would be up late the night before, so I tossed out the more traditional brunch menu and went with a menu that included the jackpot recipes I know like the back of my hand, in order to save time. Normally I would serve these dishes closer to dinnertime, but being this was a special occasion, and given the fact champagne was still coursing through my veins, I had to go with what I know.

Menu

Freshly Ground Coffee, I Mean, *Brewed*
Lemon Verbena Tea
My World Famous Lil' Smoky Cheese Ball (see page 181)
Ginger Ale
Various Juices
Pastitsio
Spanakopita (Spinach Pie)
Tula's Country-style Greek Salad
Greek Beans (see page 238)
Arty Sarayiotes Koulouraki (Greek Cookie Twists)
Tattletail's Vanilla Cupcakes (see page 182)
White Wine

PASTITSIO (MEAT PIE)

MACARONI:

1 16-ounce package of ziti macaroni
5 tablespoons of butter
3/4 cup of Parmesan cheese or Kefalotiri cheese
1/4 teaspoon of nutmeg
Salt and pepper
3 eggs, lightly beaten

MEAT SAUCE: 

1 or 1-1/2 pounds of beef
1 onion, chopped
1 crushed garlic clove
3 tablespoons of olive oil
1 small can of tomato paste
1/2 cup of red wine
1/2 can of beef broth or stock
2 tablespoons parsley
1/2 teaspoon sugar
Salt and pepper

SWEET TEA

4 boiling cups of water 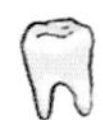

4 standard tea bags (sometimes I'll add 3 bags black tea then make the 4th peppermint or lemon)

Let it steep. Remove bags and let it sit awhile on its own before putting it in the refrigerator. Add a cup of sugar. Pour over ice with a lemon wheel. If tea becomes cloudy that's OK.

PASTITSIO (MEAT PIE), CONTINUED

CREAM SAUCE:

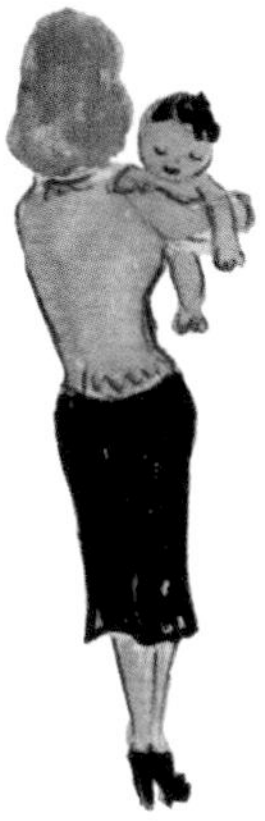

- 1/3 cup of butter
- 1/2 cup of flour
- 3 cups of milk
- 1/4 teaspoon of nutmeg
- Salt and pepper
- 1 egg

Preheat oven to 350 degrees F.

In a large pot, boil and drain your ziti, return to pot.

Melt butter. Pour over the ziti and toss.

Add 1/2 cup of the cheese, the nutmeg, salt, and pepper. Save a little of the cheese to sprinkle over the top of the dish before baking.

Toss again and set aside. Let it cool a little before adding the eggs. Toss well.

To make meat sauce, brown meat in frying pan until almost fully cooked. Drain off the fat and set meat aside.

Fry onion and garlic in oil. Add meat and remaining ingredients. Cover and simmer for 20 minutes.

To make the cream sauce, melt the butter in a saucepan. Stir in flour and cook until smooth. Add milk all at once and bring to a boil, stirring constantly.

Add nutmeg, salt and pepper. Let it cool, then stir in the beaten egg.

Add 1/2 cup of this cream sauce to the meat sauce and mix.

To assemble, use a 13 x 9 x 3 inch oven dish, buttered.

Spoon 1/2 of the macaroni evenly on the bottom, then top with the meat sauce. Cover that layer with remaining macaroni. Pour on cream sauce and spread over the entire top.

Sprinkle remaining cheese on top and bake until a little brown, about 45 minutes.

SPANAKOPITA (SPINACH PIE)

5 eggs

3 10-ounce packages of frozen, chopped spinach, defrosted (ring out any water using cheesecloth or dishrag)

8 ounces of cream cheese

8 ounces or more of crumbled feta cheese

8 ounces of small curd cottage cheese

Olive oil

2 bunches of chopped green onions, sautéed

1 tablesoon of parsley

Dill, fennel (optional)

3 tablespoons of Parmesan cheese

1 1-pound of box of phyllo pastry

In a mixer, beat the eggs until fluffy. Add everything else (except the phyllo) gradually, just until mixed. You can store the filling in the refrigerator to make the next day, if desired. Or you can make the whole pie, freeze it and bake the next day.

Melt a stick of butter. Using a pastry brush, butter the pan you will be using to bake it in. I use a 9 x 13 x 3 inch pan.

Line the bottom with half the box of phyllo, buttering between each layer. Add spinach filling and spread evenly.

Top with a little extra crumbled feta, if you have some left.

Place the remaining phyllo on top, again buttered between each sheet.

I precut the spanakopita and place it in the freezer until ready to bake. I then baptize the top with a little water and bake at 350 degrees F until brown and crispy on top, 45–50 minutes.

If phyllo starts to get too brown, cover with foil.

Pastitso

TULA'S COUNTRY-STYLE GREEK SALAD

3 tomatoes, sliced

1 cucumber, peeled and sliced

3 spring onions, chopped, or 1 small red onion, sliced

Lettuce and green peppers (optional)

5 ounces feta cheese, diced, crumbed, or cubed

Handful kalamata olives

Salt, pepper, and oregano or rigani

Handful roasted pine nuts

Arrange the tomato, cucumber, onions, lettuce, and green peppers in bowl. Top with the feta and olives and sprinkle with salt, pepper, and oregano or rigani, to taste. Toss on pine nuts.

Beat dressing (below) and pour over vegetables.

Serves 6.

SALAD DRESSING:

Mix 1/4 to 1/2 cup olive oil and 3 tablespoons of red wine vinegar or lemon juice. Salt and pepper to taste.

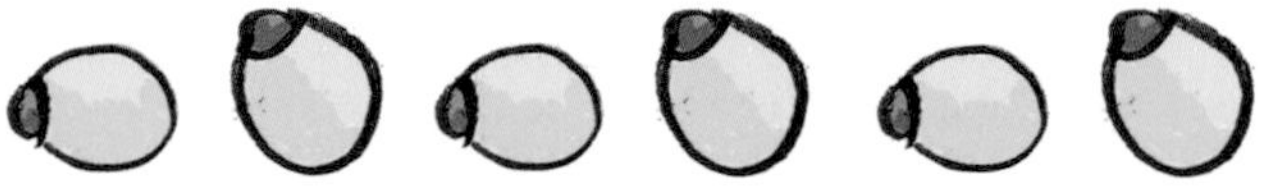

ARTY SARAYIOTES KOULOURAKI (GREEK COOKIE TWISTS)

1 pound of sweet butter

1 to 1 1/2 cups of sugar

2 eggs, yolks and whites separated

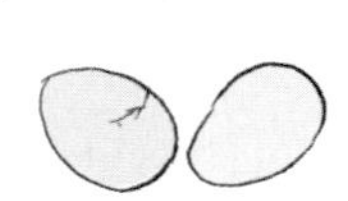

2 teaspoons of vanilla extract

1/4 teaspoon of cardamom (from seed, crushed)

2 pounds of flour or 6 to 7 cups

2 teaspoons of baking powder

1/2 pint of heavy cream

You will need egg wash and sesame seeds too.

Preheat oven to 350 degrees F.

Beat butter and sugar until light and fluffy. Add egg yolks, vanilla, cardamom.

Sift flour and baking powder together. Add to mixture with heavy cream.

Shape by taking a tablespoon or two of dough and rolling into 7" ropes (looks like a long cigar). Fold the rope in half and twist together.

Place on foil-lined cookie sheet and brush each twist with egg whites and top with sesame seeds.

Bake for about 25 minutes, or until light brown.

Other Preparations

- Instant camera for moneymaking ideas (see “The Money Jar,” page 32).
- Cardboard boxes for the kids to play in.
- It’s nice to have a couple different newspapers sitting around on this occasion because you feel lazy and newspapers and brunch seem to go together.

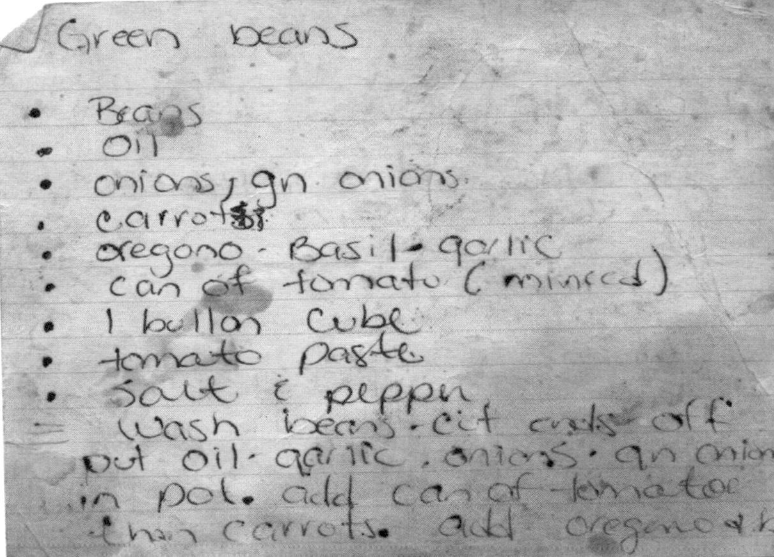
Green beans

- Beans
- Oil
- onions, gn onions
- carrots
- oregono - Basil - garlic
- can of tomato (minced)
- 1 bullon cube
- tomato paste
- Salt & pepper

wash beans. cut ends off put oil. garlic, onions. gn onion in pot. add can of tomatoe than carrots. add oregono &

PASTILLAS
DE
LORATO DE POTA
ROSADAS
HE

PROPERTY OF THE U.S

I like drugs. And when I say drugs, of course, I mean helpful pills that are legally prescribed by doctors. Why would I partake in the use of illegal substances? I firmly believe that illegal drugs are destroying the moral fiber of this nation and I would be willing to repeat this statement in any court of law where I'm on trial. Now, if the prosecution asserts that illegal substances such as marijuana are as common at my parties as punch or appetizers, well, all I have to say to that ridiculous accusation is, "Judge, I rest me's case!"

I never have drugs at my parties. I do occasionally have what I like to refer to as party enhancers. There are all sorts of party enhancers and often the differences in symptoms can be subtle. As a safety measure it is often helpful to be able to identify the specific enhancer your guest is flying on.

A Guide to Help You Keep Track

1. Dilated pupils. They seem wired, tense, jittery or wound as tight as a spring. Their hands and feet are in constant motion. They threaten another guest with a pork chop bone. This would indicate "Goofballs."
2. Pupils are contracted. The person is apathetic. Their movements are slow and relaxed. They seem "out of this world." They nod out in the eggnog. This would suggest "Zombies."
3. Bloodshot and slightly glazed eyes. Binge-eating followed by bouts of passivity. They attempt to describe all their ideas. Say hello to pot.

Alcoholics

If one of my parties was pulled over and administered a breath analyzer it would spend the weekend in jail. That's because at my parties, alcohol and drugs are encouraged, in moderation, and by "moderation," I of course mean that whatever my guests want to put in their throats is fine by me; I'm not here to judge. That's not to say I'm eager to entertain alcoholics. Even though some of my friends, as well as most of the guys I've dated, are alcoholics, I'm not

Interesting Information

- If you are purchasing hash and you notice that it has been rolled really tight, chances are that children rolled it. Maybe this will make you think twice about buying it.
- When you hear someone use the word "meds" instead of the word "medicine," chances are they're no stranger to massive doses of mind-altering psychotropic drugs. Back out of the room slowly.
- If you know you are going to be drinking or doing drugs, make sure to first organize your wallet so you don't accidentally pay the cabbie too much money.

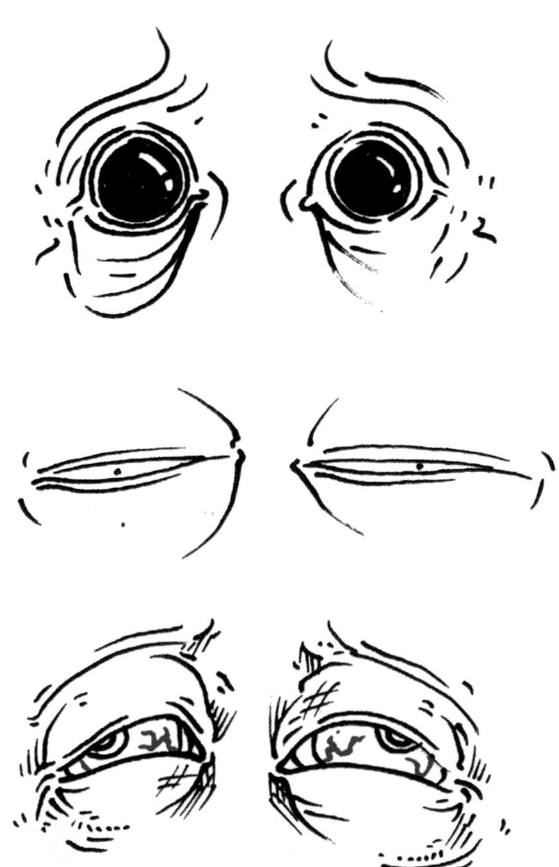

I like you.
baked beans

Young boys start drinking at an early age when feelings and emotions develop and they yearn to suppress them. This explains why so many adult men are crisis prone and emotionally blocked. This can also apply to some women. You know who you are.

a big fan of drunks at my parties. On first thought they might seem like the perfect party guests: lively, spirited, unpredictable, and they can be until that time of the night comes when they're throwing up in your dishwasher. As much as an alcoholic can rev up a party, they can kill one just as fast. Yes, it's kind of amusing when they make that beard out of cheese, but the laughs die quickly once you realize you now have nothing to dip your crackers in. And that's the problem with alcoholics at parties, they don't have any boundaries. That and they'll drink all your liquor, crash in your bed and wet it. Alcoholics tend to think they are much funnier than they actually are, and this is a major pitfall for the alcoholic. Most people know when they've lost their audience, but not the alcoholic. They'll keep plugging away long after the house lights have come up. If you decide on having an alcoholic at your party, make sure it's a large gathering. This way, until the alcoholic begins removing their clothes or dangling the cat out the window they can sort of blend in. An alcoholic at a small gathering is called an intervention. Also, alcoholics are no fun to cook for. They are not interested in food. Alcoholics like to drink. When alcoholics cook for themselves, they only think in terms of what they can do minimally and still sustain life.

On the other hand, a party won't fare any better with recovered alcoholics. They love to regale party guests with ribald stories from their "drinkin' daze," which always makes me think, "I bet you were a lot more fun when you drank."

An Alcoholic's Menu

Whiskey Dick's Baked Chicken Wings

Applesauce

GOONY BIRD

WHISKEY DICK'S BAKED CHICKEN WINGS

Put chicken wings in a pan with some oil. Add salt and pepper now (or whatever you're sober enough to reach for) so you don't forget later. Bake at 375 degrees F for about an hour. TURN OVEN OFF.

SUGGESTION

Odd numbers of food look better on a plate. Five chicken wings are going to look better than four.

Baked Chicken Wings

LINGUINI AND CLAMS

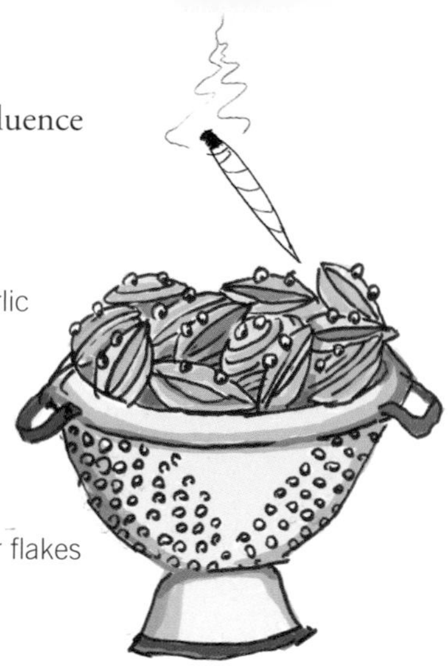

60 small fresh clams

1 tablespoon of chopped garlic

4 tablespoons of olive oil

3/4 tablespoon of parsley

Pepper

Pinch of crushed red pepper flakes

Pinch of oregano

Clam juice (optional)

1 pound linguini

Open the clams by steaming. Remove the clams and chop into pieces. Save all the juices. Save a whole clam or two just so you can use it later to garnish the dish. Sauté the garlic in oil until tanned. Add parsley, pepper, pepper flakes, and oregano. Add the clams and cook for about 4 minutes. Add the optional clam juice. Add it when you add the pepper, pepper flakes, and oregano and maybe more after you have cooked the clams, then just cook for another 2 to 3 minutes. Serve on top of linguini.

Bats in the Belfry

As a host, you will have to accept early on in the party process that some or many of your guests will have psychological problems and these need to be considered. For instance, one of your guests may be unable to remove himself from a physically abusive relationship. You need to be sensitive to this and avoid menu items such as battered chicken, whipped potatoes, beets, or sock-eye salmon. If another guest is in a codependent relationship, they might feel more comfortable being served peas and carrots, turkey and stuffing, fish and chips, linguini and clams, or pork and beans.

You might not be aware of a guest's mental disorder beforehand, only to find it flaring up just as the party kicks in. Remember, this is your party not a sanatorium. Your healthy party guests must come first. If the troubled guest cannot be talked down, ask him or her to leave. If the troubled guest refuses to leave, sedate him. If sedating him flops, coax him into a closet by either preying on his paranoid fantasies or with a chicken wing. Once the guest is trapped, block the door with furniture and call a professional.

Codependent Foods

There is much one can do to remove a urine stain from a mattress. Vinegar can remove odors, but because this is a moisture problem, I suggest dragging your mattress out into the sun. But realize you're not only airing a mattress, you're airing your dirty laundry as well.

ROOFIES

DOWNERS

UPPERS

AMPHETAMINE

WHO IS THIS?
WHY ARE YOU CALLING ME?
WHAT DO YOU WANT?
WHO ARE YOU?

Potato Salad

TIDDLYWINKS TOADSTOOL PIE

1 baked piecrust
(see page 214)

CREAM SAUCE:

3 tablespoons of butter (salted or unsalted)

3 tablespoons of flour

1 cup of light cream

Salt and pepper

MUSHROOM FILLING:

1 pound of fresh mushrooms, sliced

2 tablespoons of butter

2 small garlic cloves, crushed

3 shallots, minced

2 egg yolks mixed with 1 tablespoon of light cream

Salt and pepper

2 tablespoons of white wine

TOPPING:

1/2 cup of grated Swiss cheese

Melt the butter in a saucepan. Stir in flour and cook until smooth. Add cream and bring to a boil, stirring constantly. Sauté mushrooms in butter with garlic and shallots. Drain off any liquid. Add the mushrooms to the cream sauce and the egg mixture. Blend salt, pepper, and wine. Pour into pie shell. Top with cheese. Bake at 350 degrees for 15 to 20 minutes, until cheese is melted and crust is brown.

MR. MACE'S MUSHROOM CASSEROLE

1 can cream of mushroom soup

1 package frozen chopped broccoli

1 cup mayonnaise

1 cup grated Cheddar cheese

1 cup chopped onion

Breadcrumbs

Butter pats

Mix everything except breadcrumbs and butter in a bowl and place in baking dish. Cover with breadcrumbs and place butter pats on top. Bake at 350 degrees for 30 minutes, until brown.
Courtesy of Alan Mace.

Buttermilk Pound Cake

Pound Cake

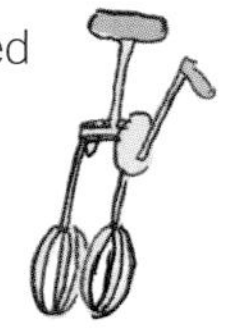

- 1 cup butter, softened
- 3 cups sugar
- 4 eggs
- 1/4 teaspoon baking soda
- 2 teaspoons vanilla extract
- 2 teaspoons lemon juice
- 3 cups flour
- 1 cup buttermilk

Cream butter and sugar together. Add eggs one at a time, incorporating well.

Add baking soda, vanilla, and lemon juice. Add flour and buttermilk alternately. Bake in a greased and floured tube pan at 350 degrees F, for one hour.

Optional: Sprinkle top of cake with sugar before baking to create a sweeter crust.

Courtesy of Jennifer McCullen

Munchies

1. Baked Tater Tots, topped with Cheddar cheese and bacon
2. Mozzarella sticks dipped in Cool Whip
3. Take the chewed-up cracker that is in your mouth and top it on another cracker and eat it
4. Peanut butter sandwich with grapes, bananas, and honey on toasted bread
5. Cold peanuts with milk
6. Toasted frozen waffles with ice cream between them
7. A glass of milk with four Milk Duds at the bottom
8. Popcorn popped in bacon grease
9. Banana with peanut butter on it
10. Coconut and peanut butter mixed together
11. Block of Cheddar cheese with mayonnaise on it
12. Grilled cheese and corn sandwich
13. Powdered sugar on any kind of cheese
14. Banana dipped in Jell-O powder
15. Potato chips dipped in ketchup or mustard or salad dressing
16. Stovetop s'mores
17. Crushed pretzels with cream cheese on toast
18. Uncooked hot dog dipped in Swiss Miss
19. Turkey sandwich with Doritos crunched inside
20. Pretzels dipped in peanut butter
21. Grape jelly with chocolate sauce
22. Cake mix milk shake made with water
23. Crisco mixed with sugar
24. Kool-Aid mix and pickle spears
25. Fudgsicle

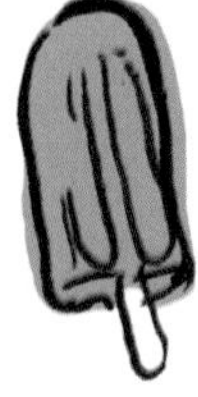

Children

As far as I'm concerned, children's parties don't really matter until the children are at least five. This is the age that gifts count. Children before that age are too young to understand the concept of presents. You can gift wrap a head of cabbage and give it to a two-year-old and they won't know the difference. I once gave a toddler a string of old colored lightbulbs and his reaction was no different from when he opened the blocks or the stuffed turtle. Of course, I say that gifts don't matter to children under five, but this is coming from a person who has given a hand-tailored cape to her rabbit. But that's different, rabbits know (see "And Rabbits," page 179).

When planning a child's party, send invitations out, because children love to get mail. Explain what activities are planned so the children know what to wear. (Pool party or hayride.) Children's parties should always have a set time limit, like, "from 2 to 2:30," because, given a child's boundless energy and the lack of yours, you will never wear them down. The more organized the party, the better, because you don't want the kids to get bored or restless.

Organizing a child's party is also a great time for your own child to begin learning how to be a good host or hostess. Make sure they greet and

THE BEST ROOT BEER FLOAT IN TOWN

Take two scoops of vanilla ice cream and put them in your favorite glass. Pour as much root beer as you can on top.
Serve with a straw and a spoon.

say good-bye to everyone and send thank-you notes, even if they just say "Thanks."

Surprise parties are wasted on young children, because they take away all the excitement building up to the date as well as the fun of planning.

If you have a backyard, take advantage of it (Sprinkler! Well!) because kids need lots of game room and running space. If you have a children's party in your home be sure you put away anything that you don't want broken or chewed or scratched or ripped or tortured or burned or drawn on or peed on or spit up on or permanently stained or tangled or stabbed. If you are incapable of managing more than two children, either have a grown-up friend help you or pay some teenagers to help.

I decorate for birthday parties the same way I did growing up, with crepe paper streamers coming from each corner of the room. It doesn't matter what age group will be attending: streamers always scream "party." Use sturdy paper plates and cups; they are the safest bet around children. They are colorful and easy to clean up.

The menu should be simple and fun. Add faces to the hamburger buns, or cookie "ears" to an ice cream scoop so the food appears as if it could come alive. If you are feeling really generous, you can make what the birthday boy/girl requests. My brother always had my mother make him duck for his birthday, but he made the rest of us eat Spanish rice so we would envy him. I always asked my mom to make a Baked Alaska on my birthday.

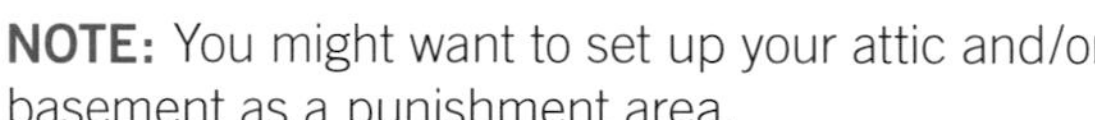

NOTE: You might want to set up your attic and/or basement as a punishment area.

Children's food needs to look like it comes alive.

Menu

Ceremony Punch for Kids
Mrs. Hog's Hot Dogs
Mr. Hog's Slaw for Hot Dogs
Mrs. Mason's Chili Sauce for Hot Dogs
Patty's Hamburger Patty
Baked Alaska

Optional Menu

Croque Monsieur
Poppy's Shake-a-Leg Drumsticks
The Perfect Party Cake

MRS. HOG'S HOT DOGS

You will need: hot dogs, hot dog buns, ruffled potato chips, timer, pan of boiled water, fork or tongs, plate, ketchup, mustard.

1. Wake up.
2. Turn the stove on.
3. Get a pan, put water in and boil it.
4. Drop hot dogs in boiling water but be careful not to splash boiling water on yourself.
5. Set timer for 3 minutes.
6. Get out hot dog buns and put on a plate.
7. Jab the hot dogs with fork, or use tongs to remove from pan. Put into hot dog buns.
8. Decorate with ketchup and mustard.

CHUCK WAGON STYLE (ALL THE WAY):

Ketchup, Mustard, Mrs. Mason's Chili Sauce for Hot Dogs, onions

Carl's Cheese Cameos

MR. HOG'S SLAW FOR HOT DOGS

1 shredded head of cabbage

2 finely shredded carrots

½ a green pepper, slivered

1 cup mayonnaise

Salt and pepper

½ teaspoon sugar

¼ teaspoon dried mustard

½ tablespoon celery seed

1½ ounces vinegar

Toss the cabbage, carrots, and green pepper together. Mix remaining ingredients to make dressing and pour over cabbage. Chill. Serve with ruffled potato chips or French fries.

MRS. MASON'S CHILI SAUCE FOR HOT DOGS

1 pound or less of ground beef

2 tablespoons of chili powder

1 finely chopped onion

½ to ¾ teaspoon of garlic salt or powder

1 can of tomato paste

1 teaspoon of salt

Put enough water in pan to cover beef. Bring to boil. The color will be an unattractive gray. Don't precook the beef. If you do, it will be larger chunks and you don't want that for this chili. After water begins to boil, add all other ingredients. Simmer for at least a half hour or more.

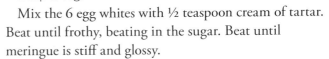

THE MERINGUE:

Whites of 6 large eggs

½ teaspoon cream of tartar

1 cup of sugar

Mix the 6 egg whites with ½ teaspoon cream of tartar. Beat until frothy, beating in the sugar. Beat until meringue is stiff and glossy.

TO ASSEMBLE:

Set oven at 500 degrees F. Place the cakes on a board, then on a baking sheet. Loosen the ice cream from the bowl and invert bowl over the cakes. Cover the cake and ice cream completely with meringue. Put the assembled cake into the broiler (if the broiler is on top of the oven) for 3–5 minutes or use a torch and torch it all over.

You can also use my aunt Joyce's brownie recipe that I wasn't supposed to give out (see page 224) to make the bottom of the Baked Alaska.

CEREMONY PUNCH FOR KIDS

Fill Punch bowl full of ginger ale. Float a carton of lime or orange sherbet on top.

BAKED ALASKA

THE ICE CREAM:

Pack an 8- or 9-inch mixing bowl or round container with your favorite ice cream and refrigerate for 8 hours or until solid. You might want to line the bowl with Saran Wrap or even foil just so when you have to remove the ice cream, it's easier.

THE TWO SPONGE CAKES:

6 eggs

1 cup of sugar

2 teaspoons of pure vanilla extract

1 cup of cake flour

1 stick of butter

Preheat the oven to 350 degrees F, and grease two 9-inch baking pans. Beat the eggs and add ½ cup of sugar. Continue mixing (about 6 minutes with a mixer). Gradually add the other ½ cup of sugar and beat until the mixture looks lemony and has a ribbon texture (about 2 more minutes). Add the vanilla and fold in the cake flour. In a double boiler, melt butter and let it cool a little before folding it into the batter. Pour into the prepared pans. Bake for 35 minutes.

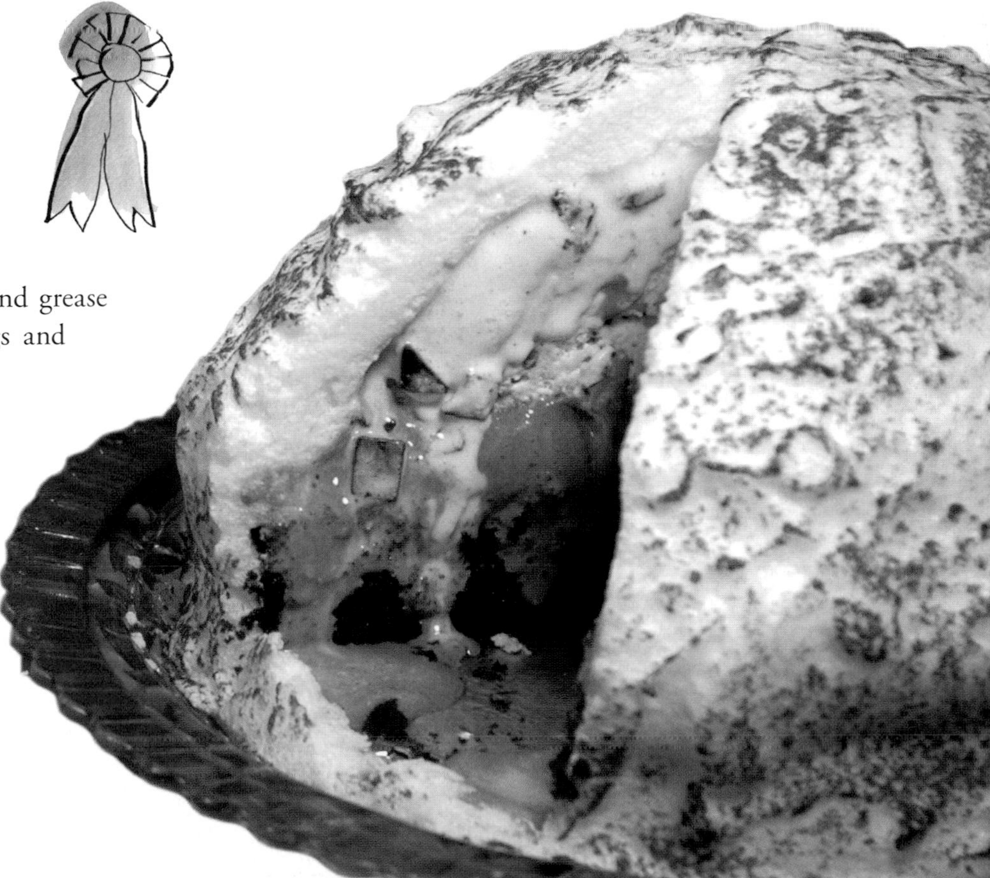

POPPY'S SHAKE-A-LEG DRUMSTICKS

½ cup of flour

½ teaspoon of salt

⅛ teaspoon of pepper

½ teaspoon of paprika

2 pounds of chicken legs

1½ sticks of butter and/or shortening

Take a brown paper lunch bag (I double mine) and mix the flour and seasonings in the bag.

Take 3 or 4 drumsticks at a time and shake them in the bag, until they are coated.

Place in a small, foil-lined pan (13 x 9½ x 2 inches) with about ⅓ stick of butter, or butter mixed with vegetable shortening.

Bake at 425 degrees F for about 45 minutes.

It's a lot of fun to shake chicken in a bag.

To prevent disputes when hosting a party for children, be sure to keep all the party favors and treat decorations the same for every child.

PATTY'S HAMBURGER PATTY

What you will need:

1 pound ground chuck

½ teaspoon Worcestershire sauce

Salt and pepper

3 hamburger buns

Optional toppings: ketchup, mustard, relish, lettuce, tomato, cheese, and onion

Potato chips

Mixing bowl

Fork

Broiler pan

Tinfoil

Timer

Spatula

Plate

1. Wake up.
2. Put ground chuck in bowl, breaking it up with a fork.
3. Add Worcestershire sauce.
4. Add salt and pepper.
5. Form meat into three patties using your hands.
6. Wash hands and dry.
7. Get a broiler pan. Cover with tinfoil. Randomly stab some holes through the foil.
8. Place patties on pan.
9. Turn broiler on and heat patties about 3 inches from heat.
10. Set timer for 6 minutes.
11. When the timer goes off, turn patties over with a spatula.
12. Set timer for another six minutes.
13. Get hamburger buns ready on a plate.
14. Place a patty on each bun.
15. Dress with ketchup, mustard, and relish or go deluxe and add lettuce, tomato, cheese, and onion.
16. Serve with potato chips.

To make these paper clip necklaces, see page 281.

CROQUE MONSIEUR

You will need:

- 2 slices of bread
- 2 tablespoons of room-temperature butter
- 2 slices of deli-style cheese
- 1 slice of deli-style ham
- Plate
- Knife
- Frying pan
- Spatula

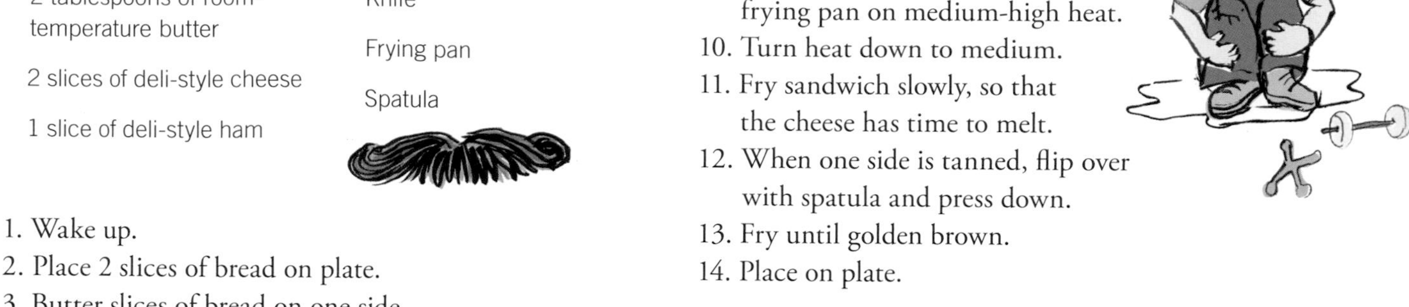

1. Wake up.
2. Place 2 slices of bread on plate.
3. Butter slices of bread on one side.
4. Place unbuttered side up.
5. Place 1 slice of cheese on top of one slice of bread.
6. Place 1 slice of ham on top of cheese.
7. Place 1 slice of cheese on top of ham.
8. Place remaining slice of bread on top, buttered side up.
9. Melt 1 tablespoon of butter in frying pan on medium-high heat.
10. Turn heat down to medium.
11. Fry sandwich slowly, so that the cheese has time to melt.
12. When one side is tanned, flip over with spatula and press down.
13. Fry until golden brown.
14. Place on plate.

Serve with French fries.

Ice cream clown clowns

THE PERFECT PARTY CAKE

Make an angel food cake from a box. This is the only boxed cake I ever make because to me it tastes just like a homemade one and you don't have to deal with egg whites. Egg whites intimidate me (for some people it's phyllo), but either way, the best part of making an angel food cake is that you get to hang it upside down on a wine bottle for an hour, and you can still do that with a boxed angel food cake.

Take your 10-inch angel food cake and place it on a plate. Slice entire top from cake, about 1 1/2 inches down. Lift off the top and put it somewhere else. Make a tunnel and scoop out the angel food cake. Now there is a wall; it will look similar to a Jell-O ring mold. Take the angel food cake that you scooped out and put it on another plate. Completely fill the cavity with either the chilled whipped filling or with an ice cream of your choice. Replace the top of cake. I like to use the cake left over from the tunnel and stuff it in the center hole. I then slather the sides and top with whipped cream.

You can include a half cup of toasted almonds to the cake cavity and then sprinkle the outside with 1/3 cup of shaved toasted almonds.

FOR FILLING:

Make whipped cream using a chilled bowl and beater.

You can dye the whipped cream and decorate it any way you want.

For chocolate whipped cream, use a chilled mixing bowl and add:

6 tablespoons cocoa

1 cup sugar

2 cups whipping cream

¼ teaspoon salt

Stir well and chill for an hour or two. Whip in chilled bowl using chilled beaters. Use for cake filling and topping.

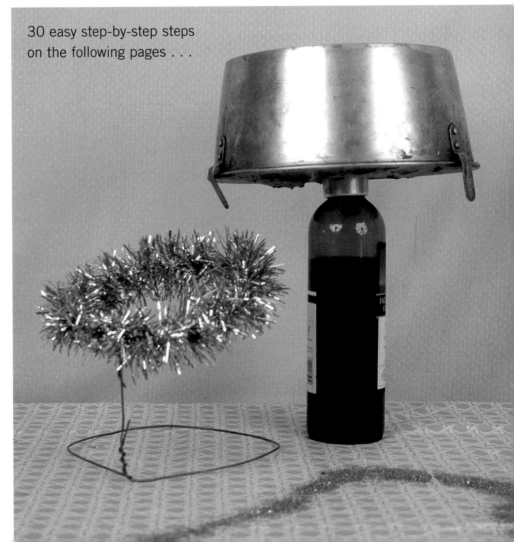

30 easy step-by-step steps on the following pages . . .

1
2
3
4
5
6
7
8
9
10
11
12
13
14
ice cream

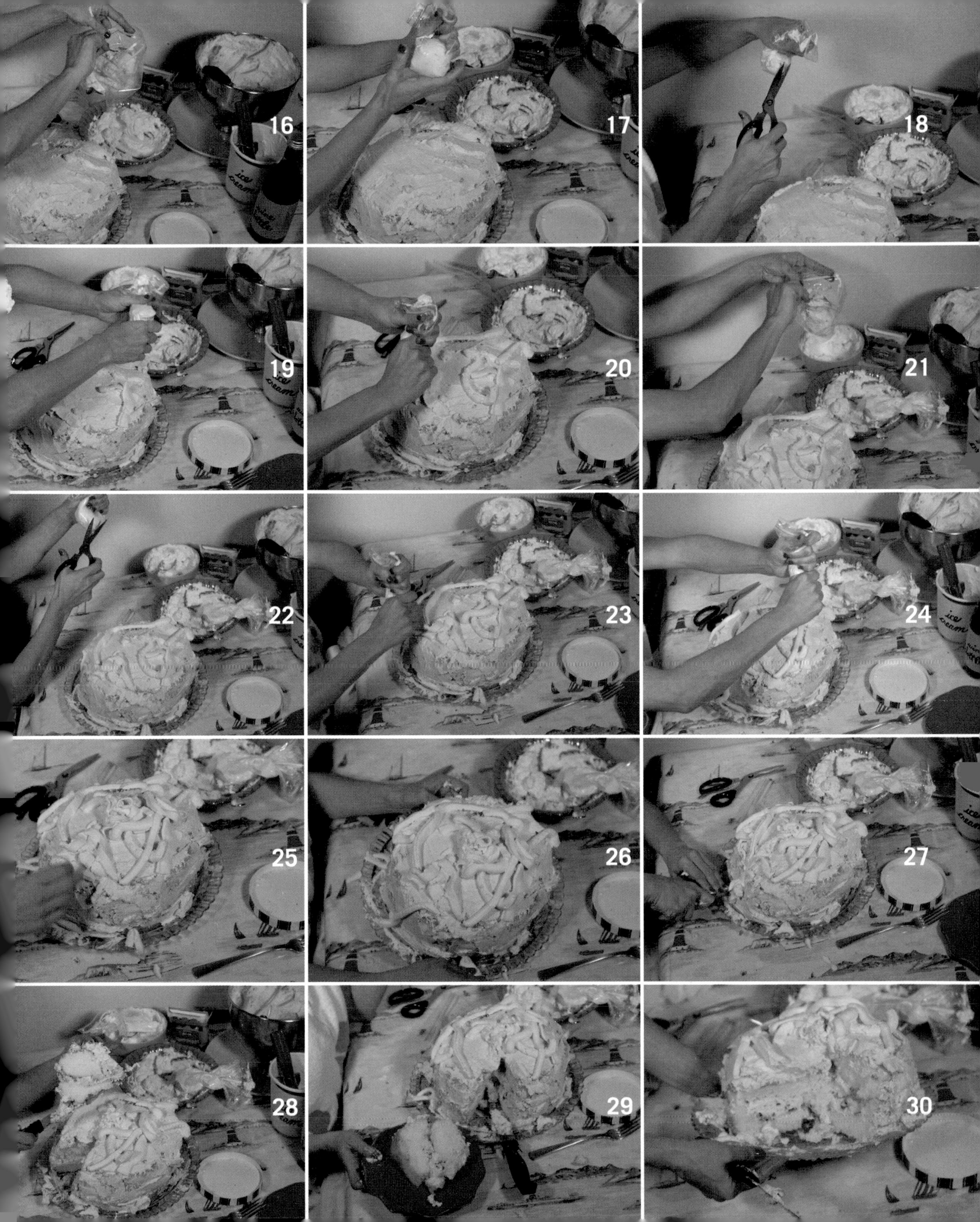
16
17
18
19
20
21
22
23
24
25
26
27
28
29
30

Children's Games

You've got fifteen to twenty children in your home and they're getting restless. By God, you better have some activities planned or they're gonna start making up their own games, like "rub doodoo on the couch" or "doodoo in the fish tank." Here is a list of children's games that are sure to entertain even the most stubborn of children.

General Party Game Safety

NOTE: If for any reason a child's clothing catches fire, prevent the child from running because this adds oxygen, causing him to burn more quickly. Roll the smoldering child on the ground or in a rug. If a youngster breaks through the ice, have him kick his feet and wriggle to a solid surface. Kerosene is an accelerant: try not to mix it with an open flame unless an escape route is cleared. Stay in single file. Don't scratch and never put that in your mouth. The eyes are the most vulnerable part of the wolf. When cornered, jab something pointy into this area.

1. MEMORY GAME Out of the children's view, place about twenty items on a table and cover the items with a blanket. Now, divide the children into two teams. In the presence of both teams, uncover the items for one minute and then cover them again. Now send the teams off to separate rooms. Adults should act as the secretary. Have the kids try to name as many of the objects as they can remember. Whichever team remembers the most wins.

2. MEMORY GAME II Have the children sit in a room together. Ask a neighbor to enter the room and let the kids take a good look without informing the kids that they will later be asked to describe him. Now, after about three minutes, tell your neighbor to leave and have the kids attempt to remember details about your neighbor. Not only is this fun and helpful for honing detective skills, but if your neighbor does become involved in anything unsavory, you now have twenty youthful witnesses who can describe him.

3. PLAY GROWN-UP Have a cocktail party. Make fake liquor using food coloring. For example, use yellow for scotch, green for crème de menthe. Pretend French fries with the tips dipped in ketchup are lit cigarettes. Have children simulate spousal abuse by arguing and, as this escalates, slapping each other. Use Tic Tacs to spit out of the mouth as if they were teeth. Use red Tic Tacs if you want to pretend they are bloody teeth. If there is an infant in the house, it's always fun to play Social Services. Have one child pretend he is going to take the baby away from another child. The pretend "mother" can fight for custody. You can always substitute a real baby with a fake baby by wrapping something baby-like in a towel. Have a child pretend he is walking in on his wife and catching her having an affair with another person.

4. GYPSY Blindfold all the children and then drive them across town. Drop them off in a place they have never been before. Remove their blindfolds and drive away. Their goal is to make it back home.

5. JR. ASTRONOMER Have the children lie in a neighbor's driveway and look up at the stars.
6. JR. U.N. AMBASSADOR Teach the kids how to say hello in different languages.
7. JR. CAT BURGLAR Lock the kids out of the house and see if they can break in.
8. JR. VACUUM SALESMAN Have the children take turns dumping things on the floor, and then demonstrating how they would clean it up.

9. TRAIN ROBBERY Make a pretend train car by setting up chairs in a line. Now have some of the children act as train passengers. Have the rest of the children pretend they are Indians and rob the passengers. If one of the "passengers" is a blond girl, encourage the "Indians" to kidnap her in hopes of making her their savage bride.
10. BUSKING Drive the party to the airport and have them entertain travelers for small change.

11. HILLBILLY HIJINX Toss a greased watermelon into the pool and have the kids try to grab for it. If you don't have a pool, use a tub.
12. P.O.W. Confine some of the children and give them a secret. Now have some of the other children escort the confined children one by one into another room. Once secured, the "guard" children will attempt to get the "prisoner" children to tell their secrets through coercive means.

13. WIGGLE WORM Have the children take turns being a worm. One child gets in bed and another makes the sound of a phone ringing. They then try to make it to the phone to answer it by dragging themselves across the room. The goal is to make it to the phone before it stops ringing. A variation on this theme is to pretend someone is breaking in and the child playing the worm has to make it to the phone in time to call for help.
14. WISHING WELL Make your friends use their pocket change. Turn your bathtub into a wishing well and let them try to earn their money back.
15. BEAUTY PARLOR Do each other's makeup and hair and talk about your problems.

16. BEAUTY CONTEST Pick up some old clothes, bathing suits, hats, and jewelry from a thrift store. Create a catwalk and have all the children dress up and play Beauty Contest. Videotape it and critique each other afterwards. Make a winning sash out of toilet paper.

17. I WANT TO SEE, I WANT TO SEE Blindfold someone and do some sort of activity in the room. Un-blindfold him and see if they can guess what you did.

18. THE GREASY BAG GAME Pass a greasy bag around and act out different scenarios. This is especially good for all ages. "Dr. Fleischacker—don't forget your lunch."

Several of the games listed here are also fun for children with a disability or handicap—no need to eliminate these children from your party guest list. If they are blind, invite them to your house a day early to familiarize themselves with the layout of your house. If they are deaf use bright, vibrant colors and play games that aren't hard to explain. You might want to invite another child with the same misfortune so they don't feel alone. I would imagine planning activities would be challenging but in a fun way.

Suggestions

- Organize coloring books and crayons using your dish drainer.
- If you place a tight rubber band around a glass, your child will be able to hold on to it better and this will eliminate drink spills.
- The more colorful clothes your child wears, the easier for you to find them in a crowd.
- Buy a book on stain removals.

Montgomery's Disguise Kit

Hello to you! My name is Montgomery and I am a worm of many disguises. Sometimes I find myself in a tough situation that I need to wiggle out of. Whether it's avoiding being dangled from the end of a fishing pole or being dropped to the bottom of a tequila bottle, I do a lot of squirming around. That's why I have put together my disguise kit, because a lot of times it's safer not to be me. Now get a wiggle on!

This kit includes bald cap, icky teeth, Coke bottle glasses, mustache, eyebrows, mole (with hair), eye patch, nicotine stain, rubber cement for scars, scabs, cork and matches (for hobo), fingernails, yellow paint (for Oriental), red paint (for Indian chief), Chap Stick (if you suck the lid onto your upper lip, it looks like you have a bucktooth).

Also includes: steel wool for a beard, vacuum cleaner hose to make antennas, and charcoal tablets to give the illusion you don't have a tooth in your head, like me, Montgomery.

Sambo

Sanchez

The Dirty Bomber

Junkie

Construction Worker

Stephen

Chop Stix

Pirate

Hobo

Chauncey

French Resistance Guy

Injun Joe

Opening Night

The show has just let out and a small troop of thespians is headed to your home for an encore, only now it's your opening night and being a hostess is just like being the star of your own sold-out show. If you've prepared correctly you can expect rave reviews! A must-see! An extended smash hit! Make sure to have the affair scripted, leaving some room to improvise. Don't be upstaged by surprises, and you'll be guaranteed to have no walkouts for this performance. Take this opportunity to cast some of your guests as backstage helpers—although the program consists of do-ahead dishes served at room temperature, you can always use an extra hand behind the curtain.

The guests have arrived and it's time to seat the house. Curtain. Appetizers to half, appetizers go! Fade on appetizers. Cocktails go. Someone asks for a "Rum Punch Dazzler." Line!? Cue main course. Main course, go! Don't rush it . . . This isn't a speed-through. Relax, just like you've rehearsed! Cue ambient music. Lights to half. Settle into tableau. Fade up on small talk. Fade out on general laughter. Strike dishes. Wait for applause. Bow. Encore! Coconut cream pie! General conversation, ad-lib. Fade out music. Strike dessert plates. House to full. And curtain!

Suggestions

- Ask someone to play meat carver.
- It's always good to keep some nonalcoholic beer in your refrigerator in case someone is on penicillin or in the program or has been banned from drinking at your parties (see "Alcoholics," page 86).
- Stock your neighbor's apartment with basics (alcohol, ice, corn chips . . .) so when you run out at three in the morning you know whose door to knock on.

Menu for this Evening's Performance:

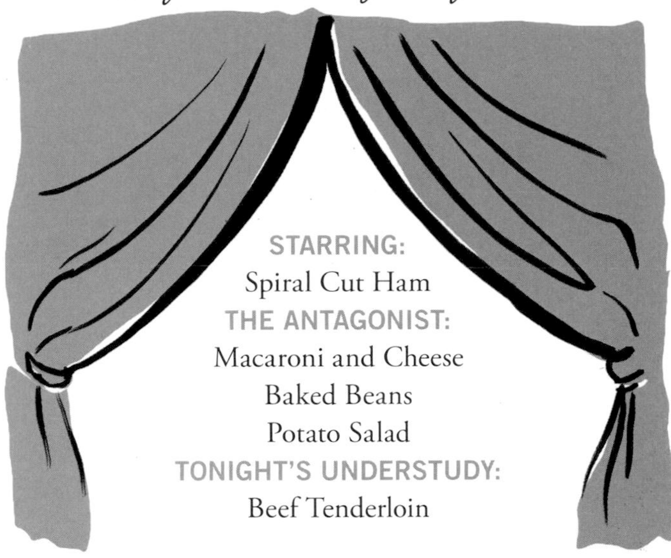

STARRING:
Spiral Cut Ham
THE ANTAGONIST:
Macaroni and Cheese
Baked Beans
Potato Salad
TONIGHT'S UNDERSTUDY:
Beef Tenderloin

Thumbnail Review

Crab Balls and Stuffed Mushrooms were scene-stealers. Good in a supporting roll: the biscuits. Nice turn as foreign dignitary: the Dijon mustard and horseradish mayonnaise. The debut of the heavyset cheese ball was surprisingly crowd-pleasing.

Award-winning Desserts

Coconut Cream Pie

Gingersnaps

Assorted Chocolates

Coffee and Tea

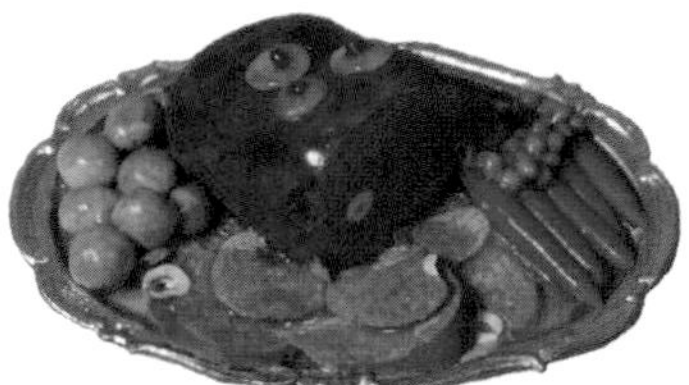

Notes on the Night's Performance

Normally, in a situation where seventeen people are coming over to my house late evening, I would plan a menu similar to the one I prepare for brunch, which consists mostly of do-ahead dishes served at room temperature. But because I was lucky enough to manipulate the help of a good friend, my do-ahead dishes were done-ahead while I was at the theater. This meant a meal that could be served warm as the guests arrived and that didn't rely on a knife to eat.

I personally wouldn't have chosen this menu because it required a lot of attention as far as keeping the food warm and fresh and because I needed a lot of help. But then this is also what I liked about it; it was different for me. Also, because this was an evening performance the menu might have been a little heavy in the cheesy sense. But it worked to our advantage because we were up all night waiting for the reviews of the show that we had just come from and my guests had performed in. This meant plenty of awake time, giving all that cheese ample time to move through the system.

COCONUT CREAM PIE

You need a 9-inch prebaked pie shell (that has been pricked) for this, and you won't want to fill it with the pie filling too soon because it can become soggy by the time you are ready to serve it.

½ cup of sugar

½ cup of flour

1 teaspoon of salt

3 cups of milk

3 slightly beaten egg yolks

2 teaspoons of vanilla extract

2 tablespoons of unsalted butter

½ cup of shredded coconut

Whipped cream

Preheat oven to 425 degrees F.

In a saucepan, combine the sugar, flour, and salt. Add the milk and stir on a low heat, until it becomes thick. Add in the egg yolks, stirring for another 2 minutes. Take saucepan off the burner and add the vanilla, butter, and coconut. I let the custard cool and transfer it to the refrigerator.

When the pie is ready to be served, I pour the filling into the shell and slather a generous amount of whipped cream all over the top. Then I toast some coconut by browning it in a pan on the stove and tossing it around using my fingers until it's toasted. Sprinkle the coconut on top. If I need to hold off on serving the pie for a while and need to cover it, I insert about four or five long raw spaghetti strands in the whipped cream to prevent the Saran Wrap from touching and ruining the look of the pie (see picture).

For Banana Coconut Cream Pie, add two peeled bananas, sliced, to the bottom of the pie shell before adding the cream filling, or before you add the whipped cream topping.

For Chocolate Coconut Cream Pie, all you have to do is melt 2 ounces unsweetened chocolate and add it to the milk before mixing it with the sugar and flour mixture.

You can make any of these pies without coconut—just leave it out.

This recipe was originally known as "The NutSnacker," by Kraft.

THE HEAVYSET CHEESE BALL

1¼ cups of whole natural almonds

1 8-ounce package of cream cheese

½ cup of real mayonnaise

5 crispy cooked bacon slices, crumbled

½ teaspoon of dill weed

⅛ teaspoon of pepper

1 tablespoon of green onion, chopped

Preheat oven to 300 degrees F. Place and spread all the almonds on a cookie sheet or in a shallow pan, pushing the almonds around until they turn color, about 20 minutes.

Mix together the cream cheese and the mayonnaise. Add the bacon, pepper, dill, and onion. Chill overnight.

On a serving platter, make two pinecone shapes with the cheese. Begin to press the almonds at a slight angle into the cheese, starting at the narrow end of the pinecone shape.

Do this in rows, continuing to overlap rows until all the cheese is covered. Garnish with fake pine sprigs, or real ones, or with rosemary. Serve at room temperature and spread on a Ritz.

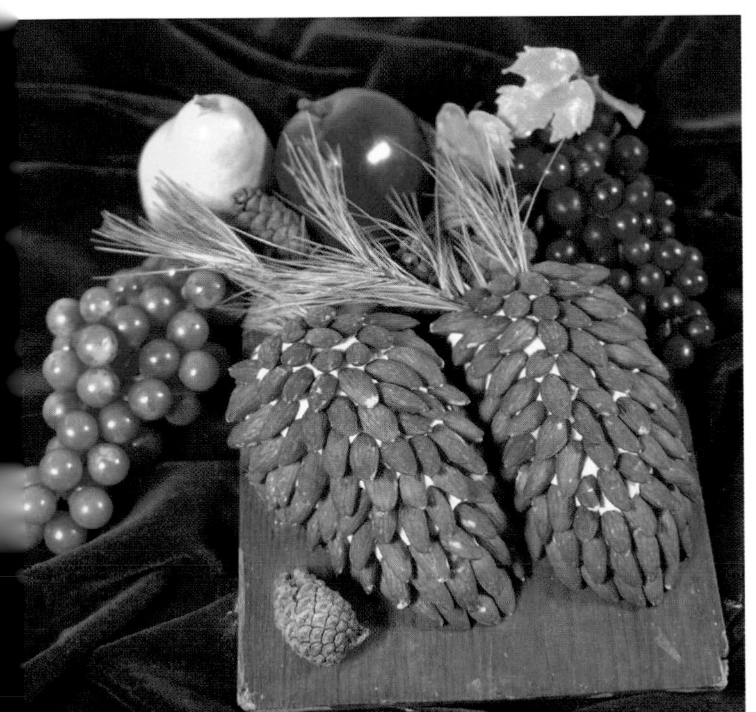

MACARONI AND CHEESE

1 box elbow macaroni

1 stick butter

1 cup grated smoked Gouda

1 cup grated white Monterey Jack cheese

2 cups grated mild yellow Cheddar cheese

1/2 cup grated Parmesan cheese

1 cup heavy cream

1/4 cup milk

Salt and pepper to taste

TOPPING:

1/2 cup grated Parmesan cheese

1 cup breadcrumbs

2 tablespoons chopped parsley

Salt and pepper to taste

8 thin pats of butter to go on top

Boil macaroni in salted water to al dente. While you are waiting for it to boil, melt together butter, cheeses, cream, milk, and salt and pepper.

Drain macaroni and put back into the pot. When cheese mixture is melted and smooth, pour over macaroni and mix well. Add to a 2-quart casserole dish. For topping, mix together Parmesan cheese, breadcrumbs, parsley, salt and pepper, and sprinkle on top of macaroni and cheese. Top with pats of butter. Bake at 425 degrees F for 20–25 minutes or until browned on top. One should be forewarned: this is a very rich dish. Not appropriate for diners with heart problems, the elderly, or breast-feeding mothers.

Courtesy of Jennifer McCullen.

STUFFED MUSHROOMS

36 baby portabella mushrooms, destemmed (save stems and chop finely)

4 scallions, chopped

1 pound Italian sausage

1 cup breadcrumbs, seasoned

⅛ cup mayonnaise

½ cup Parmesan cheese

With a little butter, sauté stems and scallions. Add sausage and brown. Drain off fat and add ½ cup of breadcrumbs and mayonnaise. Mix well and stuff mushroom caps. Place caps in baking dish. Mix remaining breadcrumbs with Parmesan cheese and sprinkle on top of stuffed mushrooms. Bake 10–15 minutes at 450 degrees F, or until tops are browned.

CRAB BALLS

3 pounds fresh crabmeat, flaked (back fin crabmeat is best)

24 saltine crackers, crushed

3 eggs, lightly beaten

3 tablespoons mustard (whole grain)

3 tablespoons mayonnaise

2 red bell peppers, finely chopped

1 bunch fresh parsley, finely chopped

Salt and freshly cracked pepper, to taste

Butter or olive oil, for browning

Mix all ingredients together. Shape into bite-size balls and sauté in hot butter or olive oil until golden brown, making sure to rotate. Serve with lemon wedges.

BRENDA THOMAS'S BAKED BEANS

Fry up some bacon and crumble it. Drain a lot of the grease, but save some for sautéing onions. Sauté 1 onion in remaining bacon grease. Add 1 big can of beans—not that big, big can, but you know, the bigger can. Add some mustard, and a splash of Worcestershire sauce. Add brown sugar. Simmer, then stir in the crumbled bacon. Optional: Cut-up hot dogs can be added.

GREEN BEANS WITH TOASTED ALMONDS

3 pounds fresh green beans

1 16-ounce package of sliced almonds

3 cloves garlic, crushed

Extra-virgin olive oil

Salt and pepper

Blanch and shock green beans and set aside. Place almond slices on sheet tray. Toast in oven at 450°F, until the nuts are toasty brown. Sauté the garlic in olive oil. When it starts to brown, add beans in small batches to the oil, and sauté. Serve beans in a bowl, layering them with toasted almonds. Add salt and pepper to taste.

GERMAN POTATO SALAD

15 red bliss potatoes

Salt and freshly cracked pepper, to taste

15 slices bacon, thickly cut (I recommend applewood smoked bacon), cubed

2 cloves garlic, crushed

2 onions, julienned

3 tablespoons flour

1-1/2 cup water

1-1/2 cup white vinegar

2 tablespoons sugar

Fresh parsley or dill

Boil potatoes with skin on. When tender, drain, peel, and slice. Season with some salt and pepper and set aside. Fry bacon until crisp. Remove bacon from pan and add to potatoes. Reserving bacon fat, add garlic and onion and sauté. When onions are translucent, add flour. When flour starts to brown and smell nutty, add water, vinegar, sugar, salt and pepper. When mixture starts to bubble, remove from heat and pour over potatoes and bacon, mixing well. Serve with a garnish of fresh parsley, dill, or freshly cracked pepper.

CREAM BISCUITS—SAVORY

3 cups flour

3¾ teaspoons baking powder

1½ teaspoon salt

1⅞ cup heavy cream

Coarse salt

Mix all dry ingredients in a bowl, except the coarse salt. Add heavy cream. Using wooden spoon or spatula, pull together until it tightens. Transfer to a well-floured surface. Form into a large ball and press out with heel of your hand until it is ¾ inch thick. Using a 2-inch round cutter, stamp out biscuits and put them on baking sheet. Form remaining dough into a ball and continue to repeat until all dough is used. Moisten tops of biscuits with some heavy cream and sprinkle with coarse salt. Bake at 450 degrees F, 10–15 minutes or until golden brown on top.

Courtesy of Daddy Mac's.

If you write someone a fan letter and request an autographed picture, you should include a self-addressed envelope. And once you have heard from this person there really is no need to write them back unless you were asked to.

Backstage Etiquette Suggestions

Most people know the basic rules of etiquette when attending a play—arrive on time, no candy wrappers. As far as backstage etiquette goes, most people seem to be a little murky on what sort behavior is appropriate. Be positive with opinions of the performance, even though no matter what you say to an actor he is not going to believe you. Actors are the most insecure people on earth, next to battered housewives. They become upset if you don't stay after the performance to praise them, but get upset if you inconvenience them by coming into their dressing room to offer them praise while they are still trying to get out of their ham costume. I always try to find something positive to say to an actor after a performance, but I don't say something like: "You looked so good on stage," or "I can't believe you have to do this four times a day," or "How did you learn all those lines?" The biggest mistake you can make when talking to an actor after a performance is praising another cast member. Trust me, they don't want to hear it. The truth is, going backstage is always awkward. I prefer to send a note off the next day or to wait and call them so we can talk about every detail of the show. If the ham in the show is your friend, let them know you won't be staying afterward, because they will assume you hated their performance if you just leave. When exiting the theater, don't talk about the show until you are a good distance away. You don't want to be overheard saying something that might hurt a thespian's feelings; you never know who's listening and how they are related to that ham in the play.

Interesting Information

It is best not to whistle backstage because the stagehands use a whistle as a cue to drop heavy sets on stage, or lift sets using sandbags as a counterweight. So if you whistle backstage and are standing in the wrong place, there is a good chance of getting a five ton set or a sandbag dropped on your head. Better yet, if you don't really have anything nice to say when going backstage, maybe you should whistle.

WHO? WHAT? WHERE?

Bailiwick Gingersnaps

"We were in the bathtub and I felt a cyst on his good testicle. I insisted on taking him to the hospital even though he protested, saying it was nothing. After a thorough exam it turned out he was right, it was nothing. On the way home he was murdered.

"I'm not allowed to talk about the case but I can say this: had I not forced him to go to the hospital he'd still be alive today."

I am sure we all have heard stories like this before. Tragic tales that could make even the most coldhearted wail. There is no bigger hospitality challenge than entertaining for the grieving. They are just so sad. One must take a practical approach. When all is said and done, entertaining for the grieving is really not much different from normal entertaining except for all the sobbing.

Often tragedy occurs suddenly, which doesn't give the host much lead time to prepare. On these occasions I think potluck is the way to go.

Most people want to contribute when someone else is grieving, but often they are unsure of what to do. I know when I hear the words, "It was a freak accident," I immediately think "I need to roast a chicken." I always encourage guests to contribute food for the table and try to subtly orchestrate the menu because I wouldn't want 12 people all showing up with 4-alarm chili, especially if the guest of honor is having trouble keeping food down.

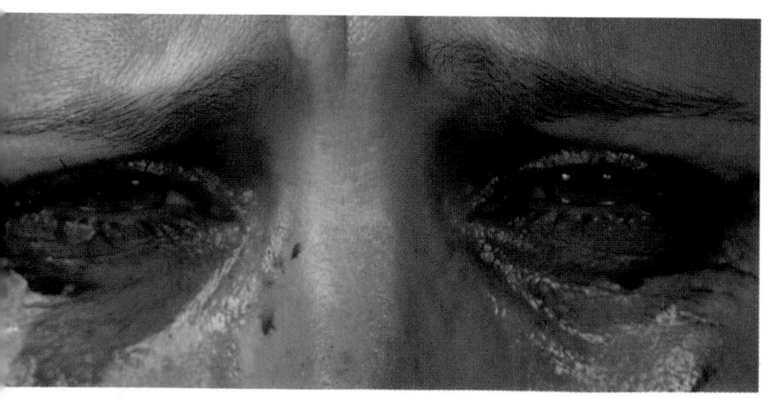

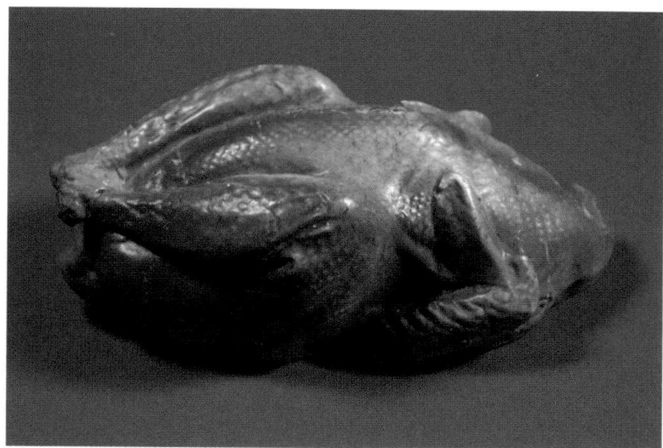

Once the food has arrived, I display it in a way so people can help themselves: it's all about the flow of the table.

It is also a good idea to have a wide assortment of alcohol on hand. Drinking kills feelings. Make sure that you crack the seal on all the liquor bottles ahead of time because mourners don't want to feel inhibited about diving in.

I always like to keep what I call a grieving kit tucked away in my closet for these occasions. It's like a first-aid kit for the brain.

THE GRIEVING KIT

It's a thoughtful idea to personalize a handkerchief for the grieving person. So if the name is Jocelyn Ellen Wortis, a nice hand-stitched "J.E.W." on a hanky would be so touching.

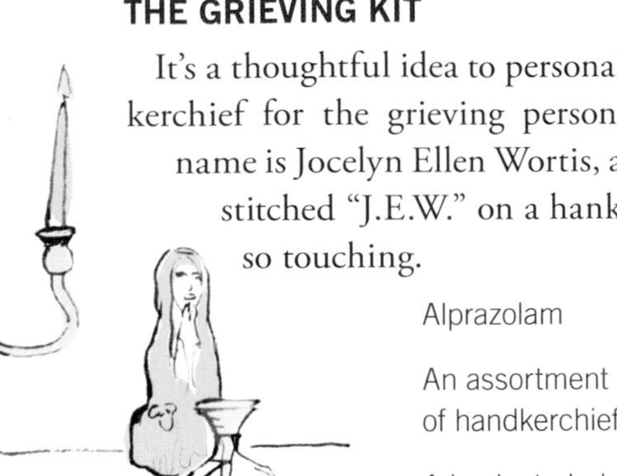

- Alprazolam
- An assortment of handkerchiefs
- A laminated picture of a religious figure or icon
- Candles
- A mix tape of sad songs
- A tuft of hair from the deceased
- Extra alprazolam

When one is in the company of the grieving, one must be considerate of the words we choose. So often we want to say something comforting to the grieving, but are stuck for something to say.

Appropriate Things to Say

My sympathy to you.

He will be missed.

He had a lot of friends.

At least they didn't suffer too much.

She lived a good life.

Be careful what you wish for.

Inappropriate Things to Say

He's better off now.

You'll meet someone new, speaking of which, I know this guy who works at the Wax and Wicker. He's got a green card!

Only the good die young.

I know exactly what you are going through, I mean, I didn't lose my husband to a boating accident, but I can imagine.

Give it 3 weeks, you shouldn't grieve more than that.

Was he drinking?

Where were you when this happened?

He told me you two split up.

Did she smoke?

He had a secret life.

A Living Will

Everyone should have a living will. You can pick one up at the post office for peanuts and it's good because all your belongings will go to someone specific instead of going to a holding area for a few years.

If you are grieving, have someone stay at your house while you are at the funeral parlor because crooks will comb the obituaries to see who has died and break into your home to steal things. The last thing I want to do is add any more stress to someone who is grieving, but you should know you are a ripe target.

If there is something someone has given you and you don't like it, get rid of it while they are still alive. Otherwise, if you don't, then you will only be hanging on to it out of guilt, and clutter piles up. Also, it just encourages them to give you more of the same.

GINA
HOT
NUTS
JENNIFER
ARTICHOKES
AU GRATIN
VICKI
PICKLED
BEETS
MICHAEL
KEY LIME PIE
MARK
BLOODY
MARY
PAUL
ZUCCHINI
FRITTERS

LOIS
HOT CHICKEN SALAD

LAURIE
DEVILLED EGGS

ANTONIA
WINE

AMY
TURKEY AND GRAVE-Y

SISTER
OUT OF THIS WORLD
POTATO SALAD

LOIS'S HOT CHICKEN SALAD

2 cups celery, chopped

2 cups cooked chicken, diced

½ cup silvered almonds

½ teaspoon salt

2 teaspoons lemon juice

2 teaspoons onion juice

1 cup mayonnaise

1 can cream of mushroom soup (undiluted)

2 cups potato chips, crushed

Pour boiling water over celery. Let set for 15 minutes and drain. Mix all ingredients together except potato chips. Place in casserole. Top with potato chips. Bake at 450 degrees F for 15 minutes. Courtesy of Billy Erb.

MICHAEL'S KEY LIME PIE

1 can sweetened condensed milk

2/3 cup key lime juice

2 egg yolks

1 premade pie shell

1. Preheat oven to 400 degrees F.
2. Whisk milk, lime juice, and eggs until well blended.
3. Pour mixture into pie shell.
4. Bake 10–15 minutes.
5. Cool in refrigerator at least 2 hours. Courtesy of Michael Ingulli.

PAUL'S ZUCCHINI FRITTERS

I don't use a measuring cup when I make zucchini fritters although I probably should. I suppose I like the crapshoot quality of cooking without specific measurements. It's exciting. Although, there is some safe ground, because whenever a recipe calls for breading and then frying in olive oil, it's hard to go wrong. Here is generally what you will need:

1 zucchini

More flour than you think you'll use

1 to 3 eggs

Salt and pepper

1 onion, chopped

A little parsley, chopped

1/4 pound of feta cheese

Garlic, sliced

The first step is to grate the zucchini, and then place it in a strainer. It's important to get as much water out of the shredded vegetable as possible. It helps to salt it, then place a heavy lid or bowl on top of it and press down. When you think you've got all the water out, keep pressing because I can tell you, you haven't. Now, in another bowl mix the flour, egg or eggs, salt and pepper, onion, parsley, feta, and garlic. Your goal here is make a light batter. Add more flour if it seems watery, or another egg if it's not binding. Place the drained zucchini into the batter and mix with your hands.

You are really going to have to get in there. Coat the bottom of a skillet in olive oil. Heat it up. For best results, make sure it is good and hot before adding fritters. Scoop a fistful of mixture from the bowl. Shape it into a small patty and place in skillet. Makes approximately 20 to 40 fritters. No one can really say for sure. Courtesy of Paul Dinello.

SISTER'S OUT-OF-THIS-WORLD POTATO SALAD

2 pounds boiled potatoes

1 cup mayonnaise

1 tablespoon Dijon mustard

2 tablespoons white wine vinegar, or fresh lemon juice (I prefer cider vinegar)

3 hard-cooked eggs, chopped

½ cup sweet red pepper, finely chopped

½ cup white or yellow onion, minced

½ cup bread and butter pickles, finely chopped

3 tablespoons fresh parsley, minced

Salt and black pepper

Crisp, fried bacon, crumbled for garnish, optional

Sweet red or gold pepper, cut into shapes (I like stars), optional

Wash the potatoes under running cold water, scrubbing well to remove soil. Fill a pot with enough water to cover the potatoes by 2 inches and boil. The preparation of the potatoes is time consuming, so it's good to start this first and, while the potatoes are cooking, get on with your prep work. When water is boiling, add the potatoes and cook until tender when pierced, about 25–30 minutes. Do NOT overcook.

Drain. As soon as the potatoes are cool enough to handle, peel them, cut into cubes of uniform size and place in a bowl (I like them about 1½ inches or chunky bite size).

In a separate bowl, whisk or stir together the mayonnaise, mustard, and vinegar or lemon juice. GENTLY toss enough of the dressing into the potatoes to cover completely. Stir in the eggs, chopped sweet pepper, onion, pickles, and parsley. I usually add 1 teaspoon of salt to start. If it's too salty, it's not good. If it's not salty enough, it's terrible. I tend to go light on the black pepper. Your choice.

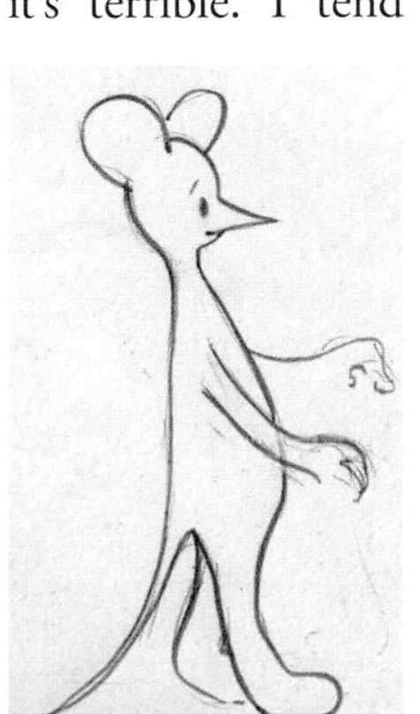

Serve the salad at room temperature or slightly chilled. Just before serving, garnish with bacon and red pepper cutouts.

Courtesy of Alan Mace.

JENNIFER'S ARTICHOKES AU GRATIN

20 ounces frozen artichokes, cooked and drained

2 tablespoons butter

2 tablespoons flour

½ cup half-and-half

1 chicken bouillon cube dissolved in ½ cup boiling water

1 tablespoon dry sherry

½ cup Gruyère cheese, grated

Salt and pepper to taste

½ cup Parmesan cheese, grated

Place artichokes in a well-greased 1½ quart baking dish.

In case you don't know: Make the white sauce by melting the butter in a saucepan. Add the flour and stir until it forms a paste. Add the half-and-half, chicken broth, and sherry.

Stir this until it thickens, then add the Gruyère cheese, salt and pepper. Melt cheese and pour over artichokes. Sprinkle with Parmesan cheese and bake at 350 degrees F for 15 minutes. Serves 8.

Courtesy of Jennifer McCullen.

GINA'S HOT NUTS

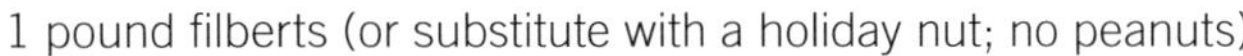

1 pound cashews

1 pound almonds

1 pound pistachios

1 pound filberts (or substitute with a holiday nut; no peanuts)

½ pound butter (softened)

2 large sprigs of rosemary without stem, pieced

Pinch of cayenne (add more if you want the nuts extra spicy)

1½ cups brown sugar

1 cup candied ginger (cut into very small cubes)

Salt to taste

Preheat oven to 325 degrees F. Bake nuts for 10–12 minutes until golden. Do not brown. In a bowl, cut up butter and add remaining ingredients. Add the hot nuts to the bowl and toss frantically. As butter melts add more sugar or other dry ingredients to taste. Let cool on a baking sheet until sugar hardens onto nut. Courtesy of Gina Vetro.

AMY'S TURKEY AND GRAVE-Y

Roast a turkey until the internal thermometer pops out. Remove the turkey from the pan and set aside. (Follow any recipe you would like for roasting a turkey.)

To make the gravy, pour off all but 8 tablespoons of fat from the turkey pan. Add about ⅓ cup of flour and cook for about 3 minutes. Add 3 cups of turkey broth (recipe below), ¼ cup of red or white wine and cook, stirring and scraping in the brown bits that are clinging to the pan. The gravy should now look thick and smooth. Add salt and pepper to taste.

TURKEY BROTH:

To make turkey broth, put 4 cups of water in a pan and add all the turkey's insides that come in that little bag that is inserted in the cavity: the heart, gizzard, neck, and wing tips.

Put 1 carrot and 1 onion in the pot as well as some celery tops, parsley, salt, and pepper. Simmer while your turkey is roasting; just keep your eye on it and add more water when you need to. Strain the broth and use it when you are making the Grave-y, above.

VICKI'S PICKLED BEETS

Boil 5 pounds whole beets until done. Peel and slice into hot sterilized jars. Bring to a boil:

2 cups of cider vinegar

1 cup of water

1 cup of sugar

Salt and pepper to taste

Pour mixture over sliced beets and seal jars. Courtesy of Vicki Farrell.

MARK'S BLOODY MARY MIX

1 teaspoon horseradish

1 teaspoon lemon juice

2 squirts Worcestershire sauce

1 shake celery salt

1 pinch black pepper

3 drops Tabasco sauce

4 ounces tomato juice

Combine all ingredients and garnish with a celery stalk.
Courtesy of Mark Ibold.

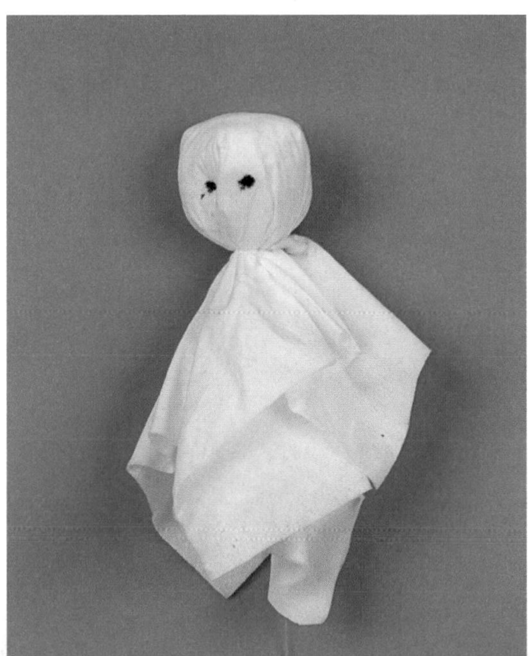

Ladies' Night

Shhhhhhh. Put your head back and shut your eyes. It's okay, don't be afraid, although this will sting a little. Imagine a beautiful outdoor water park with jet sprays spurting onto a slide. Shhhhh. Let all that luggage go. Leave it at the door. It's not invited here. Relax . . . calm, calm, hold still, fight it, fight it . . .

Hello, I'm Amy Sedaris and welcome to my Night of Beauty, an evening of tossed salad, Spa-ghetti, light drinks, and dry exfoliating. "Tossed," "light," and "dry" are the key words here. This sofa will act as my clinic: I call it Patina. That's me with the low cut uniform and pantyhose. Can you smell all that perfume? Excuse me if I get my ample bosom in your face while I take a closer look. Oh my, we've got our work cut out for us, don't we? Let's get those shoes and pants off. Why don't you fill out this index card so I'll have all your information on file, while we discuss the major pitfalls of your face. Excessive sebum, check. Pockmarks, noted. Sun damage and freckles, you betcha. And then there is that growth . . . hmmm. Why don't you relax while I first fix you a drink—a large glass of warm water and a slice of lemon to help you detoxify before I retire to my lair to assemble the right mixture of creams, lotions, emollients, and perhaps a lancing tool, so that we can tackle your . . . situation. While I'm gone, don't forget to fill out the back of the card as well, especially the part about dating status, including the last time you had relations. It matters.

Steak Diane or Yogurt Spa-ghetti

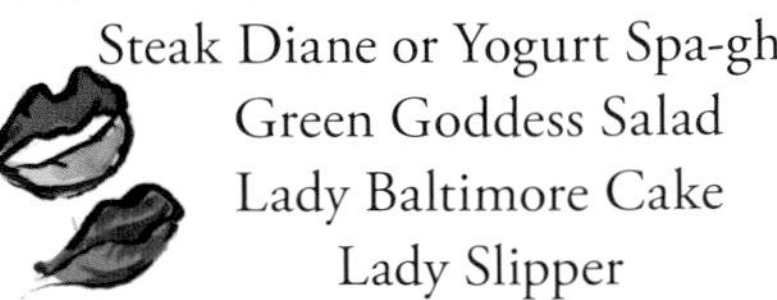

Green Goddess Salad

Lady Baltimore Cake

Lady Slipper

YOGURT SPA-GHETTI

(Inspired by the book *The Glorious Foods of Greece* by Diane Kochilas)

5 large Vidalia onions, coarsely chopped to about the size of a postage stamp

6 tablespoons olive oil

1 pound spaghetti

2 cups Greek yogurt (thick)

1 cup coarsely grated sharp cheese, preferably Kefalotiri

1/2 cup roasted pine nuts

Fistful chopped parsley

Sauté the onions in oil on medium to low heat for about a half hour, until onions are brown (caramelized). Leave them in the pan. Then boil spaghetti in salted water. Drain pasta, saving a half cup of pasta water. Mix yogurt and pasta water in a bowl, then add half the cheese and all the caramelized onions and roasted pine nuts. Toss all ingredients well. Top with remaining cheese and parsley.

I'm back. I hope I wasn't gone too long. You're not my only customer. Why don't I change your drink to something more liquory? Is the music too loud? I hope you like it: I call it ambient environmental music. I have a bootleg copy for sale. I'll give you a street price. Let's get back to your face. No time to lose. It's time for CEP: cleanse, exfoliate, purge. Bye-bye blackheads, hello red welts. Next, I'll apply a mask. I bet that feels good the way I'm rubbing on the mud and massaging your face. Good, completely coated. Now I'll place

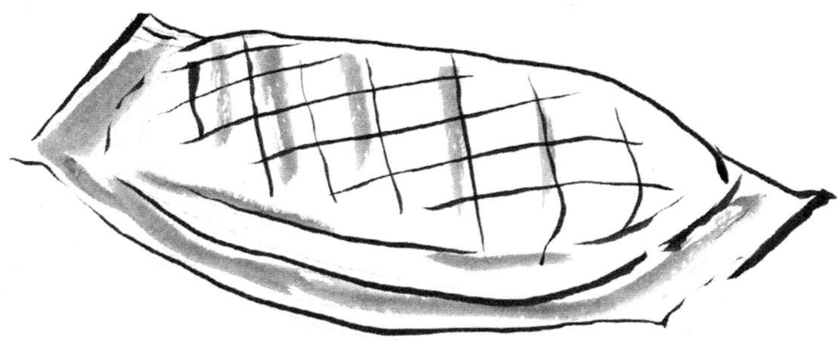

two chamomile tea bags on your eyes to rejuvenate the sockets. I'll set a timer. Generally you want to give a mask ten to twenty minutes to dry as it absorbs the many toxins from the skin and soothes it from the violent purging. For you, we're gonna go forty-five.

It's me again. I couldn't tell if you were dozing or the liquor was kicking in. Just to hedge our bets, let me fill your glass again. I'm applying warm water to your mask, which will soften and then remove all that chalky residue. What we'll be left with is squeaky clean skin and of course that growth. Next I will be spraying your face with homemade grapeseed water. This does nothing, but it's included in the cost.

It's lotion time. I will now apply a special roux of moisturizing crème that will hopefully reverse the severe drying effects of that mask. Let's just get this slathered on good and thick. There you go. Now, we'll just pat you down with a tissue to sop up some of that excess moisture. I always use cotton balls because tissue leaves embedded fibers in your skin. There you go, perfect. Now you have about the same amount of grease as when you walked in. I'm gonna go wash up and clear my roll cart and return with a fresh salad and some other healthy delights. While you are eating, I will fill out an evaluation slip and suggest purchasing some of the products I used on your face, which are for sale at street prices. Tell you what I'm going to do: I'm going to put you on something that I want you to take three times a day and it's going to make you feel better about yourself and where you're going in life. I don't do "happy endings," but I can recommend a guy who does—he works at the Wax and Wicker and he has his green card. Here's his number.

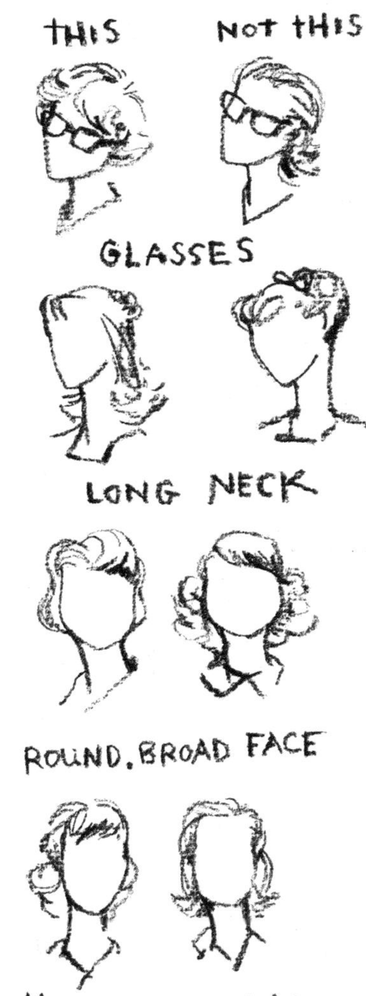

Here also is a brochure detailing some other services I provide: hair washing, waxing, foot massage. You might want to consider returning for Group Beauty Night, also known as Ladies' Lockup. Some of the events will include breast and pelvic exams on the house as well as tube tying, hair removal, and genital cleansing. You can also expect a full menu. Oh, and lastly, on the way out don't be afraid to become intimately acquainted with my tip jar.

Crabs

Crabs are light brown, small, and flat. They need your blood to survive. Crabs live in the hair of your armpits, chest, eyebrows, and eyelashes. For more information go to your local library. Drawing by Kabuki.

name [redacted]
age 27
Are you in the sun a lot? No.
How often do you wash your face? 1x day
Fav. color? None.
Sports? Basketball.
How often do you participate in sex What?
describe your body? Huh? Sorry, can't read.
What shape is your face? Round.
Have you ever kissed a boy? On the lips?
What's your fav. season? Winter.
Scars? One, on face.
Do you smoke? Nope. Except cigars.

name [redacted]
age less
sign ☮
been here before? ☒ yes ☐ no
do you wear make-up? Never
allergies? Shell fish
bath? ☐ oil ☐ powder ☐ bubbles ☒ salts
Do you eat meat? Yes
Brush or comb? Brush
lotion or cream? lotion
Do you sleep on a futon? no
Are you dieting? no
Acne scars? no

name [redacted]
age 38
Do you smoke? yes
Do you get a lot of sun? no
When is your next book due? ~~Sept~~ March 96
How do you say Beauty night in French? nuit du beauté
Do you lie? yes
Can you drive standard shift? no
What's hugh like in bed? DYN-o-Mite
How much makeup do wear? none
Do you have the Aids? no
do you have pets? yes.
what did you eat today? a ham + cheese sandwhich

name [redacted]
age 33
last time you washed your face? before London - a long time ago
what do you use? ∅
what sign are you? cusp of Leo + Cancer
Are you madly in love? I can't answer that right now.
Do you have any diseases? bad intestinal track, bad back - ringing in the ear
Did you vote? yes
3 things that make you feel good? naps, basketball, reading during the day
what is your feeling about willow trees? Irritate the nose.
owls? Boring - they kill
Medication? ∅
Soap? whatever is available

GREEN GODDESS SALAD DRESSING

1 tablespoon of lemon juice

1 cup of mayonnaise

½ cup of sour cream or heavy cream

2 tablespoons of tarragon vinegar

2 tablespoons of garlic vinegar

1 tablespoon of anchovy paste

⅓ cup of chopped parsley

¼ cup of chopped green onions

Add lemon juice to creams, then mix everything else in. Serve chilled over endives or any other lettuce, asparagus, or broccoli.

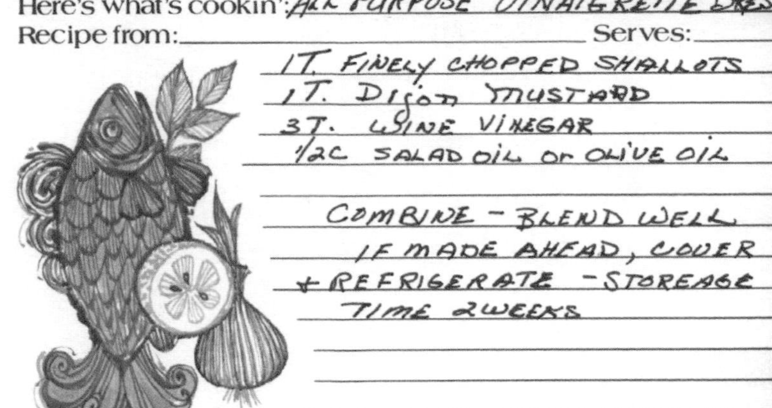

Here's what's cookin': ALL PURPOSE VINAIGRETTE DRES
Recipe from: Serves:

1T. FINELY CHOPPED SHALLOTS
1T. DIJON MUSTARD
3T. WINE VINEGAR
1/2C SALAD OIL OR OLIVE OIL

COMBINE - BLEND WELL
IF MADE AHEAD, COVER
+ REFRIGERATE - STORAGE
TIME 2WEEKS

STEAK DIANE (FOR 4)

1 pound of thinly sliced filet mignon

3 tablespoons of butter

POOF

1 tablespoon of parsley

1 tablespoon of chives

2 teaspoons of Worcestershire sauce

2 teaspoons of A.1. Steak Sauce

Brown the meat on both sides. Remove to a platter. Add remaining ingredients to the pan and stir until well blended. Pour over steaks.

CAT TOY

Put googly eyes on a tampon with no applicator. Magic marker the tail. Drive your puss-puss crrrrrazy.

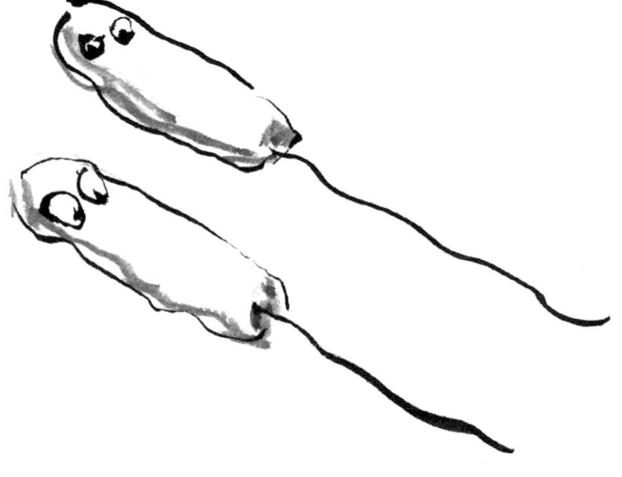

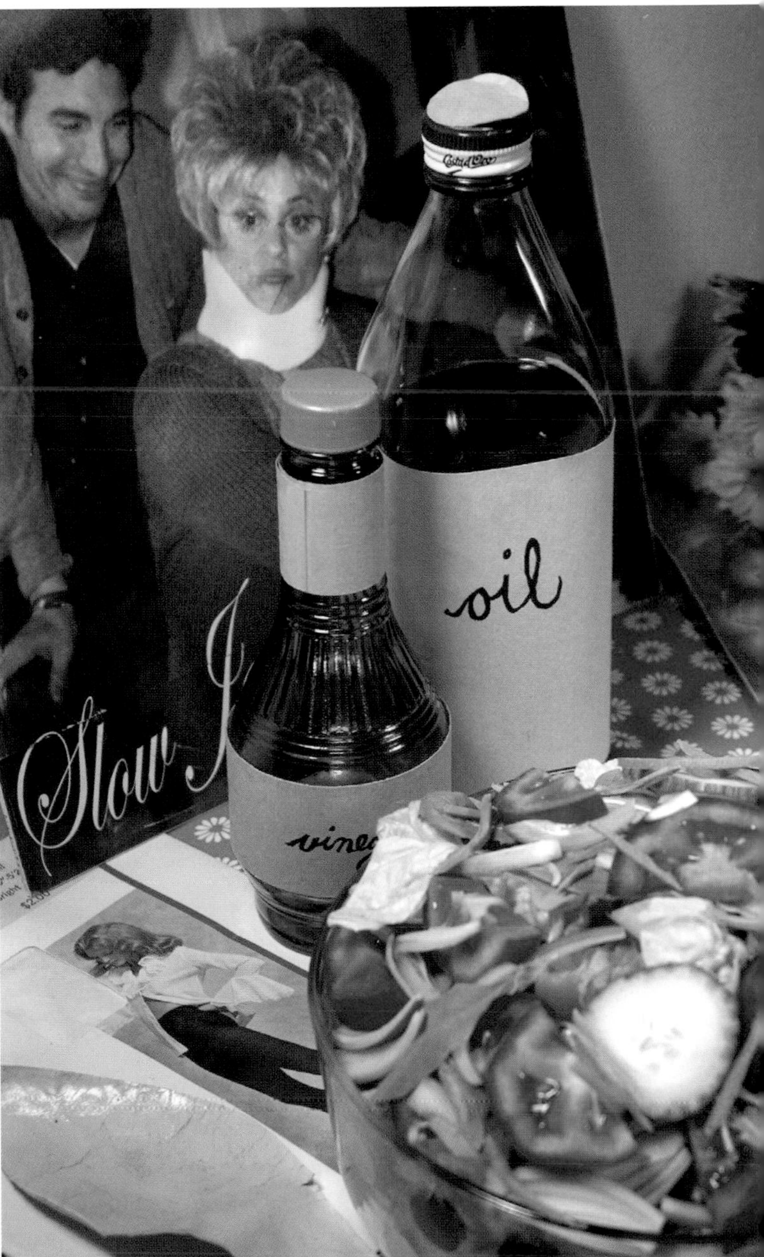

LADY BALTIMORE CAKE

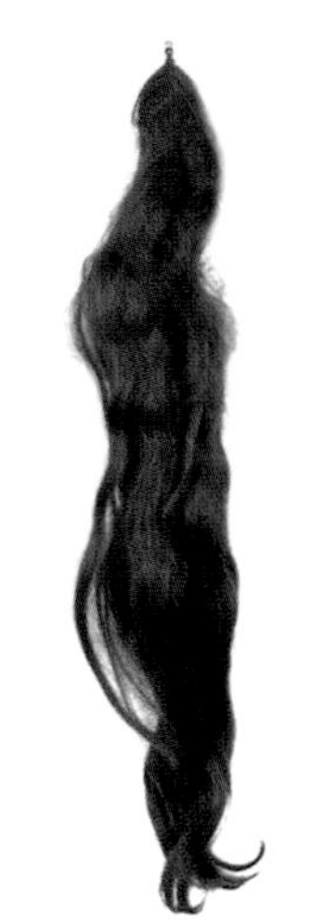

3/4 cup shortening

1 cup plus 3/8 cup sugar

6 large egg whites

3 cups cake flour

4 teaspoons baking powder

Salt

1-1/3 cup milk

2 tablespoons vanilla extract

Cream shortening with 1 cup sugar. Whip egg whites and gradually add the 3/8 cup sugar. Sift dry ingredients together. Add dry ingredients to creamed ingredients, alternating with milk and vanilla. Fold in whites at the end. Bake in two greased and lined 8-inch cake tins at 375 degrees F for 25 minutes.

FROSTING (DIFFICULT):

2 cups of sugar

Water (a little over 1/2 cup)

4 egg whites

2 teaspoons of vanilla extract

Cook sugar and water to soft ball stage (falls from spoon in thin backlashing thread).

Add a pinch of salt to egg whites and beat until stiff. Pour in syrup in a stream, beating continuously until spreading consistency.

Add to half of frosting:

1/2 cup raisins (snipped and soaked in a little liquor)

1/2 cup chopped walnuts

1/2 cup chopped figs

HAVE FUN.
Courtesy of Hugh Hamrick.

LADY SLIPPER

In a pitcher, combine some vodka, pink lemonade, and a little cranberry juice (optional: splash of maraschino cherry syrup). Stir and pour straight up in small glasses or on the rocks. Garnish with a lime and a loose cherry.

SUGGESTION

Calorie-free soda adds sparkle to iced fruit juices. Not only does it make them go further, it also reduces calories for those ladies who are watching their figures when no one else is.

Another good activity for Ladies' Night would be to have an accessory swap.

FRÄULEIN MAGIC

1/4 ounce of Egyptian musk oil

13 drops of lavender oil

1 drop of jasmine oil

Rub oil on your pulse points.

Courtesy of Nicki Lederman.

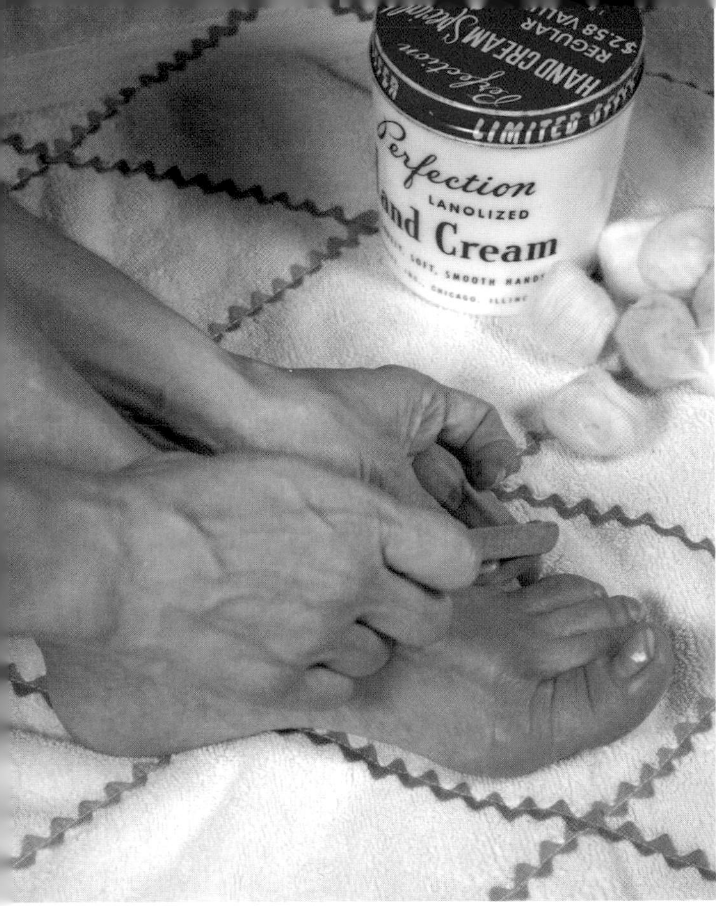

How To:

If one were to take a close, almost clinical look at your vagina, what would they find? Would they be impressed? If it's well maintained, chances are better than average that the answer will be a resounding yes. What is the best way to maintain a vagina? Believe it or not, it's as simple as warm water and a little elbow grease. There is no need to bother with douche or deodorants. Start by separating the outer lips of the vagina and tugging back the hood of the clitoris exposing all those unpleasant secretions that collect around the glands. Next, a liberal dose of clean warm water teamed with a spirited scrubbing, taking care to work the folds, and the results will speak for themselves. Our body secretions and smells are an unfortunate part of our bodies, but if you wash regularly, you will smell and taste good. Trust me, or better yet, ask my doorman.

Bloodstains, Ladies?

Use a bar of soap and wash garment under cold water or, if the stain has dried, use some hydrogen peroxide. If they are old stains, go shopping.

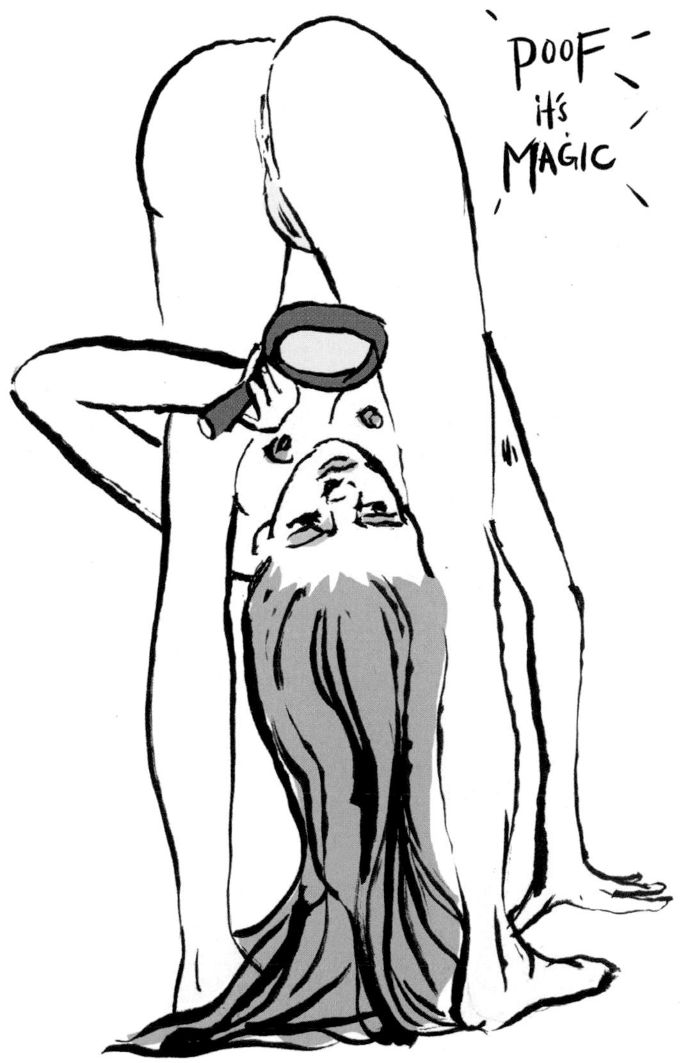

Witchy-Poo Poof Products

THE RIPE BANANA MASK

Enriching mask with banana and almond oil.

1 ripe banana

2 tablespoons of rosewater

1 egg yolk

1 tablespoon of almond oil

1 to 2 tablespoons flour

In a blender or food processor, combine all the ingredients except for the flour. Add the flour in small increments until the mask forms a smooth paste.

On clean skin, apply the mask to face and neck, avoiding the eyes. Leave on for 20 minutes and remove with warm water.

- Can be used up to 3 times a week.
- Banana helps skin find its pH balance.

Courtesy of Antonia Xereas.

WITCHY-POO LOVE POTION

Essential Oil Essentials:

Musk oil

Chocolate oil

Patchouli oil

Almond oil

POOF it's MAGIC

Clean out old perfume vial or buy some from a beauty supply store.

For a vial: 2 parts musk, 1 part chocolate, ½ part almond, ½ part patchouli.

MUST SHAKE WELL BEFORE EACH USE.

Another option is to keep all 4 essential oils separate. Just create whatever stimulates your own senses on any given day, for if you feel sexy, no one can resist you. It's a good idea to keep musk as the base note. Mix the drops on the back of your hand and then apply to neck and cleavage.

Apply Witchy-Poo when you know you will be seeing the one you lust after.

Courtesy of Callie Thorne.

WITCHY-POO'S DETOXIFYING SALT SCRUB

Use any kind of jar that is easy to scoop your hand into. Always use scrub before shaving; the exfoliation and oils will prove for a closer shave. Avoid rubbing the scrub on any cuts or scrapes, the salt will only irritate or burn them.

Ingredients:

Plain old table salt

Jojoba oil or safflower oil or apricot oil (In a pinch you can even use olive oil or vegetable oil. But never use mineral oil; it will clog your pores and dry out your skin.)

15 to 20 drops of your favorite essential oil

You want to create a consistency that is not too thick yet not too thin. Essentially this means 1 part oil to 2 parts salt. Start low with the essential oil and add more depending on how long you want the scent to last after the shower or bath.

In the shower, scrub from neck to toe to relax your muscles and to detoxify your skin. Rinse the salt thoroughly and then let the oil deeply moisturize with the heat of the shower.

For the bath, use the scrub while standing (before you get wet), then dunk in the tub and let the salt dissolve in the water while the oil moisturizes.

HINT (ONLY FOR SHOWER):

POOF

If you want to invigorate the skin and lessen the look of cellulite, mix 2 parts ground coffee with 1 part oil, and scrub away.

Courtesy of Callie Thorne.

Keeping You Abreast

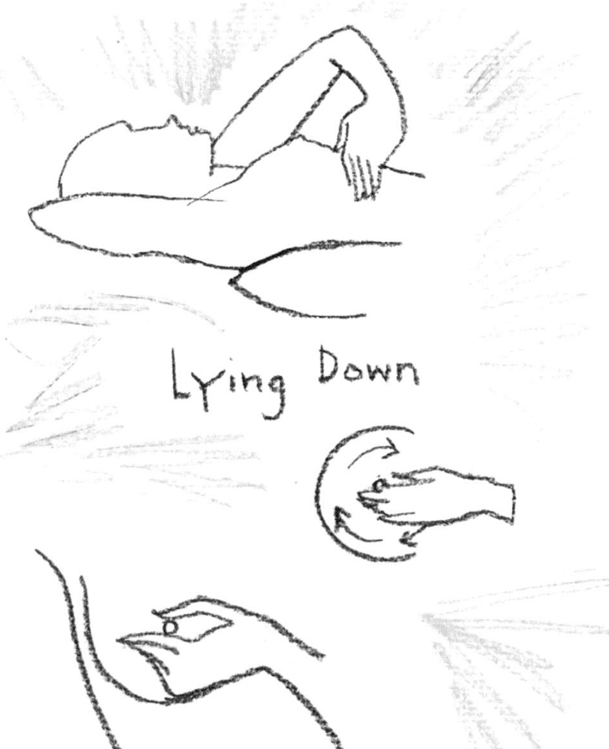

Regular
pineapple scented
Tampons

WITCHY-POO'S EGGY MASK FOR DRY SKIN

- 1 egg, beaten
- 1 tsp. olive oil
- 1 tbsp. whole milk
- 3 pinches salt
- 1 tbsp. flour

Mix up the wet ingredients until well blended. Then stir in the dry ingredients. The mixture needs to be wet, but thick enough to stay on your face. If it's too thin add more flour. If it's too dry add a little more milk.

Once you have found a good consistency, spread over clean face and neck. Leave on for 15 minutes, then rinse with warm water. Follow with your favorite moisturizer.

HINT: Add a few drops of lavender oil to tone.

Courtesy of Callie Thorne.

To keep color on your lips when your lipstick wears off, you can stain them first using a cherry popsicle (just keep one in the freezer) and/or use those little pink dental plaque tablets.

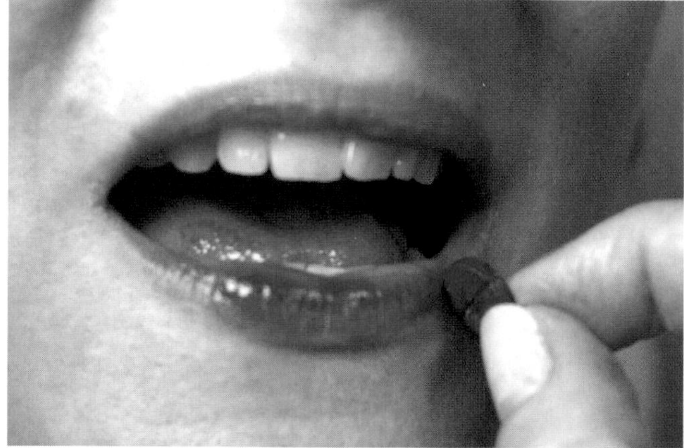

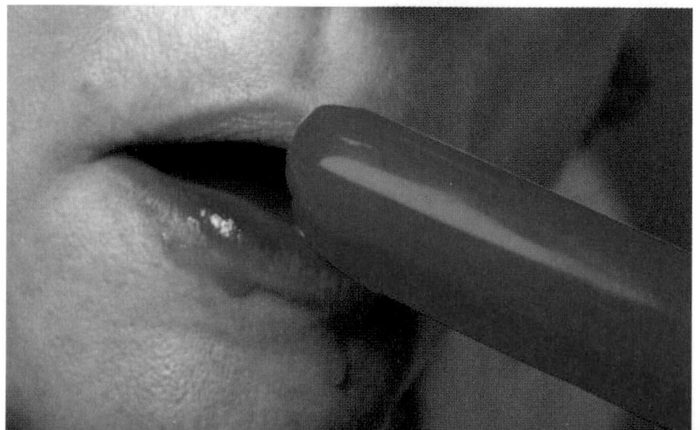

Green Toenails?

One cup of table vinegar in a Tupperware basin. Soak the toes daily and this will help get rid of the green cyano pigments created by the pseudomonas bacteria under the nail (and, of course, go see your dermatologist). For dry cracking toenails/fingernails apply household Vaseline before bed to all the nails and eat Jell-O brand gelatin (orange). Your nails will be stronger and better and glossy in two weeks. Courtesy of Dr. David Colbert.

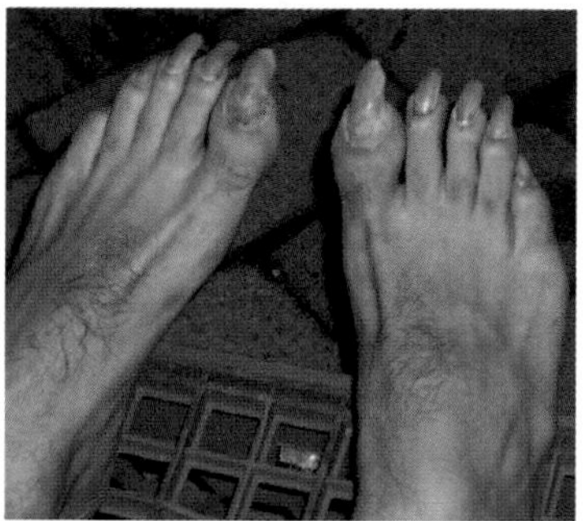

You can easily curl your eyelashes using a small espresso spoon. Press your lashes along the edge of the spoon using your thumb. The heat from your thumb will help to set the curl. Do not use a pencil.

How to Iron Your Hair

You will need an iron and an ironing board. Place either a piece of silk or a brown paper bag (based on income) between your hair and the ironing board so you don't burn it. Set your iron on low to medium and press briefly. Section hair and repeat. Courtesy of Orlando Pita, hair stylist, and Karen Thorne, astrologist.

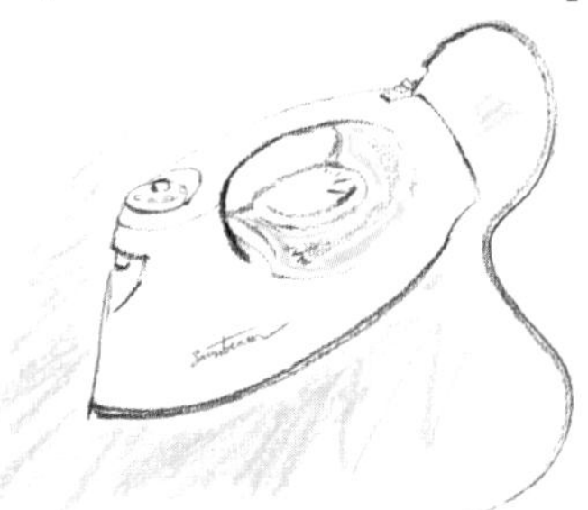

"If you feel good wearing red lipstick, regardless of what anyone says, then wear it."

—Kevyn Aucoin, makeup artist, departed

Pointers to Help You Sleep

Darken the room
Hot bath (remember a shower perks you up, a bath relaxes you)
Lavender oil or sachets (see page 267)
Red wine
Tincture of valerian root
Don't worry about staying awake

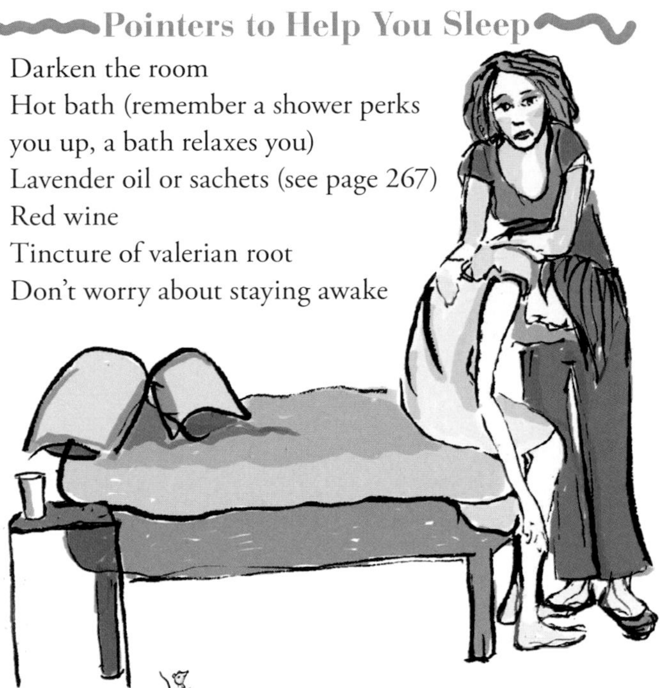

"To remove hair color from the hairline, place fresh cigarette ashes on the stain and rub off with water."
—Evan Hyisky, hair stylist

"Sleep on your back."
—Jaqueline Kennedy Onassis

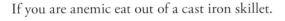

If you are anemic eat out of a cast iron skillet.

"The little curls that you place in front of your ears are called kiss curls and sometimes 'man catchers.'"
—Miss Perfidia

Make sure your wig is always secure. Just a few years ago there was a woman in Florida praying to God in hopes that her town would be safe from a hurricane and a strong gust of wind came and blew the wig right off her head.

When using hairspray on your wig, use the same amount you would on your own hair.

Tips from Beauty Expert Jim Crawford

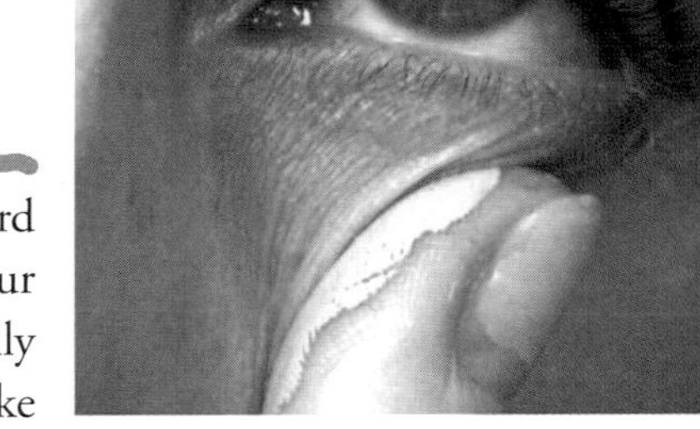

You can use old standard milk of magnesia on your face as a mask. This really works. It will appear like a liquid clay and it contains lots of minerals that help to restore and detoxify your skin. A Cuban woman told me the same thing, and her face is perfect.

Sour cream is a soothing agent and a good remedy for razor burn, so you can use it under your arms, or on your face, bikini line, or even your legs to help take away the stinging and burning.

Remember to always work in an upward motion when applying any product or moisturizer. The skin under the eye is the thinnest on the body and needs extra attention and care.

You can use the old home remedy of salt for oily skin and sugar for dry skin. Use them when removing a mask to help exfoliate.

Entertaining the Elderly

There is a lot to consider while entertaining the elderly; for one, they're old. They don't like quick movement and they can't hear very well. I don't mind pointing out some of the failings of old age, because we are all headed in that direction, unless of course we take our own lives before we become a burden. I'm not advocating suicide, oh wait, I guess I am. All right, fine, let's just all grow old together.

When I waitressed, I noticed it was common when old folks came in for the Yellow Plate Special, for them to want the music turned down and the heat and lights turned up. I try to keep this in mind when I entertain the elderly.

It's never good to stereotype. All of your guests are individuals with different needs. Except in the case of the elderly. You can pretty much count on all of them not liking loud music and being cold. Elderly people like to eat early. Plan your schedule around them. Nobody wants to prechew a roast beef at 4:00 in the afternoon, but these are the concessions you will be making when entertaining the elderly.

Bland food that is easy to chew and digest is a good idea, but that doesn't mean it shouldn't be visually cheery. Mix colors, and use festive dishware.

It's important to interact with the elderly after a big meal. This is touch-and-go time and they need all the stimuli you can muster. Keep them engaged or it's the express train to nappy-land.

Toss a balloon back and forth. Offer to treat them to a foot soak in an Epsom salt bath. Plant seeds. Read them a story or pore over a photo album and reminisce. Thread some needles for them to take home, but by all means keep them engaged.

Just as you need to childproof a home when young ones are invited, considerations need to be taken when having the elderly as guests. Make sure the rugs are secure and the traffic patterns are clear. If you have a small dog, enclose him in a room so that he doesn't get under a walker or jump up on laps.

With all the special attention needed, one might ask, why entertain the elderly? The answer is this: elderly people have much to offer. They have years of experience stored in their brains. Of course it might prove difficult getting it out. I suppose the most important reason is soon you will be in their comfort shoes, and wouldn't it be nice to be invited to a party?

If peanut appears blurry, then eyeglasses are needed.

THREE GIN-SOAKED RAISINS

This is good to have every day because it helps with arthritis.

Menu

I Remember the War Cube Steak
Canned Pork and Beans
Mom's Potato Salad
Banana
Dustbowl Junket
Glass of Champagne

I REMEMBER THE WAR CUBE STEAK

Cube steak is an inexpensive cut of beef. Melt in skillet 3 tablespoons of butter. Take cube steak and bang it with a mallet until it is riddled with pockmarks. Dip in flour. Cook as you like it. Season with salt and pepper and top with postage-stamp size butter squares.

Other foods that are good to keep in mind when cooking for the elderly:

Bananas
Raisins
Ice milk
Turnips
Tomato juice
Lentils
Escarole

MOM'S POTATO SALAD

Scrub potatoes. Boil in salted water. Drain. Put in refrigerator. When cold, peel skin off, cut into small squares. Add minced green onion, chopped egg.

Optional: 1-1/2 cups mayonnaise, 1 tablespoon mustard, 1 tablespoon wine vinegar, 2 teaspoons celery salt. Measurements vary.

Stain Suggestions

You can use 2 denture cleaning tablets to clean your Corning Ware by filling them up with water and dropping the tablets in for about 45 minutes.

Gift Ideas

- Your time.
- Offer to walk their dogs.
- Take their cat to the vet, rake their leaves, take down their Christmas tree. Discard their jack-o'-lanterns. If they know another language encourage them to practice it. Crack their ice cube trays, listen to them when they talk about the past. This will also keep them from talking about all their aches and pains. You learn more by listening than by talking, I know I already said that, but maybe you'll hear something they didn't say.
- The older they get the more they want to go to church, so offer to drop them off and pick them up.
- Comb their hair or style their wig.

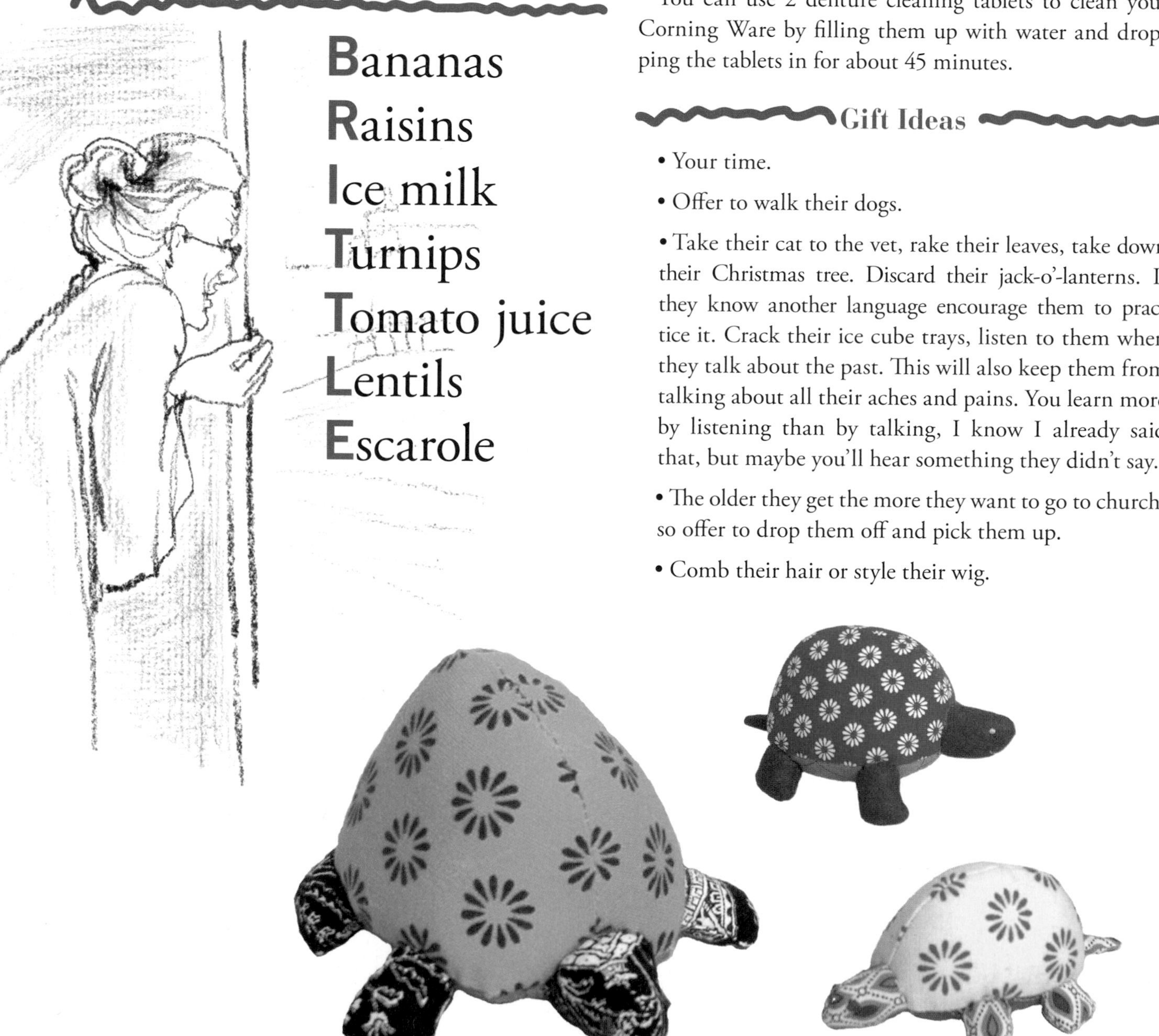

Fruit Salad

For Salt Map instructions, see page 278.

Baked Alaska

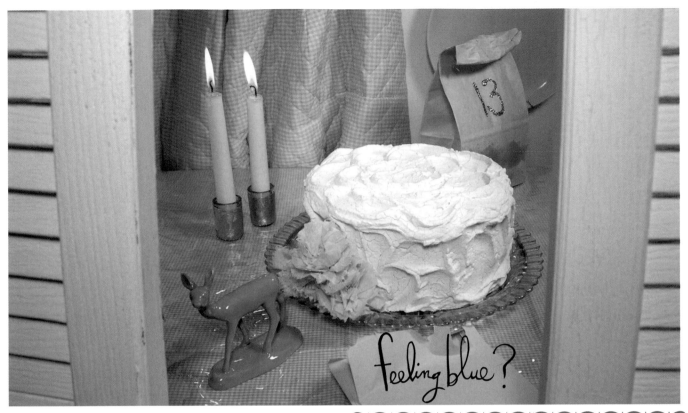

PARENT/TEACHER YELLOW CAKE

- 2 cups of flour
- 2 teaspoons of double-acting baking powder
- 1/2 teaspoon of salt
- 1 stick of unsalted butter, room temperature
- 1 cup of sugar
- 3 egg yolks
- 1 cup milk
- 2 teaspoons of pure vanilla extract

Preheat oven to 375 degrees.

Mix all of your dry ingredients except sugar in a bowl. Put aside. With an electric mixer, cream your butter and sugar until light and fluffy, add the egg yolks and mix thoroughly. Add the dry ingredients to the butter mixture, alternating with milk until thoroughly blended. Stir in the vanilla.

Bake in 2 greased and floured 8-inch cake pans for 25 minutes.

BUTTERCREAM FROSTING (SEE PAGE 182):

Frost between each layer. Then frost entire cake.

You can dye the frosting a pale cool green or light pink.

THREE WAY CAKE

WITH CUPCAKES AS SLOPPY SECONDS

- 1 eight inch layer of Yellow Cake
- 1 eight inch layer of Chocolate Cake
- 1 eight inch layer of Spice Cake

Use the extra batter to make a variety of cupcakes and frost as desired.

CHOCOLATE CAKE

Follow recipe for Parent/Teacher Yellow Cake. Add 2 melted squares of baking chocolate to the butter and sugar mixture.

SPICE CAKE

Follow recipe for Parent/Teacher Yellow Cake. Add 1 teaspoon of cinnamon, 1/2 teaspoon of cloves, and 1/2 teaspoon of nutmeg to the flour mixture.

When You Get to Play Nurse

I wanted to be a nurse because I liked the TV show *Julia* and I also liked how black nurses got to dress. Growing up, our next-door neighbor was a roaming nurse, and she would go into old people's homes and give pelvic exams because they had a hard time getting to the doctor's office. She would gather all the children in the neighborhood and show us educational sex education filmstrips. She always had these plastic see-through round stackable containers the size of crab cakes in her refrigerator to keep patients' throat cultures in (see What Not to Put in Your Refrigerator). She had a habit of putting her hands on her hips and wiggling them around. It was fun to imitate her and it felt good to know that a nurse lived next door. Maybe this is why I like to play nurse. And nothing gives you a better opportunity to play nurse than entertaining for sick people.

At first thought, it might seem like a difficult challenge entertaining sick people, and this is confirmed with a second and even third thought. But in my eyes it's an opportunity to play nurse. I'll even go as far as to wear my nurse outfit, just to lighten things up. Anybody could entertain a room full of young, attractive, healthy people, but get a room full of sick people together and you've got a tough audience. We all know someone who's ill. Whether the illness is mental, emotional, physical, or psychosomatic, these fun-starved undesirables have as much right to entertainment as the healthy.

Before your festively frail guest or guests arrive, make sure you create an environment that feels warm and safe, almost womb-like. Turn down the phone, cover your clocks, and keep the lights dim. Put away your Judy Collins tape, razor blades, and rainstorm sound machines. Get yourself in the proper mood. Accept that this party is over before it even begins, because when you are dealing with sick people seldom does the evening ever gel into anything that could even remotely be called a party. Make sure you have a complete first-aid kit in your home. Make sure the address to your home is visible from the street so the ambulance can find it easily (also good for the elderly).

I recently stabbed myself in the nose with a 3-in-1 tool and I didn't have an ice bag. I was forced to quickly create one by filling a dish towel with ice, cutting up a pair of pantyhose and tying together the loose ends to secure the ice on my face, bandit style. The one plus of my makeshift ice bag was that because it was fastened to my head, I could walk around with it and finish my scraping. If you do find you are in a situation where you need an ice bag and you've neglected to make sure one was in your kit, a frozen bag of peas will do in a pinch. This is also good to cradle between your legs for soreness.

Most importantly, when entertaining the infirm, be prepared to listen. Whether your guest had a relationship that has just gone south or a recent cranioplasty, they're going to want to talk about it. Take advantage of this time to do your own thinking. Sharpen your ability to look concerned while thinking of other things.

Steer away from jolly drinks, such as Singapore Slings, Daiquiris, or Mai Tais. You don't want anything too playful. Often these people want to spend some quality time dwelling on their problems and don't want to be reminded that there are happier things in life. You're gonna have to go to their side of the room, the basement.

It's good to serve comfort food, like Rice Krispies Treats. Leave them on a table and don't push them too hard. They're there if your guests want them.

Nonny's Rice is another good food suggestion. This recipe is perfect for comforting someone who doesn't feel safe (see page 240).

I will have my peanut bowl full, 25-cent cupcakes on the table, a nice jar of colorful candy, especially for ex-heroin addicts and alcoholics (they love colorful candy), and I'll put out lots of ashtrays. Keep a pack of cigarettes in your freezer, because these are the type of guests that will get even more depressed when they run out and there is no backup. They're apt to jump out a window. Avoid asking your guests a lot of questions, such as: "Do you want another drink?" or "Are you hungry?" The last thing these people want to do is make decisions or be interrupted during the story you've heard for the fifth time. Food and beverages should just appear.

Smell sells. I'll bake cupcakes an hour before my sick guests arrive so the house smells familiar and comforting, unless they've just broken up with a pastry chef. In that case either serve flammable food, or none at all. I also have a lot of fake meat displayed in my apartment. I find placing a sheet of tin foil on top is a good trick because they'll think it just came from the oven and it will give them a cozy home feeling. Have plenty of tissues nearby, but don't make it obvious. Never encourage tears. One time, I was in a car with a girl who was crying and driving at the same time. It was like driving in a rainstorm without wipers.

Never steal a sick person's pills. Apparently, it agitates the sick when their limited stash of doctor-prescribed narcotics is missing. Even though you'd been a gracious host, listened to their endless droning, and allowed them to stay way past an appropriate time, they scream at you over a few lousy pills. Granted, you never asked for any compensation for putting up with them for a whole evening, but I think it's understood that there should be some. Hell, what psychiatrist is going to accept four or five hydrocodone as payment for an eight and a half hour session? I was offering them a bargain.

If a person has a serious illness and cannot function without your help it will be necessary to prepare a sick room (see "Long-Term Care," page 161).

It is important to remember that most people feel uneasy spending time with someone they know is sick, especially if the person's illness is a mental illness, and this is unfortunate because sick people often feel abandoned and neglected. Once you yourself have experienced being sick and know what it's like to depend on someone's help, you'll know exactly what to do when you get to play nurse.

RICE KRISPIES TREATS

1½ bags of small marshmallows

4 tablespoons margarine

6 cups Rice Krispies Cereal

Melt margarine and marshmallows (1 bag). Add cereal and remaining marshmallows and form in a 9 x 13 inch greased pan. (Use greased waxed paper to help form mixture into pan.) Pat the mixture so it is good and tight. Let it cool and cut into squares or diamond shapes.

Long-Term Care

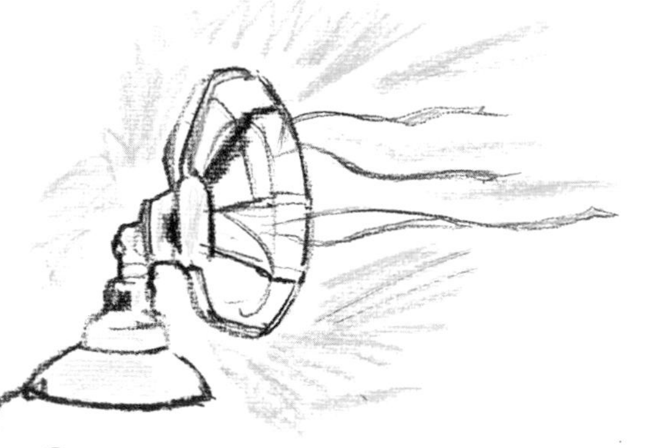

How to Fix a Sick Room

When playing nurse to a long-term patient, you will want to set up a sick room. The sick room should be clean, attractive, and empty of small accessories that are distracting. If the room has a fan, attach colorful streamers to it so your patient can see them come alive. If you have a plant or flowers in the room, remove them at night so you can freshen them up for the morning. You don't want anything dying in the sick room. If you have a TV set, don't put it high up in the corner like a hospital. Make sure the TV has a remote. On the bedside table, there should be a bell to summon help. You can make your own bedside tea bell (see page 162). Your goal is to make your patient as comfortable as possible and you can do that without draining your jars of money.

You need fresh pillowcases every day because they can get soiled (also applies to alcoholics). The bed may need extra protection so you might want to use a plastic or a rubber sheet (also applies to alcoholics). It might be a good idea to make a waste disposal bag that you can hang on the side of the bed for used tissues, banana peels, or other disposables. The bag should be taken away every day and set on fire. If you don't have a bed tray and you want to feed your patient in bed, you can make one. Find a cardboard box that looks like it would be big enough to cover their hips. Cut out sections allowing the table to fit over the patient's body. Cut small holes on the sides for handles. You can decorate the box by painting it or covering it in sticky shelf paper or cotton balls. You can make a footrest by taking that same box and putting it at the end of the bed so they can rest their feet against it. When I see those little white paper cups for ketchup in fast-food restaurants, I take a few. They're free. Next time you need an aspirin try putting it in a small white cup before you ingest it; this will really make you feel like a sick person. Also, next time you're in a doctor's office, snag a few urine sample cups. They make great gifts and are fun to have on display in your bathroom.

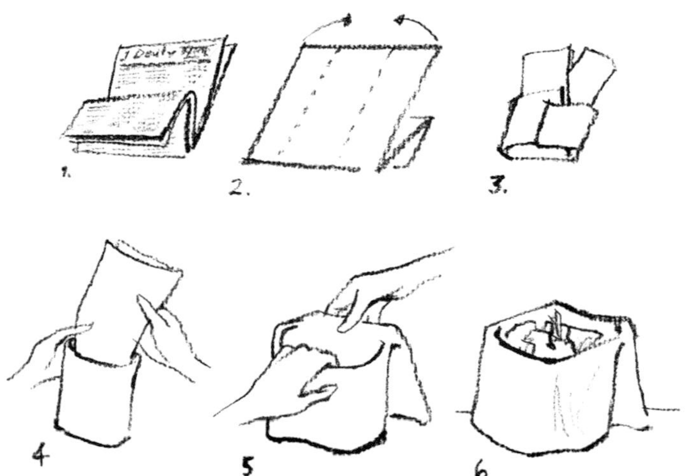

As far as food goes, you might be following doctor's orders, but regardless, try to make the food colorful and as easy to eat in bed as possible. Put something attractive on the tray, like a flower with googly eyes on it or a pinecone that's been dipped in glitter.

Try to be as entertaining as possible because if a sick person gets bored they might try to entertain themselves and often they don't have the strength to do this. Read to them, give them books on tape, sharpen pencils, decorate clothespins, make jewelry out of potatoes and carrots (see "Jewelry Making," pages 280–281), toss a balloon back and forth. If your patient is a sick woman, you can boost her morale with lipstick and colorful nails. If your patient is a man, try a shave and a new hairstyle.

- When you are going to see a doctor, wear loose-fitting clothes so it's easy to roll up your sleeves.
- When going to see a dentist, remove your lipstick.

A nurse told me once that patients tend to do better around the same time they were born, so if you were born at night chances are you will feel better at night.

- Pez holders are great for holding hydrocodone, just pull back the head and take what is being presented to you.

call the Police

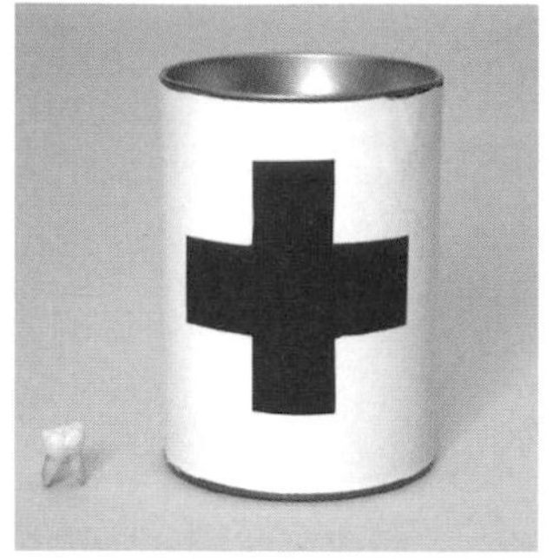

THE TEA BELL

Find a metal can with a tight lid. Put a tooth in it. Cover the can back up and shake it when you need something or when you need help. You can make the can pretty by painting it, or use sticky shelf paper. Other suggestions for the contents are: dice, dried beans, marbles, dimes, or buttons.

- To feel how frustrating it must feel to not be heard when needing help, take the contents out of the can and shake it. It's a horrible feeling.

Gift Suggestions for the Bedridden

- Stamps
- Sack of oranges

Change your medicine chest from herbal remedies to something that works—fast-acting, no-nonsense pharmaceuticals.

SLEEP AIDS

Exchange valerian root for **BENZODIAZEPINES.**

ENERGY AIDS

Exchange ginseng for **AMPHETAMINES.**

MUSCLE RELAXANTS

Exchange lobelia for **DIAZEPAM.**

ANTIANXIETY

Exchange skullcap or kava root for **ALPRAZOLAM.**

Gypsy

It's easy to admire the lifestyle of gypsies, a colorful and spirited people with the ability to pull up stakes and hit the road at a moment's notice. Usually that notice is served by either the authorities or angry townspeople, for gypsies also tend to be a filthy, dirty, thieving people. That's the word on the street, anyway. When you are called upon to take your party on the road, be it to a picnic, a friend's house or a relative stuck in bed, it helps to think like a gypsy. You must pack lightly, but efficiently. Just like a hobo, another lovable scamp, you'll need a completely portable party that can be wrapped in a handkerchief and tied to the end of a stick. You can never count on finding what you need once you arrive at your destination, so you must be covered. One time I lugged everything needed to prepare a three-course meal to a friend's house, with the exception of cinnamon. She assured me that she had some. Soon after I arrived and started cooking I discovered that what she thought was cinnamon was actually cayenne pepper. My rice pudding tasted like a sweet Spanish risotto. We still aren't speaking.

Many times I go to people's homes to cook for them because they seldom cook for themselves. I never expect these people to have the things they say they have. They could confuse a bay leaf with a vanilla bean only because they both come in jars. They might mistake shaved wax

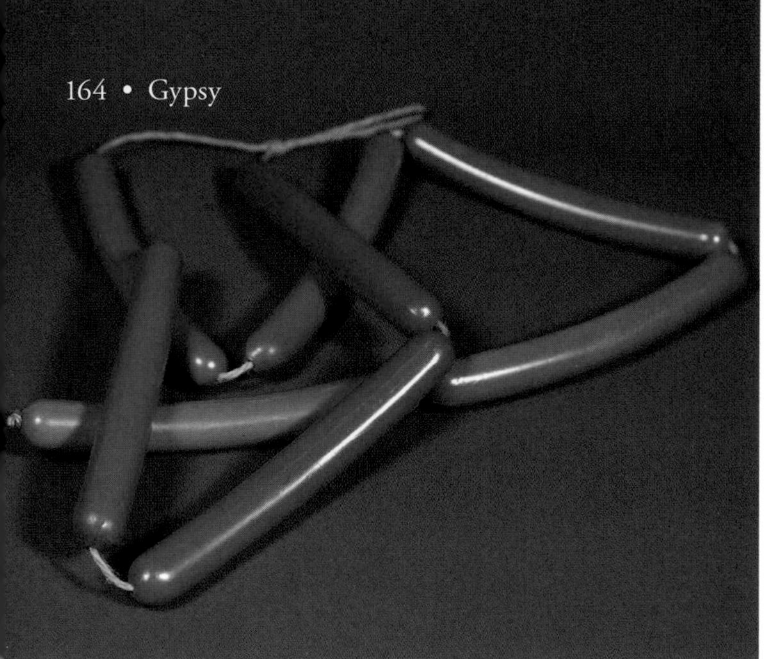

for coconut, or mashed potatoes with ice cream. The list goes on. They are often clueless about the kitchen, so when cooking in others' homes, be sure to bring knives, pans, ladles, cutting boards, foil, Saran Wrap, paper towels, and dish soap. Don't assume the butter they have in their refrigerator is fresh or actually butter. Bring your own fresh ingredients. Also think about the containers you're using. You might not want to put potato salad in a sandwich bag or use film canisters for ketchup and mustard; this will make the food less desirable. Respect your food. Also, respect your containers: you don't want to put a stool sample in a coffee cup.

If you are one of the people who doesn't know how to cook, and someone is coming over to your house to cook for you, be courteous enough to empty your sink of dirty dishes. Maybe straighten up the house a bit, and check that you have toilet paper. Gypsies and hobos don't ask for much.

Because gypsies are known to have tin cups and cans hanging off their belts I have included some simple outdoor recipes you can make using these rustic utensils.

When hand-washing the delicates, add a 1/2 cap of chlorine bleach to a basin full of creek water to keep the whites white.

BILLY GOAT TIN CAN POTATO STEW

First thing you want to do is put your name on the can so you don't confuse it with somebody else's can.

Find two zipper-size pieces of bacon to line the bottom of the can. On top of the bacon, layer all the vegetables you can gather, like onions, tomatoes, carrots, celery, potatoes, and green beans. If you are fortunate enough to come across ground beef you'll want to add this as well.

Place can on an open fire and cook for 25 minutes, adding a little water or wine if it's cooking too fast. This works best when the can has some sort of lid, so look for a can that has its lid still connected.

POTATOES COOKED IN A TIN CAN

Take one of the larger cans off your belt and fill it with some dirt. Find a potato and bury it in that dirt so the potato doesn't touch the sides of the can. Place on top of an open fire and cook for 45–55 minutes. This also works best when the can has a lid or some tin foil placed on top.

PICKPOCKET'S POCKET STEW

Take a piece of foil and wrap it around beef, potatoes, onions, and carrots and place in the embers of a campfire. Cook for 25 minutes. This is good for other combinations as well, like hot dogs and onions, and hot dogs and hot dogs.

TOAST ON A STICK

Place a piece of bread on the end of your stick and hold it over an open fire until it looks tanned.

"HIT THE TRAIL" TRAIL MIX

Mix any combinations of nuts, berries, and seeds to take on your journey. Place in bandana and tie to a stick. May also include chocolate morsels.

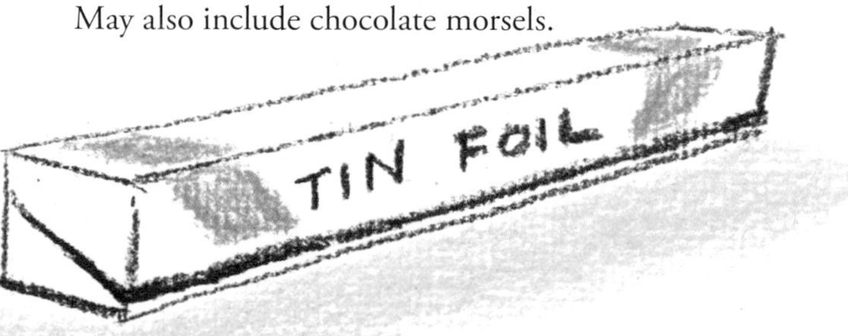

GIMME SOMEMORES

You'll need chocolate bars, graham crackers, and marshmallows. Make a sandwich with the chocolate and graham crackers. Toast a marshmallow. Put it in the sandwich on top of the chocolate and press.

SALAD ON THE RUN WHEN RIDING THE RAILS

Steal an apple off a tree, cut the top off and core it. Fill the hole with nuts and raisins and chocolate morsels and then replace the top.

If you are going to be traveling with a large group, it is best to meet up at dinner so you have something to talk about. Skip breakfast; you'll just get roped into touring caves and shallow-water snorkeling.

The Nature Trail

- Vodka is distilled from potatoes.
- Sassafras plant is used in making root beer.
- Mushrooms don't need sun to grow. The Spanish Lady mushroom is called such because it resembles a flamingo skirt. It grows like a counter on trees.
- Snakes can't hear.
- Black snakes are nice—they eat rats and keep copperheads away.
- Worms don't have legs.
- Only female wasps can sting.
- Bears walk on their toes and heel.
- Moss always grows on the north side of a tree.
- Maple wood doesn't splinter.
- Rhubarb leaves make a light-green-colored dye.
- Saffron makes the brightest of golds.
- Dandelion greens make magenta.

THE GYPSY (BANDIT STYLE, ON THE ROCKS)

1½ jiggers of vodka
1½ teaspoons of orange juice
1½ teaspoons of fresh lemon juice
½ jigger of Bénédictine liqueur

Shake with ice and strain. Pour over rocks. Garnish a chilled glass with an orange slice.

- If you form a teepee with your hands over your nose, you'll block your view and simulate the perspective of a prey animal's eyesight, kind of.
- Actors and gypsies are a lot alike. They always come sniffing around at dinnertime for a free meal or a glass of wine.
- Poison ivy—leaves of 3 let it be, leaves of 5 will get you high.

Gift Ideas for Gypsies

Compass
Can opener
Shoe inlays
Hairpins
Waterproof matches
Trail mix
Corkscrew
"It's not your fault" lice comb

For more of a gourmet gypsy recipe, see Oxtail Ragout on page 256.

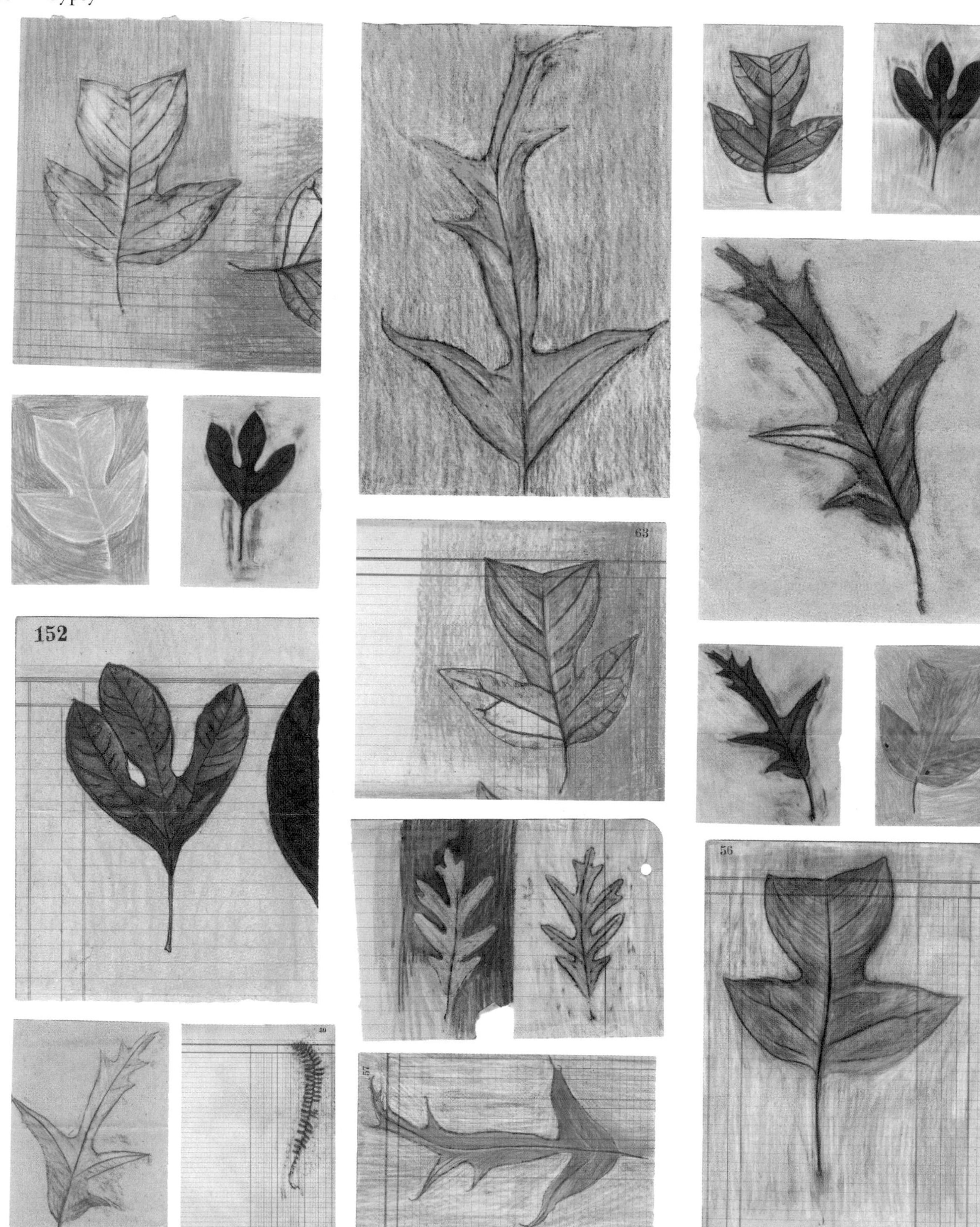
152
63
56

Price Chompers

Growing up, every fall my brothers and sisters and I would turn the basement into a movie theater and charge the children in the neighborhood 25 cents to watch the *Wizard of Oz* or *To Kill a Mockingbird* when they would be shown on television. We'd serve simple snacks and beverages, and then kick everybody out once the movie ended. This laid the groundwork for what was eventually to become Price Chompers, a discount in-home movie theater experience.

As far as I'm concerned, entertaining and television never go together. I immediately shut down if I'm at someone's house and a guest flips on the TV "to catch the score" or to see a favorite celebrity on a talk show. If the television is going to be on, then that should be the focus of the evening. The best part of Price Chompers is it's a wonderful way to entertain if you're not in the mood to talk. If you know a lot of people that you like but have a hard time finding something in common with, then watching a movie is perfect because it gives you something to talk about afterward.

I like to have Price Chompers in the fall when the weather starts to change. This is the perfect time to turn my home into a discount movie theater. I always have a theme and plan to show at least a couple of films. If it's the month of October and Halloween is near, I pick scary movies. Or maybe I'll have a special selection of Jane Fonda movies and call it "Jane Fondling Nights." I may even serve fondu.

To prepare for Price Chompers, I set up my living room with comfortable chairs and get out my TV dinner trays. If you have a pull-down movie screen that is great because it really gives the room a movie theater feel. I like to make my own movie tickets to sell to my friends at discount prices. Admission is open to all, although I do ask ticket buyers to arrive freshly shampooed because it's my experience that most discount venues tend to smell like dirty hair.

As guests arrive, I dim the lights and play organ music to make their entrance seem dramatic. I set up an easel announcing what films will be screened and use my ironing board as a concession stand where I sell budget candy, popcorn, and drinks.

PUMPKIN PIE

Directions are on back of can of pumpkin. Follow that. Make festive silhouettes using some cookie cutters. Place on the pie after it's been in the oven for 15 minutes.

Before the feature starts, I show "appeteasers" to warm up the audience. This can be anything you've collected that can be projected and is only a few minutes long. It could be highlights from a family vacation, a clip from a favorite TV show, footage of an in-home operation, or something educational like propaganda films. After the "appeteasers" program, I have a five-minute intermission where I serve the type of meal that doesn't require one to see it to eat it. Remember, your guests will be eating in the dark. At the climax of the movie, just before the important facts are revealed, I like to start vacuuming just to remind the audience that this is, after all, a discount theater.

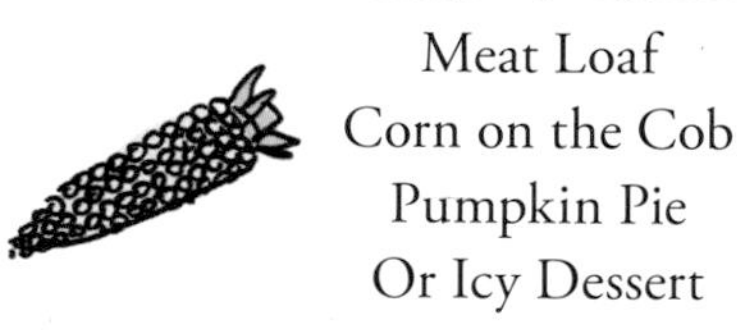

Meat Loaf
Corn on the Cob
Pumpkin Pie
Or Icy Dessert

CORN ON THE COB

Boil corn in water for just 2 minutes or so. Roll in stick of butter. If you boil with a little sugar the corn won't be tough.

MEAT LOAF

Meat loaf has a lot of variations so be creative and change it up.

- 1-1/2 pounds of beef
- 3 tablespoons of Parmesan cheese
- 2 eggs
- Parsley
- Salt and pepper
- Worcestershire sauce
- 1 onion, chopped
- 1 garlic clove, crushed
- Mix about 2 cups of breadcrumbs with 3/4 cups of milk
- Ketchup
- Slices of red onion (keep intact so they are large disks)
- Red wine, eyeball it, about 1/2 cup (optional)

Mix everything together in one big bowl. Mix it really well using your hands. Add as much ketchup as desired to this mixture. Form into a loaf or ring pan, or make a shape and bake it in a large pan. Top meat loaf with the red onions and bake for 45 minutes at 350 degrees F. You can substitute bacon slices for the onion. All ingredients can vary.

ICY DESSERT

Cut an orange in half, scoop out the insides and replace with your favorite ice cream or sherbet. You can't put it down . . . literally.

These Are a Few of My Favorite Moments in Movies that Involve Food

In *The Autobiography of Miss Jane Pittman* when Jane and her family are eating rice pudding out of bowls using wooden spoons, the sound the spoon makes against that bowl is one of my favorite sounds. I like to recreate it when I make my rice pudding (see page 52).

In the movie *Trilogy of Terror* it's obvious Karen Black's character knows nothing about cooking when she goes into the kitchen, takes out that cookie sheet, places some chicken on the sheet and cuts it up, and then puts the sheet in the oven and turns it on.

Best example of preplanning a meal is in *Coming Home* when Jane Fonda has Jon Voight over for dinner. The minute she walks in she takes a blender of margaritas out of the freezer, blends it some more, pours it in pre-prepared chilled glasses, explains the device that has been cooking the meal all day (Crock-Pot), and walks into another room where the table has been preset.

A perfect example of what 15 minutes before a party is like for a hostess is in the opening of Mike Leigh's movie "Abigail's Party." A perfect example of unexpected guest is in the Cassavetes movie, *A Woman Under the Influence* when Gena Rowlands entertains a table of firemen.

Meat Loaf Wreath

SUGGESTIONS

Clubs

I love clubs. Well, mostly I like starting them up. I am currently the president of four clubs. As president, I've discovered one must be very selective when accepting members. Attempting to join one of my clubs is no different than trying to join a private country club. Sometimes there is a long waiting list. Occasionally it's restricted. If you fail to get into one of my clubs, don't try to force your way in, start your own club. If I am confident you are not going to be accepted into my club you can be sure I am going to subject you to a lengthy and complicated application process, because the only thing I like as much as starting up a club is sending encouraging rejection letters. Here is a sampling of rules a member of one of my clubs might have to adhere to:

- Nonrefundable initiation fee
- Regular and generous contributions to my "vacation fund jar" (see page 187)
- No pets, unless it's mine
- No running unless you have scissors in your mouth
- No horseplay
- Must show pass
- No radios, TV, or lyrics to listen to
- Bring your own towels
- No guests, unless it's been okayed
- No instruments
- Bookshelf-building ability
- All long hair must be worn under a cap, especially if it's gray
- What happens in the club must stay in the club

ARNOLD PALMER

1/2 cup iced tea

1/2 cup lemonade

Chipped ice

A lemon wedge really drives it home.

When I was younger, my clubs were a good place to learn how a true democracy worked (see "The Money Jar," page 32). Everyone in the club had the freedom to voice an opinion and the majority ruled. Now, I don't have time for democracy. The only way for a club to achieve anything is through a strict dictatorship. When the goal for the group is to create "felt woodland creatures," an iron fist produces the quickest results.

Clubs are a good way to help strengthen weaknesses. If you are shy, join a club. If you want to read more, join a book club. If you want to manipulate people into doing free work and give you money towards your vacation fund, start a club, or in my case, a lot of them.

One of my oldest current clubs is called the Crafty Beavers. We mostly spend time "herbally enhancing our moods" and then making things out of pinecones. Because the Crafty Beavers has a closed membership, I started a splinter club called Creative Daze. It is similar to the Crafty Beavers in that we spend a lot of time enhancing our moods and then making stuff out of pinecones.

Anyone can start up a club. You need a president, a treasurer, refreshments, a space, and of course, members. It's also nice to have a mascot. The mascot for Creative Daze is a worm named Montgomery (see "Montgomery's Disguise Kit," page 112). You also need bylaws and rules so you know how to punish those members who don't follow rules. Excommunication is often effective. Try to avoid starting clubs that are essentially just a hangout for divorced bitter people. Let these people start their own club. I tried starting a sad sack club where members sat around discussing how sad they were feeling. The club was a

huge success until other people started talking. I quickly dissolved this club. Sad.

If your club is meeting at your home, it's important to provide some nourishment. I try to serve dishes that are simple to prepare, don't take a lot of time to serve, and are easy to eat, so you can quickly get back to the club activity. For this reason, I like to prepare a meal that doesn't require knives and can be served entirely in individual large bowls.

No Squirrels

Menu Suggestions

Rigatoni with Pesto
Baked Chicken Thighs or Quarters
The Club Club Salad
Aunt Joyce's Brownies (see page 224)

PESTO SAUCE

2 cups of fresh basil leaves

3 minced garlic cloves

2/3 cup of grated Parmigiano-Reggiano

1/4 cup of pine nuts

Salt and pepper to taste

2/3 cup of olive oil

Place all these ingredients into a food processor (I use a small one). Blend until thoroughly mixed. Makes one cup.

BAKED CHICKEN THIGHS OR QUARTERS

Coat a baking pan with oil. Coat the chicken thighs or quarters (legs with thigh) with some olive oil, a little lemon, salt, and pepper and lay in the bottom of the pan. Sprinkle with oregano and dot with butter. Bake at 400 degrees F for about an hour depending on how much chicken you have. Serve it in a bowl with a salad and maybe some small roasted potatoes.

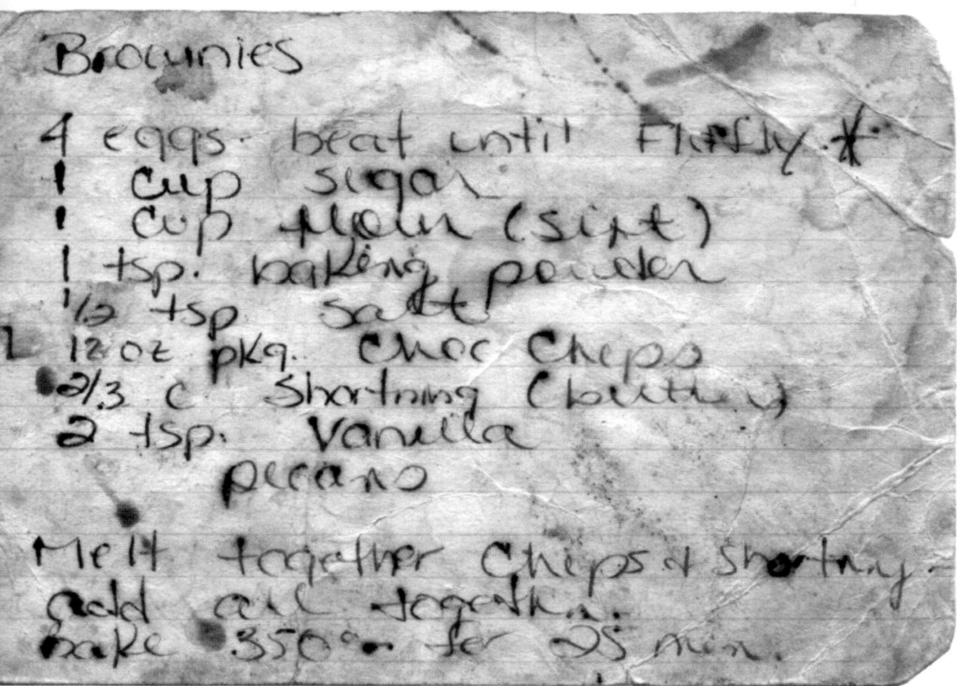

Brownies

4 eggs - beat until Fluffy *
1 cup sugar
1 cup flour (sift)
1 tsp. baking powder
1/2 tsp salt
1 12 oz pkg. Choc Chips
2/3 c Shortning (butter)
2 tsp. Vanilla
pecans

Melt together Chips & Shortning.
add all together.
bake 350° for 25 min.

Who? what? Where?

Start a fake cake (see page 279) decorating club—either make your fake cake at the meeting or bring it with you and sit around and decorate it.

OR

Start a pinecone club. Decorate pinecones and drop them off at your local nursing home so nurses can decorate bed trays with them.

THE CLUB CLUB SALAD

- Arugala, romain, or just red leaf lettuce
- Sliced red onion
- Sliced cherry tomatoes
- Roasted pine nuts
- Salt and pepper
- A little crumbled French feta
- Olive oil and red wine vinegar dressing

Sometimes I put in julienned carrots. If serving pesto, I omit the pine nuts.

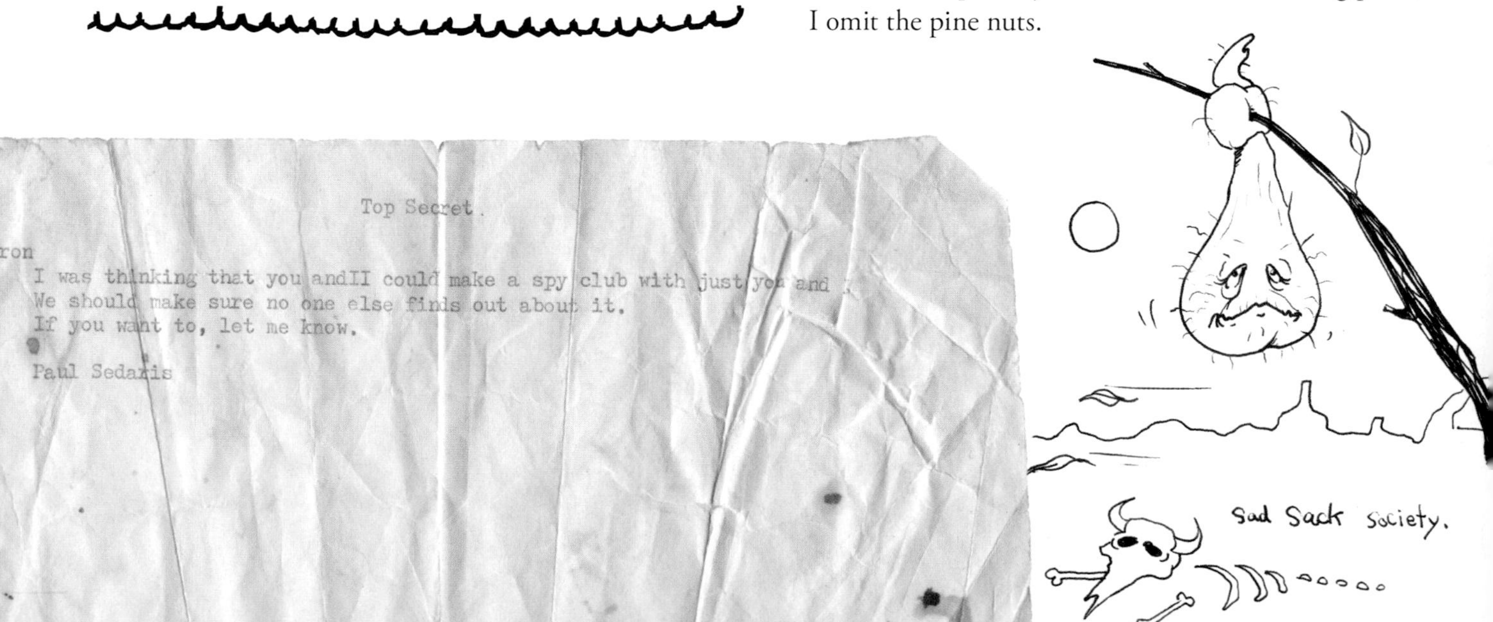

Top Secret

Deron

I was thinking that you andII could make a spy club with just you and
We should make sure no one else finds out about it.
If you want to, let me know.

Paul Sedaris

Brownies

JUST DUSTY
NO Squirrels
a "Hare" above the rest!

I have a rabbit. I don't want to say too much about it because talking about your pet is like talking about what you were doing at the age of seven, or your spiritual trip to India. No one really cares. It's like speaking on the phone with somebody while they are describing what their cat is doing. My rabbit is a big part of my life, and I like to include her at all my get-togethers. I know, for people who don't have a pet, lavishing large amounts of time and energy on our four-legged friends might seem ridiculous. That doesn't stop me from making my rabbit the center of my focus. In fact, my apartment is completely designed around my rabbit. I have chosen paint colors based on their names alone: straw, dandelion green, carrot orange, leaf grass, marsh brown. My couch is covered with a cloverleaf print. My liquor cabinet was built to resemble a small tree so that my apartment has a woodsy feel to it. My rabbit Dusty loves being scratched, so much so, that for Valentine's Day I went and had acrylic nails put on just so I could give her the ultimate massage. For Easter, she gets overflowing vegetable baskets and a tray of wheat grass. For her birthday she got wall-to-wall mushroom-cap-colored carpet in our bedroom. I even became an honorary rabbit educator. I have a badge and everything. This allows me to go to schools, sanatoriums, and homes to teach people about rabbits.

If you have a pet and are going to entertain, it's important to make sure your home is free of that scent that sometimes accompanies our pets. Nobody wants to deal with an overbearing odor of a litter box just as they sit down to enjoy a Fudgsicle. Make sure you have allergy medicine (preferably prescribed) in your cabinet just in case a guest is allergic. If a guest does have a reaction and their face puffs up, take advantage and grab a snapshot. You can use the photo along with the caption: "Have a swell Christmas," as a card, which you can then send to all your friends during the holidays.

If you, by any chance, happen to have a dead animal in your freezer awaiting a spring burial, remove it while entertaining. Ask the lady next door if you can store it in her freezer for just a night or two.

KATIE'S SMACK SNACKS FOR RABBITS

1 cup rolled oats, finely ground—a coffee grinder works best

1/4 cup rabbit pellets, finely ground

2 medium-size bunches of parsley

1/2 a carrot

1/2 a banana

1/4 cup and 1 tbsp water

Preheat oven to 325 degrees F and line a baking sheet or stone with wax paper (baking stones actually work best). Grind oats and pellets down to a powder and set aside. Puree parsley, carrot, banana, and water. This should become fairly liquefied, so you can add more or less water depending on the consistency. In a bowl, mix puree and dry ingredients together. Knead until a stiff dough is formed. Dough will be somewhat sticky. Place ball of dough between two sheets of wax paper and roll to about 1/8 to 1/4 of an inch thick. Cut into small squares and place on baking sheet.

Bake for about 30 minutes (don't let them brown too much), then turn off the heat and allow the snacks to sit.

Courtesy of Katie Richardson.

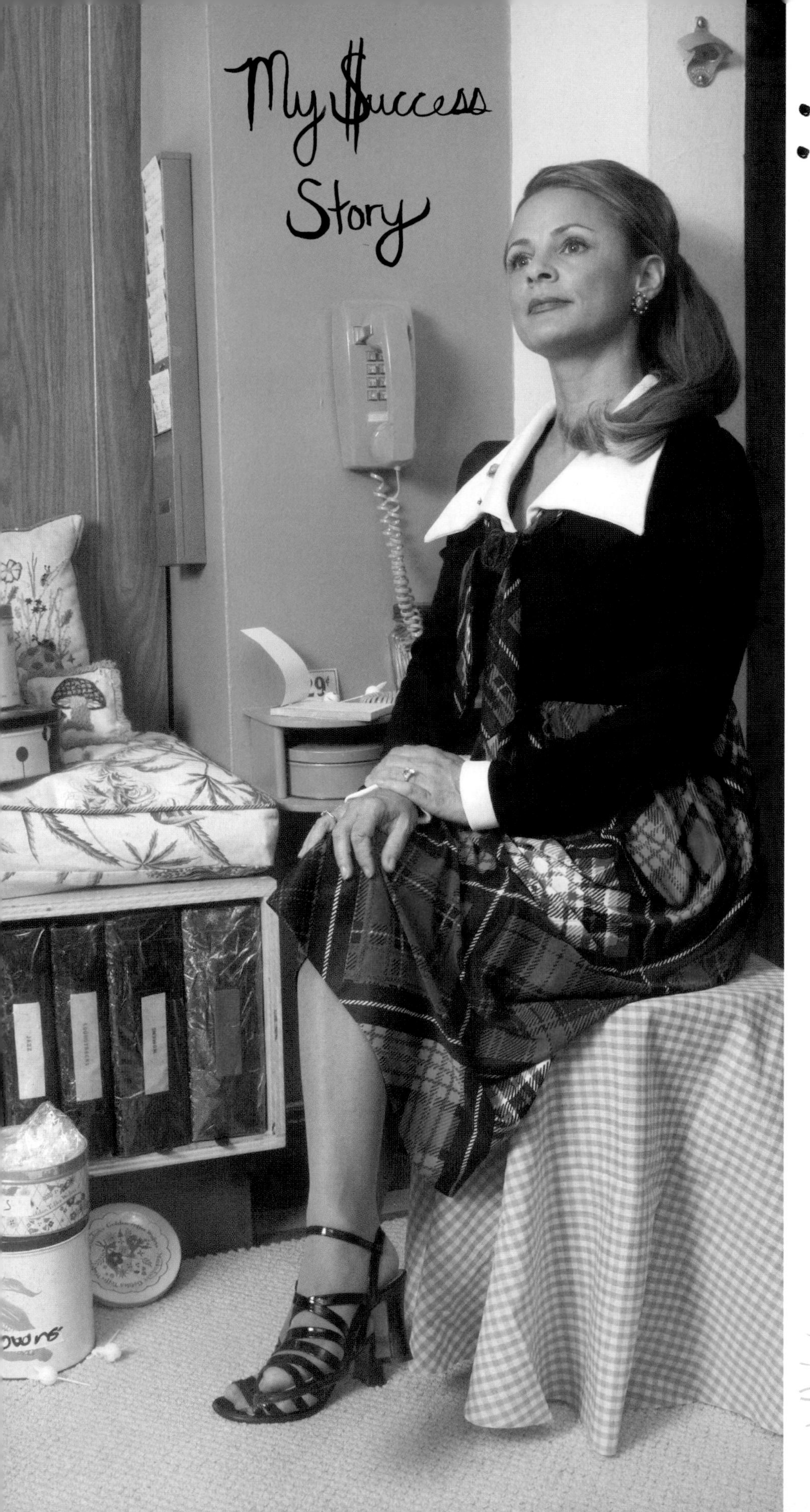

- Rabbits can live 7 to 9 or 8 to 10 years. Face it, it's a crapshoot.
- Rabbits are not in the rodent family because, unlike rodents, they have a second set of upper incisors (peg teeth).
- Rabbits are prey animals, which means they are always thinking, "I'm going to be eaten." They can be literally scared to death, which is why rabbits and children are not a good combination.
- Rabbits are strict vegetarians.
- A rabbit's closest relative is the horse, but whenever they ask to borrow money their phone calls are never returned.
- A rabbit's droppings are really easy to pick up. I don't even have to wash my hands afterward and they are a great way to spruce up a salad.
- You will always need electrical tape for chewed-up wires.
- Rabbits don't like "loud" anything.
- Rule number 6 in Girl Scouts is "Be kind to animals."

$ Who wouldn't want their picture taken with a rabbit? Big-ticket-price item at dinner parties. And remember: whatever you charge for a single person, double it for a couple.

NO FREELOADERS

Often it's been asked of me why I started my cupcake business. Well the answer is my first rabbit, Tattletail. The day I brought her home I looked down at her and said, "You, young lady, are going to have to get a job if you want to stay here. Read the sign, no freeloaders." So I began selling my products in her name and I would take the profits and put them in her money jar. I would then use that money (allowance) for her room and board and toiletries, and then later it went toward a $1,500 hand-painted, velvet-lined cedar coffin for her ashes. After my grieving process, a new rabbit hopped into my life and I looked at her and said, "You, young lady, are not going to be a trust-fund bunny living off Tattletail's jar money." So now I run the company in her name, Dusty (under new management), and started a new jar. I spent the rest of Tattletail's money on what I needed for my grieving kit (see Alcohol and Drugs).

I later expanded my business from just cupcakes to include my own Lil' Smoky Cheese Ball, a combination of cheeses shaped into a ball and then rolled in nuts.

LIL' SMOKY CHEESE BALL

- 2 cups of shredded smoked Gouda
- 16 ounces of cream cheese
- ½ cup of butter
- 2½ tablespoons of milk
- 2½ teaspoons of steak sauce
- 1 cup of chopped nuts

Bring all ingredients to room temperature. Add milk and steak sauce to cheeses and butter and beat until completely blended. Chill overnight. Turn it into a ball the next morning. Roll it in the nut mixture. Serve it room temperature, spread on a Ritz.

TATTLETAIL'S VANILLA CUPCAKES

Turn oven on to 375 degrees F.
You will need:

Unsalted butter, sugar, eggs, vanilla extract, baking powder, salt, flour, milk

Put 1 1/2 sticks of butter in mixer and beat at medium speed until somewhat smooth. Pour in 1 1/2 cups of sugar and beat well. Add 2 eggs. I like to crack the eggs on the side of the bowl while it is moving, which can be really stupid. I like to take chances. Yes, I have had to throw away my batter because I lost eggshells in the mix. Yes, it was a waste of food and yes, I know how expensive butter is, but what can I say? I'm a daredevil. Mix well. Add: 2 teaspoons of pure vanilla, 2 1/2 teaspoons of baking powder, 1/4 teaspoon of salt, 2 1/2 cups of flour, and 1 1/4 cups of milk. Beat until it looks like it is supposed to and pour into individual baking cups, until they are about 2/3rds full. Bake for 20 minutes or until golden brown. Should produce 24 cupcakes; I get 18 because I'm doing something wrong, although my cupcakes were voted 2nd best in the city by *New York Magazine.*

TATTLETAIL'S VANILLA BUTTERCREAM FROSTING

In a bowl combine: one box of confectioners' sugar, one stick of unsalted butter, one teaspoon of pure vanilla extract, and ¼ cup of milk or light cream and beat for a while. Really whip it, don't be afraid to get in there. I occasionally add food coloring and sometimes substitute pure almond extract for vanilla.

If you do choose to add pure almond extract instead of vanilla, you're on your own. I don't know the measurement for it, but I do know it's less than the amount of vanilla you would add.

DUSTY'S CHOCOLATE BUTTERCREAM FROSTING

Unsweetened chocolate

1 box of confectioners' sugar

1 tsp of pure vanilla extract or 1/4 tsp pure almond extract

1 stick unsalted butter

1/4 cup of half-and-half

Melt 2 squares of unsweetened chocolate and stir into the above. Beat all ingredients together in a bowl until light and fluffy.

HUGH'S SHELLS

Medium shell macaroni

1/2 pint cream

Parmesan cheese, more than the Gorgonzola cheese

Bel Paese cheese, small piece

Gorgonzola, small chunk

Shiitake mushrooms, large handful

Small bulb of radicchio

Salt and pepper

Butter

Sauté shiitake mushrooms in butter.

Cook shells al dente. Rinse in cold water, drain.

In large bowl, combine cream, grated Parmesan cheese, grated Bel Paese, and crumbled Gorgonzola. Take the drained shells, shiitake mushrooms, sliced radicchio, salt, and pepper and put in a buttered dish. Bake for 20 minutes at 400 degrees F.

Courtesy of Hugh Hamrick.

FARMER'S SALAD

Combination of salad greens—dandelion highly recommended

Tomatoes

Cucumbers

Red onion

Cold Roasted Potatoes in Their Jackets (see page 53)

Avocado

Sunflower seeds

Raisins (optional)

Olive oil and red wine vinegar

Salt and pepper to taste

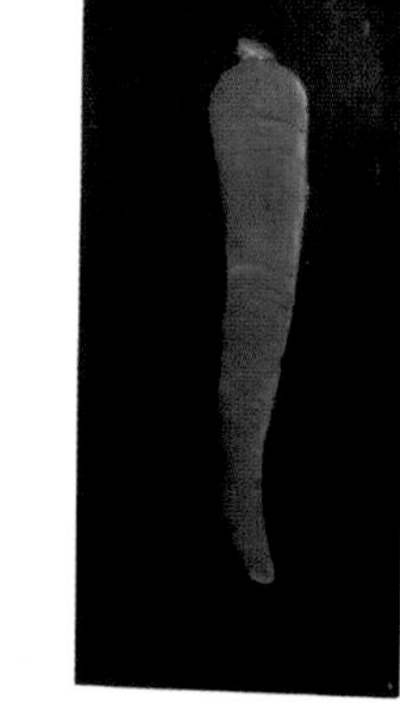

Toss well.

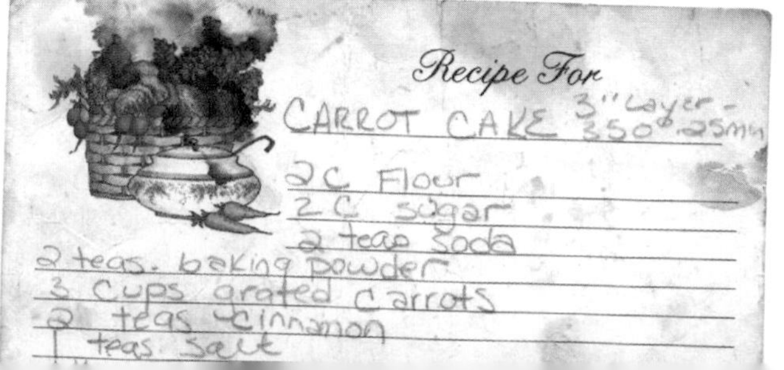

Recipe For
CARROT CAKE 3" Layer – 350° 25 min
2 C Flour
2 C sugar
2 teas Soda
2 teas. baking powder
3 Cups grated carrots
2 teas cinnamon
1 teas Salt

FENNEL AND ARUGULA SALAD

Create a salad using arugula lettuce, shaved fennel, and Parmesan cheese. Top with oil and vinegar dressing.

PROPER RABBIT HOUSING

A cage should be at least four times the length of the rabbit when he is fully stretched out (this generally means a cage at least 4 feet long).

It should be high enough to permit the rabbit to stand upright on his tip-toes and stretch upward.

The cage floor should be flat and not made of wire; wire-bottom cage floors can create or contribute to foot problems. Rabbits do not have padded heels the way people do. Their heel bone is directly up against the skin—like a human's elbow. Wire floors can cut into the heel and create a path for infection. If you have a wire-bottom cage, cover the floor with plain, clean, corrugated cardboard.

For many reasons (fleas, ticks, parasites, extremes of weather, predators), the safest place to keep a rabbit is indoors, and a 30" high, 4' x 4' puppy exercise pen makes

an ideal indoor rabbit environment. A large dog crate with a metal or plastic-pan floor is a suitable alternative. Using corrugated cardboard to cover the floor gives the rabbit something nontoxic to dig at and chew, and it is easily replaced whenever necessary.

Outdoor cages or hutches must be carefully protected from the elements. Rabbits are extremely sensitive to high heat and humidity. Provide shade from hot summer sun, and provide adequate shelter from wind, rain, snow, and ice in other seasons. In subfreezing weather, check daily to make sure your rabbit's water is not frozen, and provide plenty of hay or straw for bedding and insulation against the cold.

Rabbits kept outdoors in wire-bottom cages or hutches are at especially high risk for fly strike. Feces that are permitted to accumulate on the ground under the hutch attract egg-laying flies. If there is any fecal material stuck to the rabbit, this also attracts flies. The fly eggs hatch into maggots, which literally eat the rabbit alive. Rabbits kept outdoors should be checked frequently to make sure they are free of fecal material (and maggots!). Feces around the rabbit cage or hutch must be removed regularly and frequently.

Rabbits are, by instinct, immaculately clean. In an effort to keep their quarters clean, they will normally select one corner of the cage for urination and defecation. Identify which corner the rabbit has chosen, and put a litter box there. The litter box should have sides that are 4–5 inches high. Line the litter box with a section of newspaper and fill it with grass hay, such as timothy.

Courtesy of Mary Cotter, House Rabbit Society chapter manager.

LHS HUMMUS RECIPE —

INGREDIENTS:

1 – 15 OZ CAN CHICK PEAS — DRAINED

½ LEMON OR LIME, JUICE

1 SPRIG FRESH PARSLEY - CHOPPED

* 1 LARGE CLOVE OF GARLIC - CRUSHED

1½ TABLESPOONS OLIVE OIL

2 PINCHES COARSE BLACK PEPPER

PUT ALL INGREDIENTS IN FOOD PROCESSOR AND BLEND UNTIL SMOOTH/UNIFORM

* FOR ADDITIONAL ZEST ADD ANOTHER HALF OR ONE SMALL CLOVE

SERVES 2–4

Almost everyone has lost a pet at one time or another. I like the traditional method of burying them in the backyard, but I live in a city and I don't have a backyard. You can always flush them down the toilet, but make sure you are on good terms with your plumber because these things tend to go awry. I have now found what I consider to be a great way to not only dispose of a pet, but to memorialize them as well: first, have them cremated (any veterinarian can do it), then retrieve the ashes and place them into a customized grieving sack. You can make your own sack using felt and customize it according to your loss.

I'M Sorry
I'M SO SORRY

Gift Giving

Giving a gift can express many things—Congratulations! Get well soon. Remember me? I'm so sorry, it will never happen again. Happy Secretary's Day! Happy Graduation. Happy Birthday. I didn't mean it, it was the spiced rum talking. The best presents come from the heart and say something simple: "I like you."

No matter how hard you try, you cannot purchase affection with presents unless you are willing to drop some serious coinage, but you can show thoughtfulness and creativity. Sometimes the way you present a gift, say, with genuine enthusiasm, is much more important than the amount of money you spend, unless of course, again, you are trying to buy somebody's love, then it's all about the price tag. Cha-ching. The card you give along with your gift is important in the presentation. Did you just sign your name to a store-bought card? Or did you put a little effort in and make a card from scratch and write a little something personal?

Gift wrapping is another chance to make your present unique. My younger brother wrapped all his presents in carpet one Christmas.

Some people put very little energy into buying a gift and then use the excuse, "Well it's the thought that counts." These lazy people tend to give gifts that end up in your hallway stairwell or on your "reduced for quick sale" display table (see "The Money Jar," page 32). They're the same people who start their Christmas shopping on Christmas Eve and don't travel with an address book (see "For a College Graduation," page 189), any aspirin, or suntan oil.

Money can make a nice gift, but once you start sending family members checks for their birthdays, you'll have to do it for the rest of your life because they will be looking for it for the rest of their lives. It's like feeding a dog from the table. A good way to give money is to donate to a charity of the person's choice. When friends say they want to donate money to a charity of my choice, I always suggest my vacation jar. I keep my vacation jar screwed under my kitchen cabinet above the sink so when I wash dishes I can stare at it and fantasize about the places I might go, and all the ways I can convince people to donate money to it.

OTHER CREATIVE WAYS TO SEND MONEY

- A card pocket to hold dimes.
- A special envelope for paper money and checks.
- Offer someone a shopping spree.
- Make a "coupon" book full of passes and gift certificates such as movie or theater tickets, fast-food gift certificates, or lotto tickets.
- Only older sisters give traveler's checks, because traveler's checks are very practical.

- People who have lived through a war tend to give bonds. They never want to give up the fight.
- Make your own gift certificates, like: "good for one back massage with full release," or "good for one cheese ball." Or, "I'll be your slave for a day." This is a good idea if you are low on money.
- If you have a friend or loved one in the hospital, and you want to assure that they will be taken care of, supply the nurses—especially the ICU staff—with baked goods, chocolates or a Crock-Pot of soup or stew.
- Re-gifting is tricky. This is when you receive a gift you don't like and then rewrap it and try to pass it on to someone else. Usually it's pretty obvious. Did you really think your aging aunt would appreciate those skates? Or your toothless cousin would enjoy that box of saltwater taffy?

Compliments

If you can't afford a gift, give a compliment. This is an easy way to make somebody feel better. If someone gives you a compliment, accept it. Nobody wants to hear "Don't tell me—tell my gynecologist," or "Thanks, but you're not exactly the *Piedmont Times* book review," or "Oh please, I just rewired it."

If you receive a gift and you don't have something in return, accept it graciously. Nobody wants to hear your backhanded compliments: "Thanks for the hook rug you made me. I don't know how you do it, Dale. I couldn't find any time to even think of gifts what with all the work we're supposed to be doing on the Teesdale project. Well, I guess one of us has been slacking off, and the other one of us has a new hook rug."

Gift Suggestions

See other gift ideas in the chapter.

For a Single Man

Identification bracelet

Shiitake log

New strap for his sports watch

Neck chain

Blazer buttons or tools

Sponges and socks

Rock concert tickets

Gifts for a Divorced Man Who Works in an Office

An easy-to-care-for terrarium

Place mats

Frozen chicken thighs

The Holy Bible

Paint chip wheel

Hangers

Oven mitts

Comb

For Preteen Girls

Gold balls for pierced ears

Animal pin

Colored cotton balls

Stationery

Subscription to a magazine

Tin can bank

Diary

Apron with turtles on it

A book about horses

For a High School Graduation

Potted plants

Bridge or guitar lessons

Corkscrew

Radio

Hair dryer

Money

Wristband

Instant camera

For a College Graduation

Evening scarf or Fuck It Bucket (see page 290)

Briefcase

Set of beer mugs

Clam steamer or Crock-Pot

New tires

Wall clock

Binoculars

Belt

Pen set with initials

Address book (When going on trips with other people, bring your own address book if you want to send postcards. Nothing is more annoying than traveling with someone who didn't think of that. The point of sending a postcard is that you thought enough to bring their address with you.)

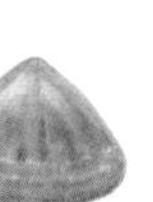

For a Priest

Cooked turkey and roast beef

Color TV* or Calf Stretcher (see page 292)

Golf clubs

Pistachios

Pot holders

*The best time to choose a color TV is on Saturday morning when the cartoons are on. That way you can tell which TV has the best color for your money.

For a Nun

TV set

Suitcase

Cheese

Soap

Sausage links

Shower caps

Raisins

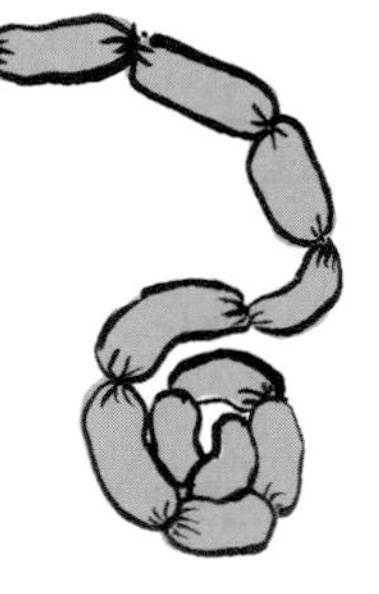

Single Girl in Her Mid-Forties Living Alone

Pink toilet paper

Stamps

For Early Menopause

A pin made from a broken china plate

Drapes or curlers

Hand mirror

Earring tree

Rose lotion

Rolling pin

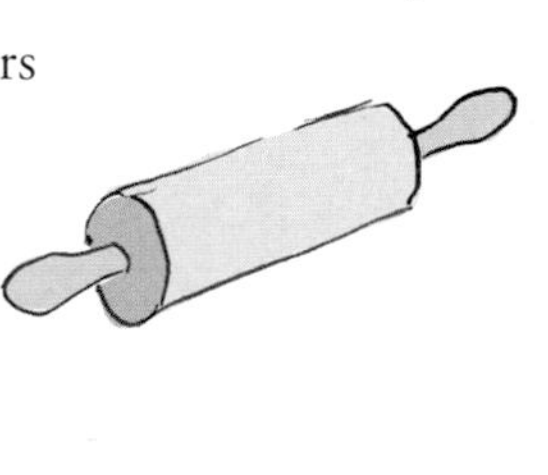

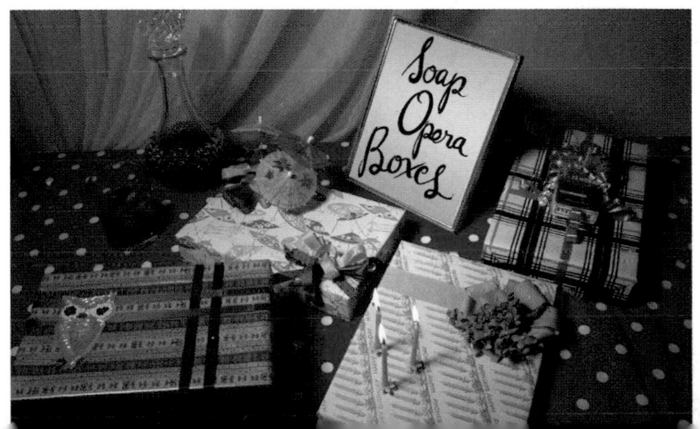

Homemade Children's Gift Ideas for a Rainy Day

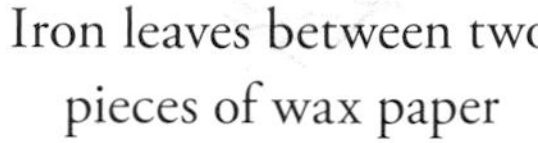

Iron leaves between two pieces of wax paper

Matchbox puzzle

Make your own flash cards

Your own disguise kit (see page 112)

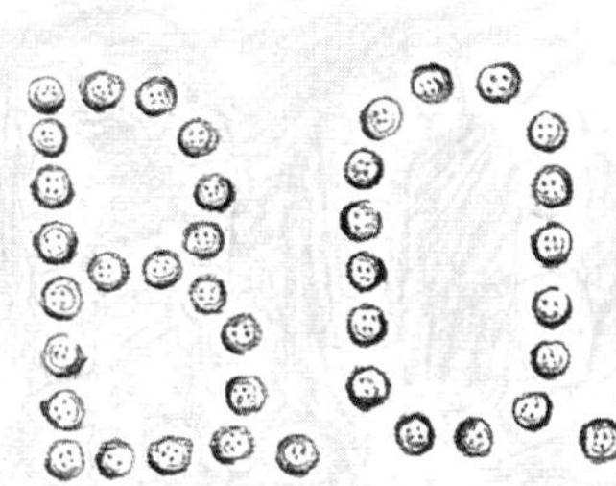

Homemade decoration for their school bags or pocketbook. Outline your initials in chalk first, and then sew the buttons along the lines. Be careful when tossing it in the dryer because it can get noisy.

I Like You For Children

- Bank
- Wallet with pictures of scientists and movie stars
- Popcorn popper
- Paint set
- Breakaway china
- Inflatable briefcase
- Magnifying glass
- Box filled with old wigs, clothes, and character glasses
- Push toys are good for two-year-olds

Housewarming Gift Ideas

- Key chain
- Band-Aids
- Stamps and a stamp holder
- Flashlight with extra batteries
- Homemade bookends (see page 277)
- Timer or peppermill
- Phone book covers (see page 286)
- Personalized matches
- Wood-burning kit
- Scissors
- Clothesline
- Hard line (in case of a blackout)

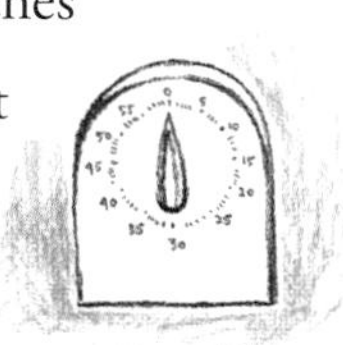

Offer to clean the apartment or house before they move in or clean their oven. My brother did both of these things for me before I moved into my apartment and continues to clean my oven when he comes to visit me.

NOTE: Never bring a gift to an event where the recipient would be stuck carrying it around. They don't want to lug it around any more than you do—it's an inconvenience.

Never Give These

Kittens

Birds

Sterling silver pinecones to struggling newlyweds

Gag gifts

Tan colored socks

3 turtles

Sexy lingerie for your son's girlfriend

If you live with someone, don't buy them music if you don't want to hear it.

Suggestions for Gift Giving

- Send flowers to your mother on your birthday (a guaranteed tear dropper).
- Make a list. I like to ask the people I will be giving gifts to for a list of things they desire. We always did this as children—my family still does. And I never understood why people thought it was inappropriate after a certain point. It's helpful and it prevents you from getting or giving someone a bullshit present. Lists are good to give to bad shoppers. Just because it's on a list doesn't guarantee anything, so you're still surprised. Also if you are making a list and giving one to several different people don't repeat an item on the list—you might want to cater it to the person you are giving the list to. You're not going to ask your 8-year-old niece for a check any more than you're going to ask your 80-year-old grandmother for some chronic and a decent bong, unless her connections are still good.

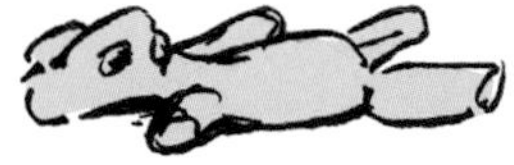

If you owe someone money give them something, even if it's just half the amount, just so the person who lent you the money knows you haven't forgotten your debt. Because trust me, they didn't forget about it. And never buy lenders a gift instead of giving them money. They don't want an expensive journal or a paperweight and they might not be into charities and scented candles—they want their money.

- Keep a record of what you have given people in the past so you can refer to it when their birthday rolls around again and you don't give them the same gift.
- In Girl Scouts, we would always get a name from Social Services of a family that was in need for a Thanksgiving dinner and we would provide that family with a meal. Or for Christmas we would give presents to the family using all our dues money. This is still a fantastic gift idea. Call Social Services and get the name of a needy family. If you are too busy or scared to go into poor peoples' neighborhoods, pay someone braver than you to deliver it.
- Don't make the mistake of telling people you collect something specific like frogs or *Star Trek* paraphernalia because once you do you'll get them for the rest of your life. Most collectors like to seek these things out for themselves. That's the fun of collecting. And try to avoid giving drinkers liquor all the time because if everybody follows suit it actually makes them feel bad.
- Take good care of the person you have listed on a medical form as a contact "in case of emergencies," because that's going to be a full-time job for them when that phone call does come.

When I meet someone for the first time and I think that I will be seeing them over a period of time, like a manicurist or cashier, I immediately ask when their birthday is and then I go home and jot it down and never mention it again until it's their birthday. Make a quick association in your head until you get home. It's a nice surprise. This goes for any anniversary as well. Note: Sometimes this backfires on me, especially if they weren't thinking of the anniversary of their mother's death, then it changes everything.

Cooking for One

Some people are alone by circumstance—they've lost a loved one, or are enduring a breakup, and others, like me, are alone by choice. I don't mind being alone. I don't need to fill up every moment of my day with companionship. I don't need warm human interaction. I don't need to be gently caressed while he whispers those sweet tender words in my ear, "I love you Amy, and you'll never be alone." Well, he's a liar. So I'm alone and that's okay. Besides, that's the way my imaginary boyfriend Ricky prefers it. He's got me all to himself. Ricky and I have had a successful relationship now for over 12 years. Sure, we've had our ups and downs, but the point is we work. He gets me.

I think it's good for a person to spend time alone. It gives them an opportunity to discover who they are and to figure out why they are always alone.

I do truly look on an evening alone with excitement. Usually I'll cook one of my simple yet tasty 15-Minute Meals in 20 Minutes (see "15-Minute Meals in 20 Minutes," page 196) such as shell steak with a side salad. If I want to treat myself, I'll put an hour and 15 minutes into it and make a shell steak with a side salad and toss a baked potato in the oven. After eating and doing the dishes, I might whip up a batch of cupcakes for delivery. I'll flip on the fake fireplace, and listen to the phone ring. I might put on some slow jams and take in a short story. I'll spend time massaging my rabbit. Perhaps I'll get involved with a project I won't finish and then rock myself to sleep.

popcorn
S

Table for One

Popcorn
BBQ Chicken (see page 208)
Steamed Green Beans with Butter and Salt
Buttered Egg Noodles

I Like Us

Optional Menu

Pork Chop
Whipped Potatoes with Turnips or Garlic
Avocado Salad or Spinach and Mushroom Salad
Cookie
Milk

POPCORN

Turn burner to high. Pour about a half inch of popcorn into a steel-bottomed pan (I like using Revere ware for this).

Pour enough olive oil to cover your kernels. You don't want an oil slick visible on the surface.

Cover pan and wait for first kernel to pop. Change burner to medium heat, and shake pan back and forth on burner until most popping ceases. Remove from heat and transfer into a bowl that is big enough to hold all your popcorn.

Season popped corn with salt.

I eat popcorn about 3 times a week. It's good for you, just ask your dentist.

Conn (the man who designed the title page for my book) recommends popping your kernels in bacon fat, so every year on his birthday I give him a jar of bacon fat, a good gift idea.

PORK CHOP

Panfry pork chop in olive oil and a little butter. Salt and pepper.

WHIPPED POTATOES WITH TURNIPS OR GARLIC

Peel and slice red potatoes and turnips. Cut into large cubes, boil, drain, mash with a fork. Add butter, salt and pepper, and a little milk if desired. If you want garlic mashed potatoes then add 2 garlic cloves when boiling your potatoes. Drain, mash with fork. Add butter, salt and pepper, and a little milk if desired.

A potato ricer is fantastic for this.

AVOCADO SALAD

Whisk about 1/8 teaspoon each of salt, pepper, and prepared mustard into olive oil (preferably Spanish). Add some fresh lime juice (to taste). Pour over sliced avocados.

SPINACH AND MUSHROOM SALAD

Fresh spinach, 1 bunch scallions, trimmed and sliced; 1/4 pound fresh mushrooms, sliced; olive oil; lemon juice; salt and pepper

Put spinach and scallions in a bowl, top with mushrooms and the dressing, toss and serve.

Too Hot to Cook?

Then don't. Cook at someone else's house or order in.

When ordering takeout, have your order planned. Nothing is more annoying for an employee at a busy restaurant than listening to a caller ask a room full of people what they want, and then going back and forth with endless inane questions like: "Does that come with cheese?" "What kind of cheese do you have?" "I'm sorry can you say that again?" "Do you have grilled onions?" "Can I have French fries instead of the salad?" "Do you have sweetened or unsweetened iced tea?" "OK, scratch that, I'll just have the . . . You know what—I'll call you back."

A Gift Suggestion for Someone Who Orders in a Lot

Make a menu folder and fill it with menus from all the local restaurants that deliver in their area. This also makes a nice housewarming present.

Live Alone?

- Change the décor of your apartment with every season so it seems like you have more homes.
- For single servings of lasagna use mini loaf pans (5¾" by 3"). Normal size lasagna noodles fit snugly in the pan when cut in half. You can cover the pans with foil and freeze. Bake one when you want. This is also a good gift idea for other single-dwellers.
- If you can't live without meatballs on hand, freeze them as you make them. Place them on a cookie sheet and put them in your freezer until frozen. Then toss them in a plastic bag, they will stay separated. Heat and serve when desired. This also works well with manicotti.
- Make a half cake. Bake an eight inch one-layer cake. Cut in half, frost one side, top with the other and frost. Now you've got yourself a 2-layer half cake. Knock yourself out, fatty.

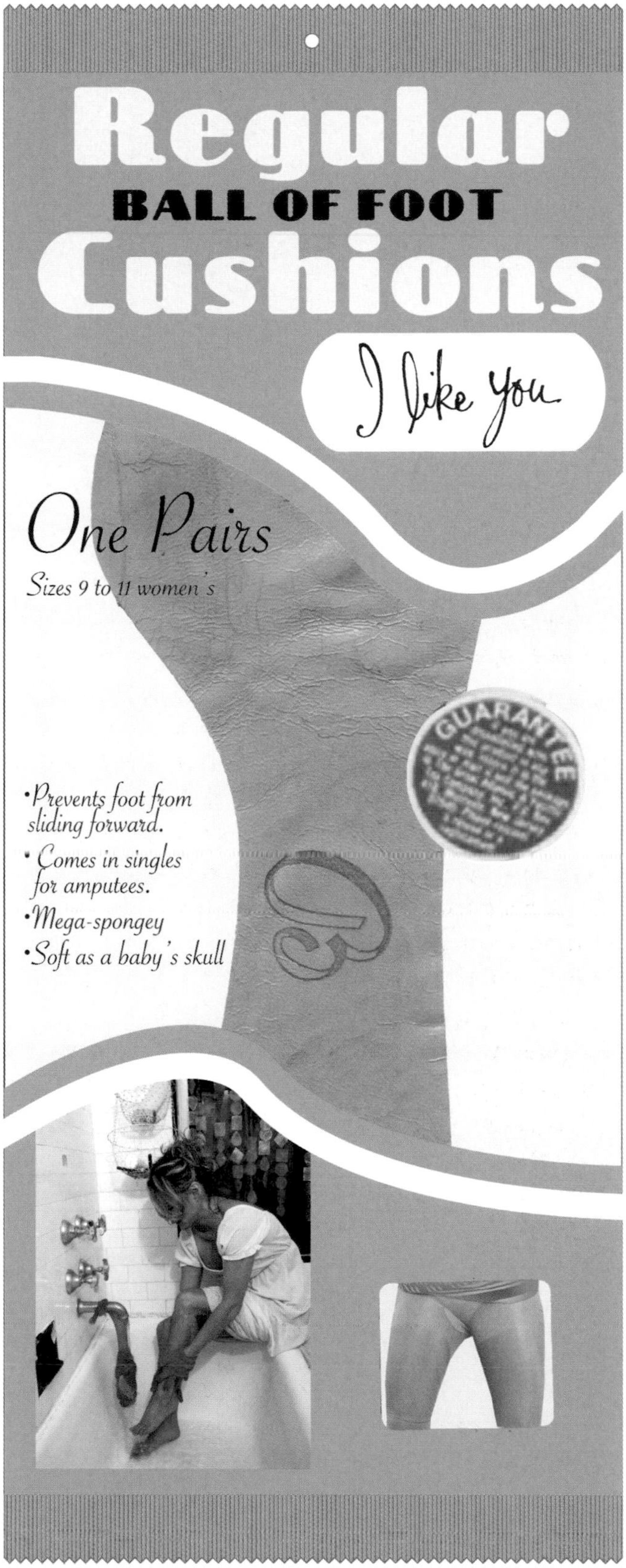

Regular
BALL OF FOOT
Cushions

I like you

One Pairs
Sizes 9 to 11 women's

GUARANTEE

- *Prevents foot from sliding forward.*
- *Comes in singles for amputees.*
- *Mega-spongey*
- *Soft as a baby's skull*

Fifteen-Minute Meals in Twenty Minutes

In a hurry? Are patience for hospitals?

STEAK AND SALAD

Cover broiler pan with foil. Jab a few holes and sprinkle coarse sea salt all over it. Rest your steak on top and broil, turning once. Broil to desired temperature. Top with pepper and a pat of butter.

Serve with salad of your choice.

DIMPLETON'S PANFRIED STEAK

Take a N.Y. strip steak and dimple it (embed it) with crushed peppercorns. Heat a skillet and brush it with a little olive oil or butter. Panfry the steak on both sides until it is done to your liking. Remove the steak. Add a little butter, red wine, and onion to the drippings and cook for a little bit. Pour over your steak.

Crushing the peppercorns on the floor: Fill a dish rag with peppercorns. Place on floor and beat with a mallet. You might have to invite your downstairs neighbor up for this.

TILAPIA AND SAUTÉED SPINACH

Sprinkle salt and pepper on both sides of tilapia.

Put a little olive oil in pan and sauté fish, never flipping over. Cook until you start to see the edges of the fish begin to turn white and the center gets a little pink, about 6–8 minutes. Sprinkle a little lemon on top and put in a 500°F oven for 3–4 minutes. Serve with spinach.

SPAGHETTI WITH BUTTER AND PEPPER

Boil spaghetti, melt butter, toss together with some salt and pepper.

SPINACH

Sauté minced garlic in oil, and add fresh spinach. Cook down by tossing around the leaves. Don't add any water, but add a little lemon (this will darken the leaves a little), and some salt and pepper.

Al dente means "to the tooth."

I like making dishes that I can eat out of the pot, standing up, over the stove. The following macaroni dishes are good for this.

PESTO AND CORKSCREW MACARONI

Pesto Sauce (see page 175). Boil corkscrew macaroni, drain. Add pesto and toss.

When you make this batch of sauce, save some and freeze it so all you have to do is melt it when you need it. My aunt Joyce kept pesto in her ice cube tray covered with see-through wrap and would just pop one out when she wanted some.

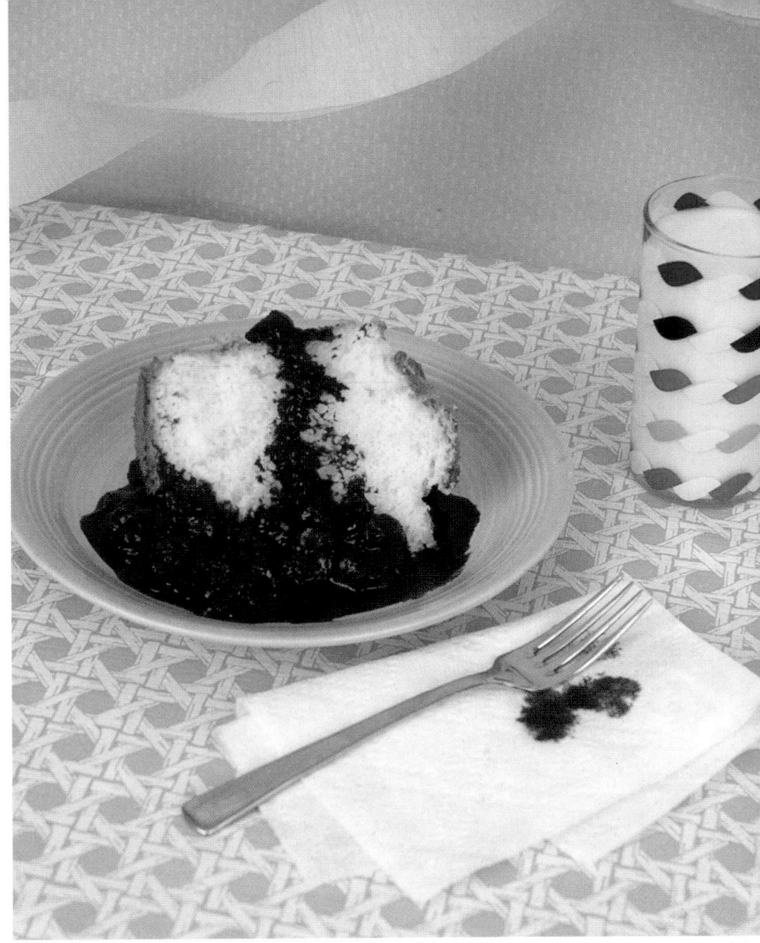

RIGATONI, BUTTER, AND GRATED KASSERI CHEESE

Boil rigatoni, toss with melted butter and grated Kasseri cheese. Salt, pepper. Parmesan cheese optional, as well as roasted pine nuts.

HUELLA'S LIGHTLY PANFRIED FISH FILLETS

3 fish fillets

Shallow bowl of milk

Shallow bowl of flour

Shallow bowl of beaten eggs

Shallow bowl of breadcrumbs

3 tablespoons of butter

Lemon

Dip the fillets in the milk, then dredge them in flour. Dip fish in egg, then roll in breadcrumbs. Melt 3 tablespoons of butter in frying pan. Fry fish. Squeeze lemon on top.

Courtesy of Hugh Hamrick.

JACKPOT RECIPES

SELL BY
MILK
Quality Controlled
MILK
VITAMIN D
HOMOGENIZED
PASTEURIZED
QUART (946 mL)
ORIGINAL
Total
Authentic Greek Yogurt
7oz (200g)
SOUR CREAM
Premium Deli Salads
Potato Salad
10/16/05
Potato Salad

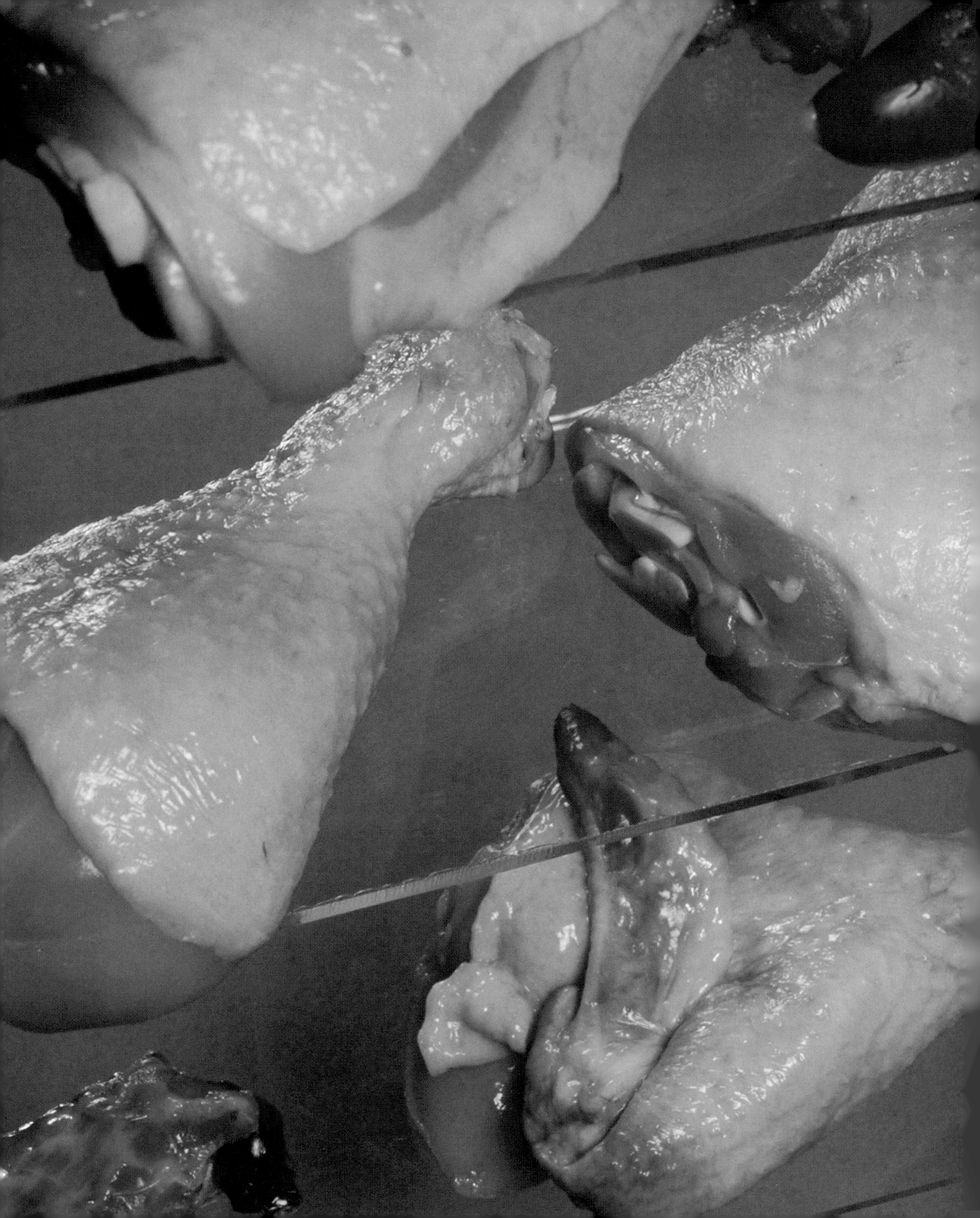

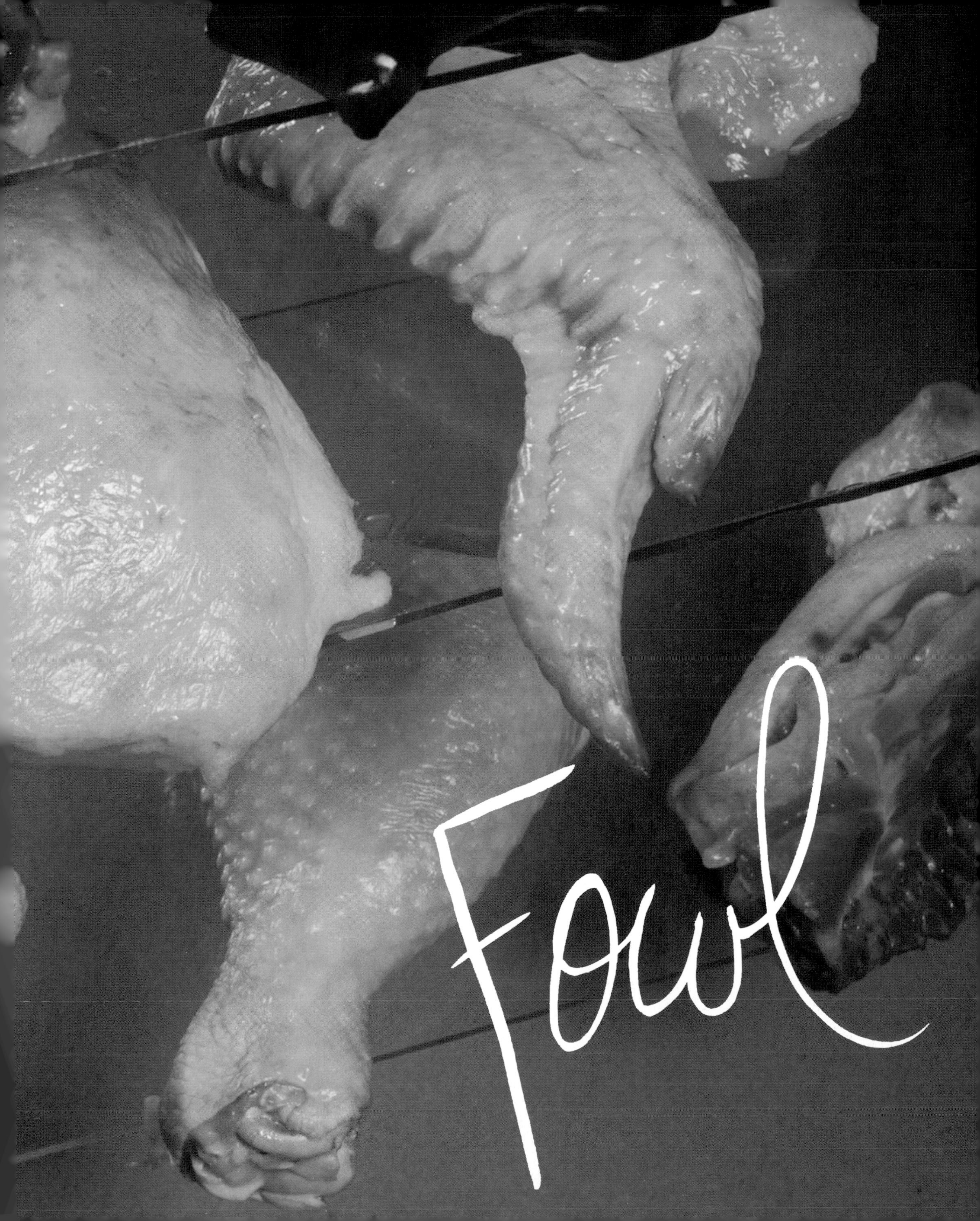

Fowl

SOUTHERN FRIED CHICKEN

Chicken parts, legs and thighs

Buttermilk

Salt, pepper

Paprika

Flour (if you add 2T of cornstarch to the flour it will make the chicken more crispy)

Lard

Soak chicken in buttermilk seasoned with salt, pepper, and paprika overnight. Dredge the chicken pieces in flour and shake off any excess. Place chicken pieces skin side down into the heated lard in skillet. Don't overcrowd the pan, fry in batches. Cook about 10 minutes on each side or you can fry for less and bake it off in the oven for about 30–40 minutes at 350 degrees F.

When you remove the chicken from the skillet drain on crumpled-up paper towels, not flat ones.

Part of this recipe was inspired by *The Gift of Southern Cooking* by Edna Lewis and Scott Peacock.

CHICKEN OF THE TAVERNS

1 chicken, cut up, or pick of the chick

1 stick of butter

2 tbsp of oil

Juice of 1 lemon

Salt and pepper

1 2-pound can of whole tomatoes

1 onion, thinly sliced

1 tsp oregano

1 tsp marjoram

1 tsp savory

1 bay leaf

½ cup of red wine

Parmesan cheese or Kefalotiri

Wash chicken well. Combine butter and oil in a pan, and heat. Pour half of oil mixture into a shallow baking pan and rest chicken pieces in it. Mix strained lemon juice in remaining mixture and baste chicken. Sprinkle the chicken with salt and pepper.

Bake at 400 degrees F for 30 minutes.

Put tomatoes and remaining ingredients in a pot. Cook for about 25 minutes and bring to a boil. Pour over chicken (after that ½ hour). Reduce oven to 350 degrees F. Continue baking for 1 hour.

Serve over spaghetti. Top with grated cheese.

Courtesy of Tiffany Sedaris.

BROWN BASMATI RICE AND CHICKEN

6 chicken thighs, or cut-up chicken

Butter

1 cup brown basmati rice

2½ cups water

Salt and pepper

Place chicken in an oiled baking dish. Dot with butter. Add ½ cup of water and bake for 20 minutes at 350 degrees (uncovered). After 20 minutes add 2 cups of water and 1 cup of rice. Stir around with the chicken, cover and bake at 400 degrees for 1 hour. Season with salt and pepper.

Serve with a salad.

KOTOPOULO PILAF (CHICKEN AND RICE)

6 chicken thighs, or cut-up chicken

Garlic powder

3–4 T of tomato paste

Salt and pepper

Butter

2½ cups of water

1 cup of raw rice

Rub chicken with garlic powder, place in an oiled baking dish or casserole dish. Coat with tomato paste.

Sprinkle with salt and pepper, dot with butter, add ½ cup of water, and bake at 350 degrees for 30 minutes, covered, turning chicken once.

Add remaining water, salt and pepper. Stir carefully to make sure that all rice sinks to the bottom of the dish. Increase to 400 degrees and continue baking for 30 minutes.

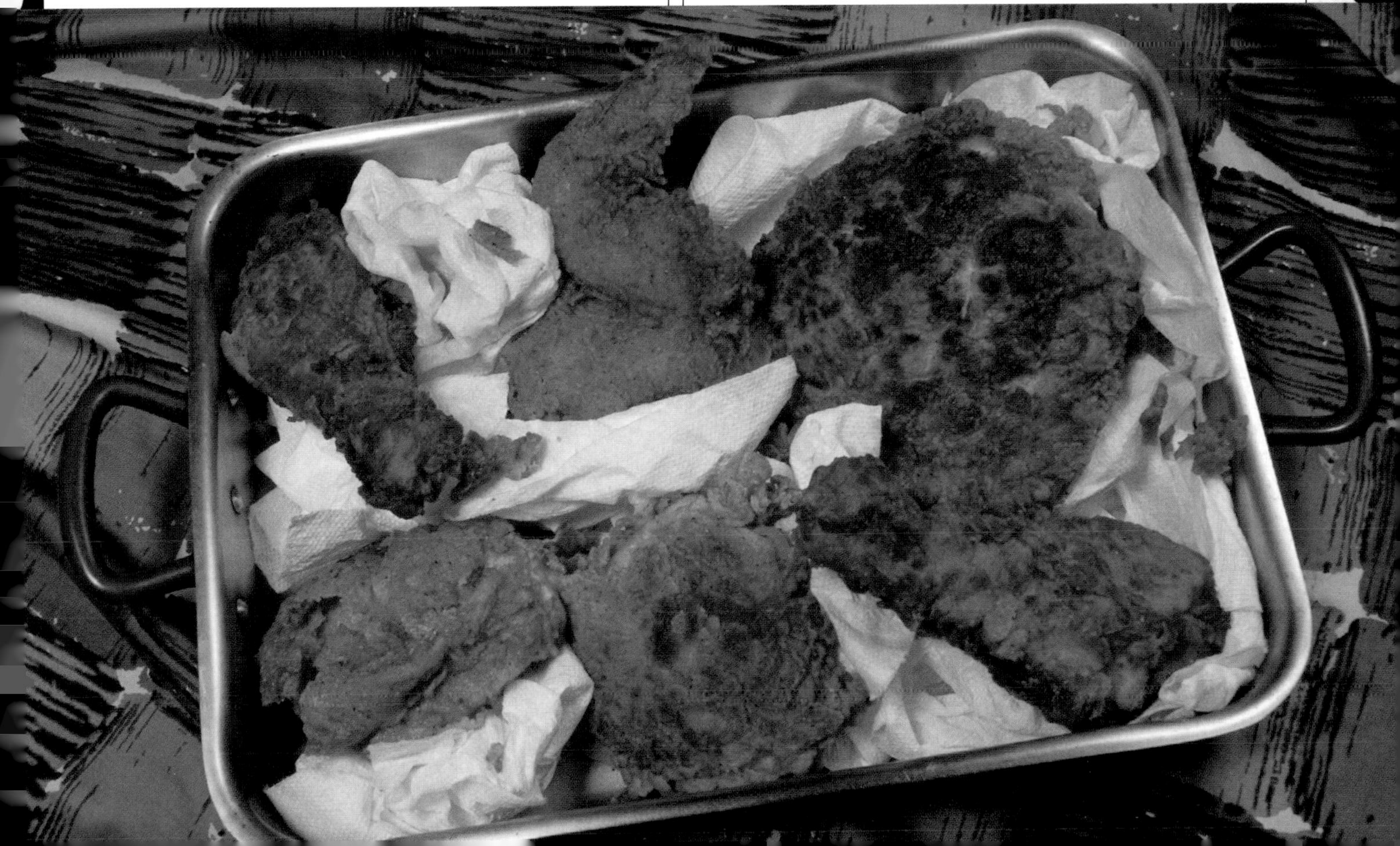

CLAYTON'S CHICKEN

You will need a clay vessel for this.

Follow the directions on the back of the clay vessel as far as preparing it to be ready for use. Immerse the pot in water for as long as the directions say. This has everything to do with getting the chicken just right.

Insert some chopped onion and garlic, and salt, pepper in the bird's cavity, then truss it, rub the outside of the chicken with olive oil, lemon, salt, pepper, and garlic. Drain the vessel (this will make sense to you after you have read the back of the clay pot's directions). Lay slices of lemon on the bottom and set chicken on top of that, with the lid on. Put the pot in an unheated oven, set oven at 450 for about 45 minutes.

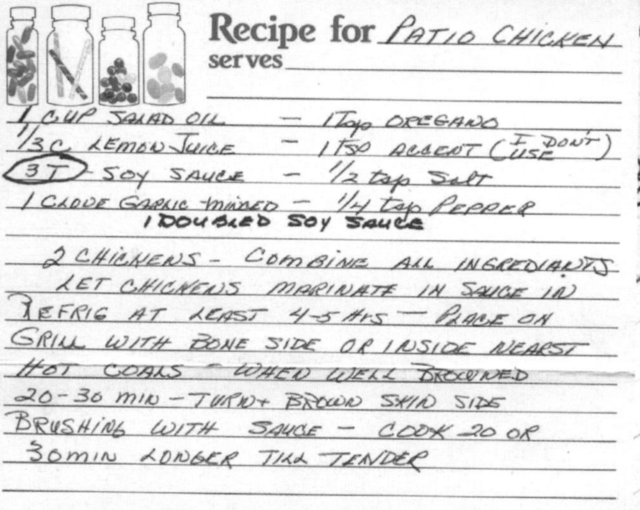

Recipe for PATIO CHICKEN
serves

1 CUP SALAD OIL — 1 Tsp OREGANO
1/3 C. LEMON JUICE — 1 TSP ACCENT (I DON'T USE)
3 T - SOY SAUCE — 1/2 tsp Salt
1 CLOVE GARLIC minced — 1/4 tsp Pepper
I DOUBLED SOY SAUCE

2 CHICKENS - COMBINE ALL INGREDIANTS LET CHICKENS MARINATE IN SAUCE IN REFRIG AT LEAST 4-5 HRS — PLACE ON GRILL WITH BONE SIDE OR INSIDE NEAREST HOT COALS - WHEN WELL BROWNED 20-30 MIN - TURN + BROWN SKIN SIDE BRUSHING WITH SAUCE - COOK 20 OR 30 MIN LONGER TILL TENDER

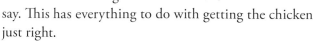

©CREATIVE PAPERS BY C.R.GIBSON

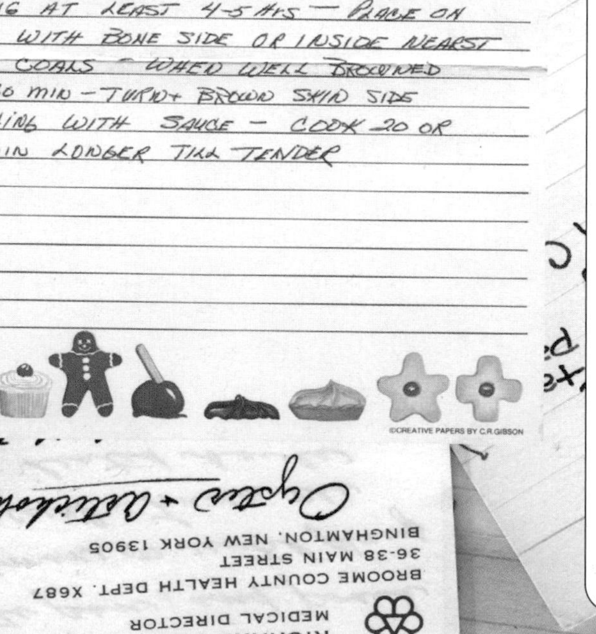

OFFICE OF:
RICHARD E. SULLIVAN, M.D.
MEDICAL DIRECTOR
BROOME COUNTY HEALTH DEPT. X687
36-38 MAIN STREET
BINGHAMTON, NEW YORK 13905

CHICKEN PARMESAN

- 1 bell pepper, chopped
- 1 onion, chopped
- 1 stalk of celery, chopped
- 1 garlic clove, chopped
- 4 T of olive oil
- 1 can of crushed tomatoes (14-1/2 ounces)
- 1 cup of chicken broth
- 1 T of tomato paste
- 1 T parsley
- 1 t of sugar
- 3/4 t of dried basil
- Salt and pepper to taste
- 4 chicken cutlets, about 3/8 inches thick
- 1 large egg
- 1/4 cup of flour
- 2/3 cup unseasoned breadcrumbs
- 2 T of butter
- 1-1/2 cups of shredded mozzarella
- 2/3 cup of freshly grated Parmesan cheese

Sauté the pepper, onion, celery, and garlic in 1 T of oil in a saucepan over medium heat for about 5–7 minutes. Stir in tomatoes, tomato paste, parsley, sugar, basil, salt and pepper. Simmer covered over low heat for 20 minutes. Then uncover and continue cooking for another 20 minutes until the sauce has thickened.

Pound out your chicken with a mallet until 1/4 inch thick.

Beat your eggs in one bowl and put your flour and breadcrumbs in separate bowls.

Dip your chicken in the flour until completely covered, then in the egg, and then in the breadcrumbs.

Heat butter and 2 T of oil in a skillet over medium heat. Add chicken. Cook turning once until light brown, about 3 minutes a side.

Heat oven to 350. Remove chicken from skillet with a slotted spatula to a shallow baking dish. Sprinkle mozzarella evenly over chicken. Spoon the sauce evenly over the mozzarella cheese. Sprinkle the Parmesan cheese evenly over the sauce.

Drizzle a little olive oil over Parmesan cheese. Bake uncovered until the chicken is tender and the cheese is golden brown, about 30 minutes.

CHIP CHOP CHICKEN POT PIE

You will need:

- Puff pastry sheets (I buy mine)
- 1 4-pound chicken
- Several onions
- 3 stalks of celery
- 1 cup of sliced carrots
- Several potatoes
- 1 box of frozen peas
- 6 tablespoons of flour
- 3 cups of chicken stock
- 6 tablespoons of butter, plus extra butter on hand
- Tabasco sauce
- Fresh parsley, if desired
- Salt and white pepper

Boil a 4-pound chicken with onion and celery tops to make a broth. When chicken is done pick meat from the bone and set the meat aside. Enhance the broth the best way you know how to make it a good chicken stock. You'll need about 3 cups.

In boiling water, add about 1 cup of sliced carrots and cover. Remove using a slotted spoon after 4 minutes. Set aside. Cut potaoes in small cubes and simmer in pot for about 7 minutes. Drain and set aside. Sauté a large onion in butter and set aside.

Make a cream sauce using butter, flour, and 3 cups of the broth. Add 6 drops of Tabasco sauce, salt, and white pepper.

In a large bowl combine carrots, potatoes, onion, box of frozen peas, and 1 cup of chopped celery ends with the chicken and gravy. Add about a fistful of fresh parsley if desired. Toss really well, adding salt and pepper to taste.

Line a baking dish with ½ of the puff pastry dough. Pour in all the chicken mixture. Dot with some butter and a little milk. Put the other puff pastry crust on top and rub top with a little milk. Bake at 450 degrees for 30–40 minutes, until brown.

CHICKEN SNATCHATORE **SERVES 4–6**

- 8 pieces chicken (1 chicken cut up)
- 3 T olive oil
- 1 sliced onion
- 1 bell pepper, cut into strips
- 2 minced garlic cloves
- 1/2 cup dry white wine
- 1/2 t dried oregano
- 1 t dried thyme
- 2 T minced fresh basil
- 1 bay leaf
- Salt and pepper to taste
- 1 can peeled tomatoes, drained and chopped up
- 8 Italian or Greek style black olives (optional, add in the last min. before adding the veg. mixture to the chicken)
- 4 oz. fresh chopped mushrooms (optional, add when you are adding the onions)

Heat 2 T of oil in a large electric skillet (or regular skillet if you don't have one) over medium heat. Place as many pieces of chicken in skillet without overcrowding and brown, turning just once. Remove chicken to a flame-proof Dutch oven. Repeat this until all your chicken pieces are browned. Add the leftover tablespoon of oil to the skillet and get that hot. Add the onion, pepper, and garlic. Stir and cook for about 6 minutes. Add the wine and reduce for 1 minute. Add the tomatoes, oregano, thyme, salt and pepper, bay leaf and simmer. Put the chicken back into the skillet, cover, simmer for 30 minutes. Transfer the chicken to a serving platter. Reduce the onion and pepper mixture in skillet, stirring until it is thick, about 4 minutes. Spoon this mixture over the chicken and top it with the fresh basil.

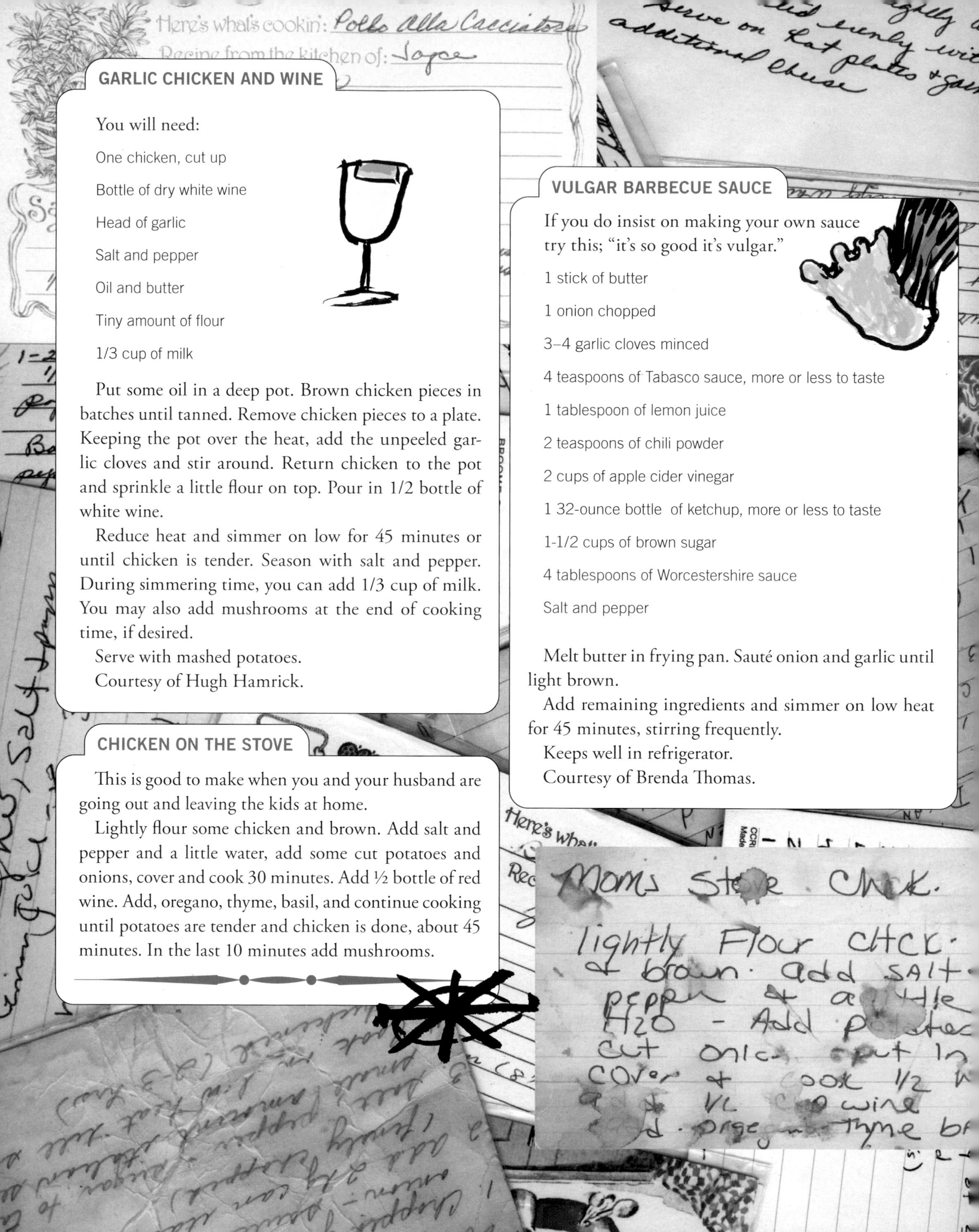

GARLIC CHICKEN AND WINE

You will need:

One chicken, cut up

Bottle of dry white wine

Head of garlic

Salt and pepper

Oil and butter

Tiny amount of flour

1/3 cup of milk

Put some oil in a deep pot. Brown chicken pieces in batches until tanned. Remove chicken pieces to a plate. Keeping the pot over the heat, add the unpeeled garlic cloves and stir around. Return chicken to the pot and sprinkle a little flour on top. Pour in 1/2 bottle of white wine.

Reduce heat and simmer on low for 45 minutes or until chicken is tender. Season with salt and pepper. During simmering time, you can add 1/3 cup of milk. You may also add mushrooms at the end of cooking time, if desired.

Serve with mashed potatoes.

Courtesy of Hugh Hamrick.

VULGAR BARBECUE SAUCE

If you do insist on making your own sauce try this; "it's so good it's vulgar."

1 stick of butter

1 onion chopped

3–4 garlic cloves minced

4 teaspoons of Tabasco sauce, more or less to taste

1 tablespoon of lemon juice

2 teaspoons of chili powder

2 cups of apple cider vinegar

1 32-ounce bottle of ketchup, more or less to taste

1-1/2 cups of brown sugar

4 tablespoons of Worcestershire sauce

Salt and pepper

Melt butter in frying pan. Sauté onion and garlic until light brown.

Add remaining ingredients and simmer on low heat for 45 minutes, stirring frequently.

Keeps well in refrigerator.

Courtesy of Brenda Thomas.

CHICKEN ON THE STOVE

This is good to make when you and your husband are going out and leaving the kids at home.

Lightly flour some chicken and brown. Add salt and pepper and a little water, add some cut potatoes and onions, cover and cook 30 minutes. Add ½ bottle of red wine. Add, oregano, thyme, basil, and continue cooking until potatoes are tender and chicken is done, about 45 minutes. In the last 10 minutes add mushrooms.

1/2
bottle
white
wine

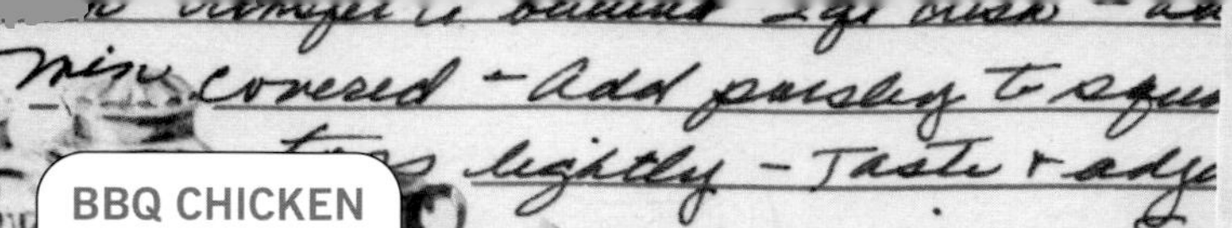

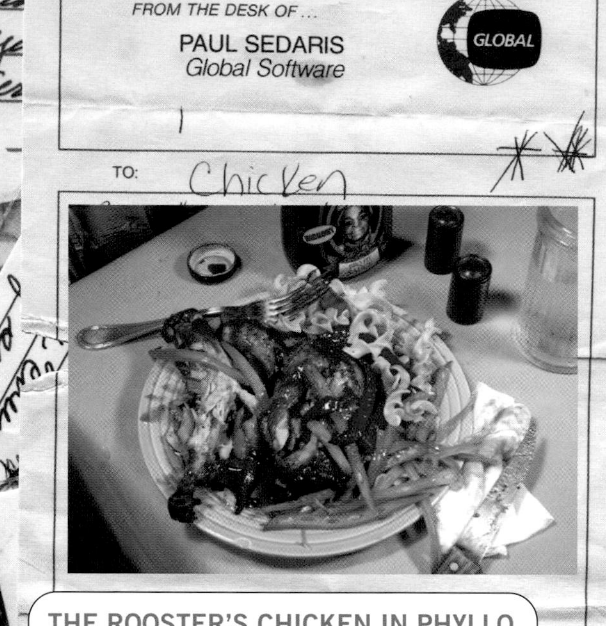

BBQ CHICKEN

Everyone swears that they can make the best BBQ chicken. The key to good BBQ is the sauce, but to me, making your own BBQ sauce is like making your own Chinese food or pizza, why bother? It's never going to taste as good as when you buy it. My recipe for BBQ sauce is as follows: I simply mix two different brands of the same kind of sauce, different prices, and then top with green, yellow, and red bell peppers for color.

I then melt ½ stick of butter with 2 cloves of garlic and baste my chicken. I place the chicken in a preheated oven (to 350) and bake for about 45 minutes. I then pour my combination sauce on and peppers over the chicken and cook for an additional 20 minutes. I try to do some degreasing and serve it with noodles and green beans and sometimes sweet potatoes and corn bread. Here is an additional way to make great BBQ chicken:

Get yourself a bottle of my brother's Can't Kill the Rooster BBQ sauce and use liberally. So good, people have been known to drink it. Also good for marinating chicken.

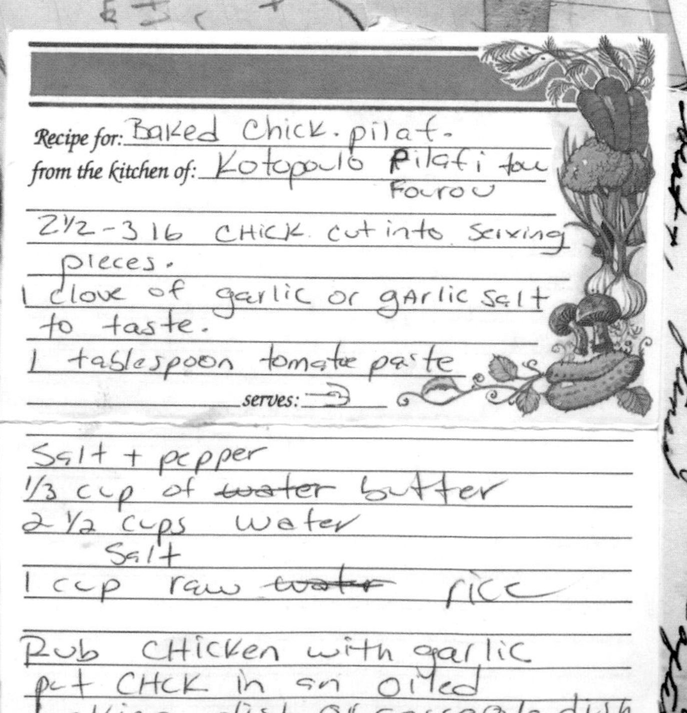
Recipe for: Baked Chick. pilaf.
from the kitchen of: Kotopoulo Pilafi tou Fourou

2½-3 lb chick. cut into serving pieces.
1 clove of garlic or garlic salt to taste.
1 tablespoon tomato paste
serves:
Salt + pepper
1/3 cup of ~~water~~ butter
2½ cups water
Salt
1 cup raw ~~water~~ rice

Rub chicken with garlic
put chick in an oiled baking dish or casserole dish

THE ROOSTER'S CHICKEN IN PHYLLO

I've seen my brother Paul make this so many times. He pounds his chicken breast using a plastic coffee cup that he got at the beach and he defrosts his phyllo by placing it on top of a toaster under a cabinet light, and it always turns out just the way it is supposed to.

4 boneless chicken breasts

1 garlic clove, cut in half

½ lemon

2 teaspoons oregano

Salt and pepper to taste

½ pound Kasseri cheese, cut into 8 thin slices

16 sheets of phyllo dough (I use more and just butter more layers for each piece of chicken)

Divide each chicken breast in half. Rub chicken with garlic and lemon. Sprinkle with oregano, salt, and pepper. Center a slice of cheese on each chicken portion and roll up neatly. Line a cookie sheet with foil, brush with melted butter, and set aside.

Unwrap phyllo, and cover with wax paper and damp paper towel to prevent drying out. Brush a single phyllo sheet with melted butter. Top with a second sheet and brush with butter. Wrap one chicken roll in phyllo and brush liberally with melted butter. Continue procedure for all rolls. Bake at 350 for 1 hour.

wooden spoon

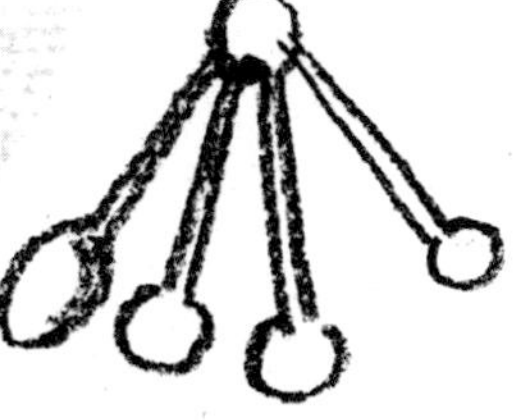

measuring spoons

cutting board

pastry brush

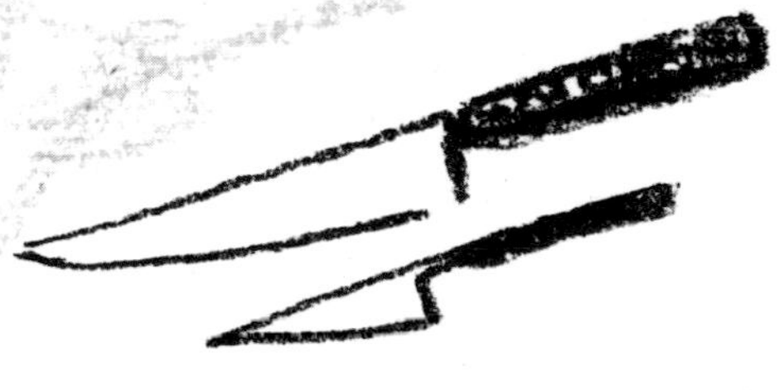

knives

pie plate

baster

Colander

tongs

Sponges

1/4 TEASPOON
Use for their beauty as well as flavor to stud ham, pickled peaches and lemon slices. Add to tomato juice, spiced sweet syrup, pot roast or meat marinade.
DINGBAT & CO.
HUNT VALLEY, MD 21031
PACKED IN U.S.A.
Soda

the Cavity Hole

MUSSER'S POTATO CHIPS
GENERAL OFFICES
MOUNTVILLE, PA. 17554

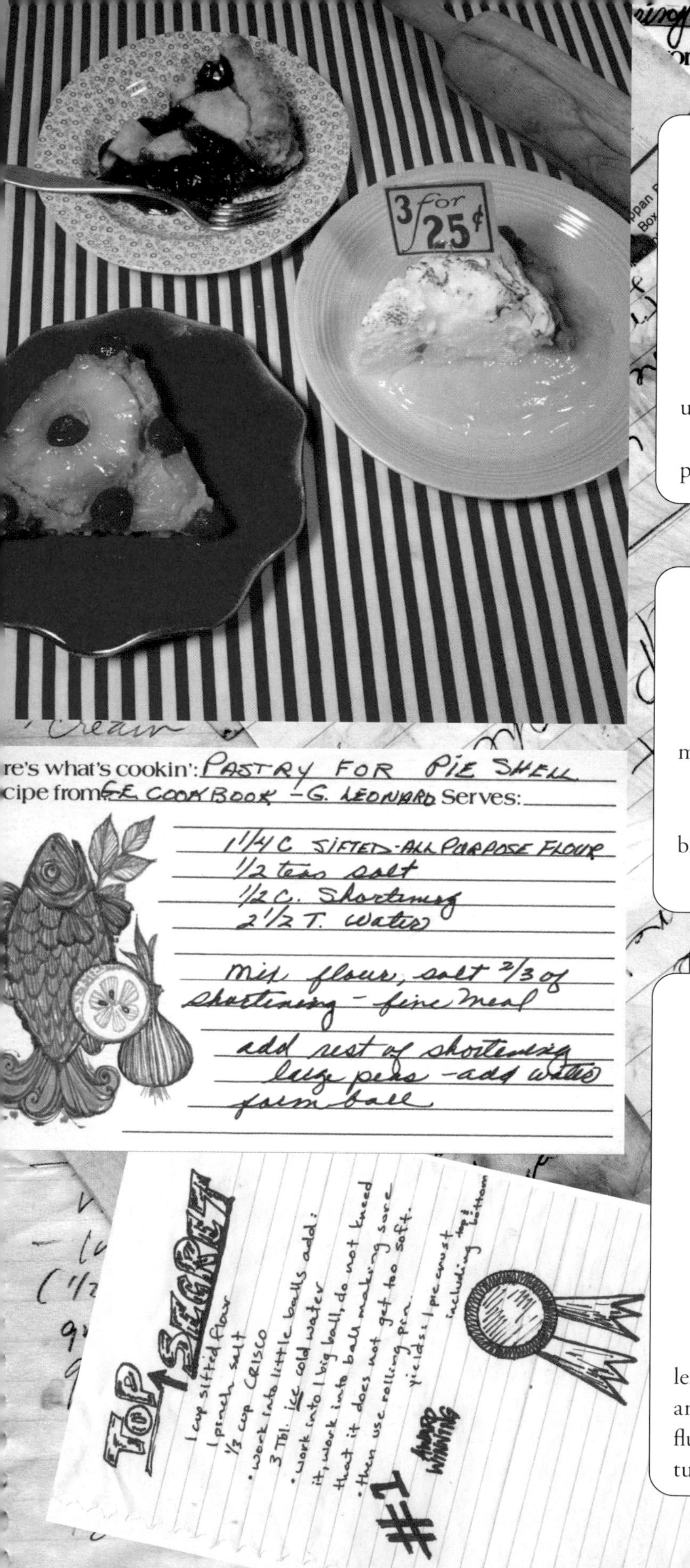

3 for 25¢
re's what's cookin': PASTRY FOR PIE SHELL
cipe from: G.E. COOKBOOK – G. LEONARD Serves:
1 1/4 C SIFTED-ALL PURPOSE FLOUR
1/2 teas salt
1/2 C. Shortening
2 1/2 T. water
mix flour, salt 2/3 of shortening – fine meal
add rest of shortening large peas – add water form ball
TOP SECRET
1 cup sifted flour
1 pinch salt
1/3 cup CRISCO
• work into little balls add:
3 Tbl. ice cold water
• work into 1 big ball, do not knead it, work into ball making sure that it does not get too soft.
• Then use rolling pin.
yields: 1 piecrust including top & bottom
AWARD WINNING
#1

GRANDPA LEONARD'S PIECRUST (MAKES 2 CRUSTS)

2 cups all-purpose flour, sifted

1 t salt

½ cup shortening

¼ cup shortening

¼ cup water

Mix flour, salt. Cut shortening with pastry blender until fine meal.

Cut ¼ cup shortening into flour so it looks like large peas. Sprinkle water over mixture and form into a ball.

BLUE RIBBON PIECRUST

1 cup sifted flour

1 pinch salt

1/3 cup Crisco

Work into little balls, do not knead it. Work into ball, making sure that it does not get too soft.

Then use rolling pin.

Yields 1 9-inch piecrust including top and bottom for blueberry pie.

Courtesy of Ann McCullen.

BLUEBERRY PIE

4 cup fresh or frozen blueberries

3 tbsp. flour

1 cup sugar

1/8 tsp. salt

1 tbsp. butter

1 tbsp. lemon juice

2 tsp. vanilla extract

Optional: 2 tsp. cinnamon

Mix flour, sugar, and salt in a bowl. Add blueberries, lemon juice, and vanilla—toss well. Pour into pie shell and dot with butter. Cover with top crust. Crimp or flute and cut several vents. Bake at 425°F for 10 minutes, turn down to 350°F and bake for 30–45 minutes.

PILOT PANCAKE'S PECAN PIE

Buckle your seat belts.

1 unbaked pie shell

2 cups pecans, chopped into pieces, plus enough whole pieces to go around the edge

3 eggs, lightly beaten

1 cup sugar

½ cup light Karo corn syrup

½ dark Karo corn syrup

2 T melted butter

1 T pure vanilla extract

1 T Maker's Mark bourbon

Preheat oven to 350.

Mix together the last 7 ingredients.

Add chopped pecans and pour into the unbaked pie shell, reserving 8 T of the liquid.

Place whole pecans around the edge of the pie shell and drizzle the reserved liquid over the whole pecans.

Bake in the center of a 350-degree oven for 50–55 minutes.

ANTONIA'S CHERRY PIE

PASTRY DOUGH:

Mix in large bowl:

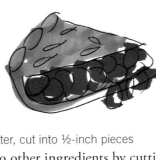

2½ cups all-purpose flour

1 tsp. white sugar

1 tsp. salt

Add:

2 sticks cold unsalted butter, cut into ½-inch pieces

Cut the fat directly into other ingredients by cutting in opposite directions with two knives, one held in each hand. When you are through some of the fat should remain, the rest should be reduced to the consistency of course crumbs.

Drizzle over the flour and fat mixture:

⅓ cup plus 1 tbsp. ice water

Using a rubber spatula, cut with the blade side until the mixture looks evenly moistened and begins to form

ANTONIA'S CHERRY PIE (CONTINUED)

small balls. If the dough has stuck together, you've added enough water, if not, drizzle 1 to 2 more tbsp. ice water. The dough should have a rough quality, not smooth. Divide the dough in half, press each half into a round flat disk and wrap in plastic. Refrigerate for at least 30 minutes and up to several hours.

Roll half the dough in to a 13-inch round disk using a little flour to ease the rolling. Fit it into a 9-inch pie pan and trim the overhang to ¾ inch all around. Refrigerate. Roll the other half into a rectangle and cut into strips for lattice. Refrigerate.

Preheat oven to 425°F.

PIE FILLING:

Combine in a large bowl and let stand for 15 minutes:

2 to 2½ pounds pitted sour or Bing cherries

1¼ cups sugar for sour cherries or ¾ cup for Bing cherries

3 tbsp. cornstarch

1 tbsp. strained fresh lemon juice

1 tsp. vanilla extract

¼ tsp. cinnamon

Pour the mixture into the bottom crust and dot with:

2 to 3 tbsp. unsalted butter, cut into small pieces

Cover the top with lattice and then seal the edge, trim, and flute. Brush the overhang and top crust with cold water. Sprinkle with sugar. Bake the pie for 30 minutes. Place a baking sheet beneath it, reduce oven temperature to 350°F and bake until thick juices bubble through, 25–35 minutes. Let cool completely on a rack before serving.

JERRI'S HOT FRUIT

Heat can of fruit on stove.

Chill.

Serve room temp.

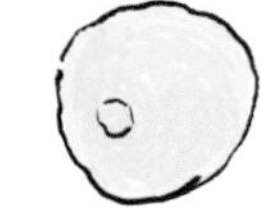

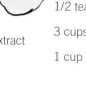

YELLOW SHEET CAKE FOR DECORATIVE CAKES

3 cups flour

1 t baking powder

1 stick unsalted butter

2 cups sugar

2 eggs

1-1/2 cups of milk

3 t pure vanilla extract

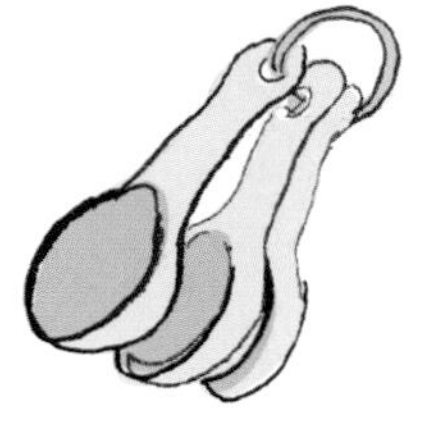

Mix flour and baking powder together and set aside. Cream butter and sugar together. Add eggs one at a time to the sugar and cream mixture. Then alternately stir in dry mixture and milk. Add vanilla and mix well.

Pour batter into two 9-inch rounds, or a 9 x 13-inch baking pan. Bake at 375 degrees F for 25 to 35 minutes until a straw from your broom comes out clean.

CHOCOLATE SHEET CAKE FOR DECORATIVE CAKES

2 cups flour

2 cups sugar

1 teaspoon baking soda

1 teaspoon salt

1 cup water

1/2 cup vegetable oil

1 stick unsalted butter

2/3 cup cocoa powder

2 teaspoons vanilla extract

2 eggs

1/2 cup sour cream

In a large bowl, mix together flour, sugar, baking soda, and salt. Melt butter and mix in water, oil, cocoa, and vanilla. Pour wet mixture over dry ingredients and mix well. Whip eggs and sour cream lightly, add to chocolate mixture and again mix well. Pour into a greased and floured sheet tray, 9 x 13 inches, or two 9-inch rounds. Bake at 375 degrees F for 20–25 minutes. Check by sticking a toothpick or broom straw in and if it comes out clean, it's ready.

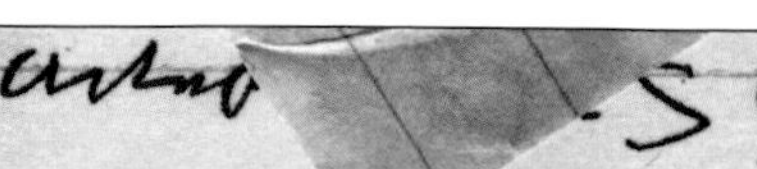

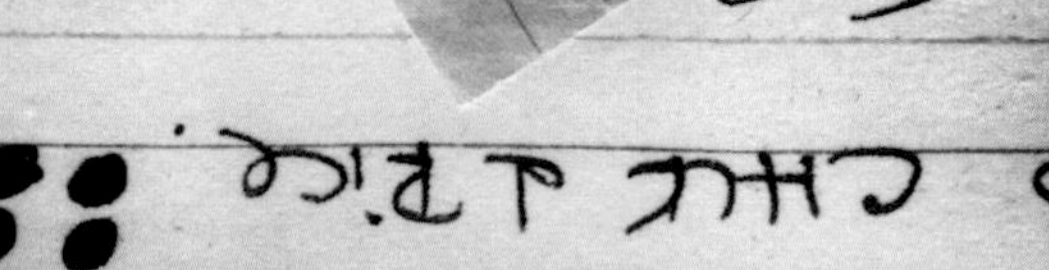

LEMON CAKE FOR LINO

1/2 cup of butter

1-1/2 cup of sugar

2 eggs

1 teaspoon of lemon extract

1/2 teaspoon of vanilla extract

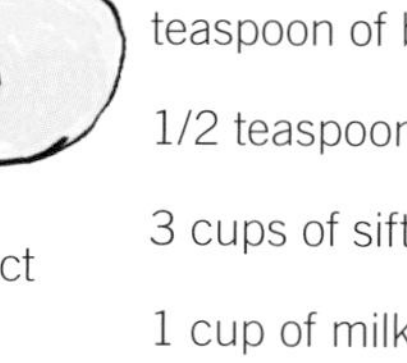

1 tablespoon plus 3/4 teaspoon of baking powder

1/2 teaspoon of salt

3 cups of sifted cake flour

1 cup of milk

Preheat oven to 350 degrees.

Mix ingredients together like you would for any standard cake.

Grease two 9-inch cake pans, bake 18–20 minutes.

LEMON BUTTERCREAM FROSTING:

1/2 cup of butter

4 cups of powdered sugar

1/4 cup of fresh lemon juice

1/4 teaspoon of vanilla extract

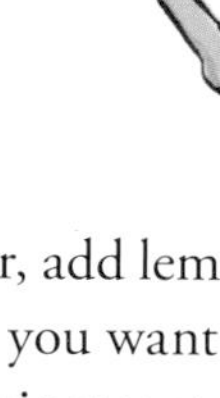

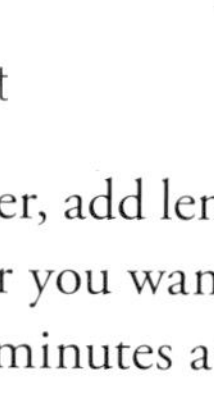

Beat all ingredients together, add lemon-colored food coloring till you see the color you want.

Beat in mixer for about 2 minutes at high speed.

Frost your cake.

CARROT CAKE WITH CREAM CHEESE TOPPING

2 cups flour

2 cups sugar

2 t soda

2 t baking powder

3 cups grated carrots

2 t cinnamon

1 t salt

1-1/2 cup oil

4 eggs

Mix oil and eggs. Add carrots. Mix dry ingredients and add to carrot mixture. Pour into 3" x 8" greased cake pan or sheet pan. Bake at 350 degrees for 25–30 minutes.

CREAM CHEESE TOPPING:

1 8-oz. package cream cheese

1 stick of unsalted butter

2 t pure vanilla extract

1 box confectioners' sugar

1 cup chopped nuts

Beat and spread on cake. Top with chopped nuts.

Sheet Cakes

You will need:

2 eggs

2 sugar cubes

Lemon extract

Crack eggs in half and discard top part of shell, white, and yolk (or use for the cake). Clean the two bottom shells well, removing the skin that lines them; this will allow for longer burning. Soak sugar cubes in the lemon extract, place one cube in each shell and pour one capful of extract over the cube. Ignite. Scary.

Cut-up Cake Ideas

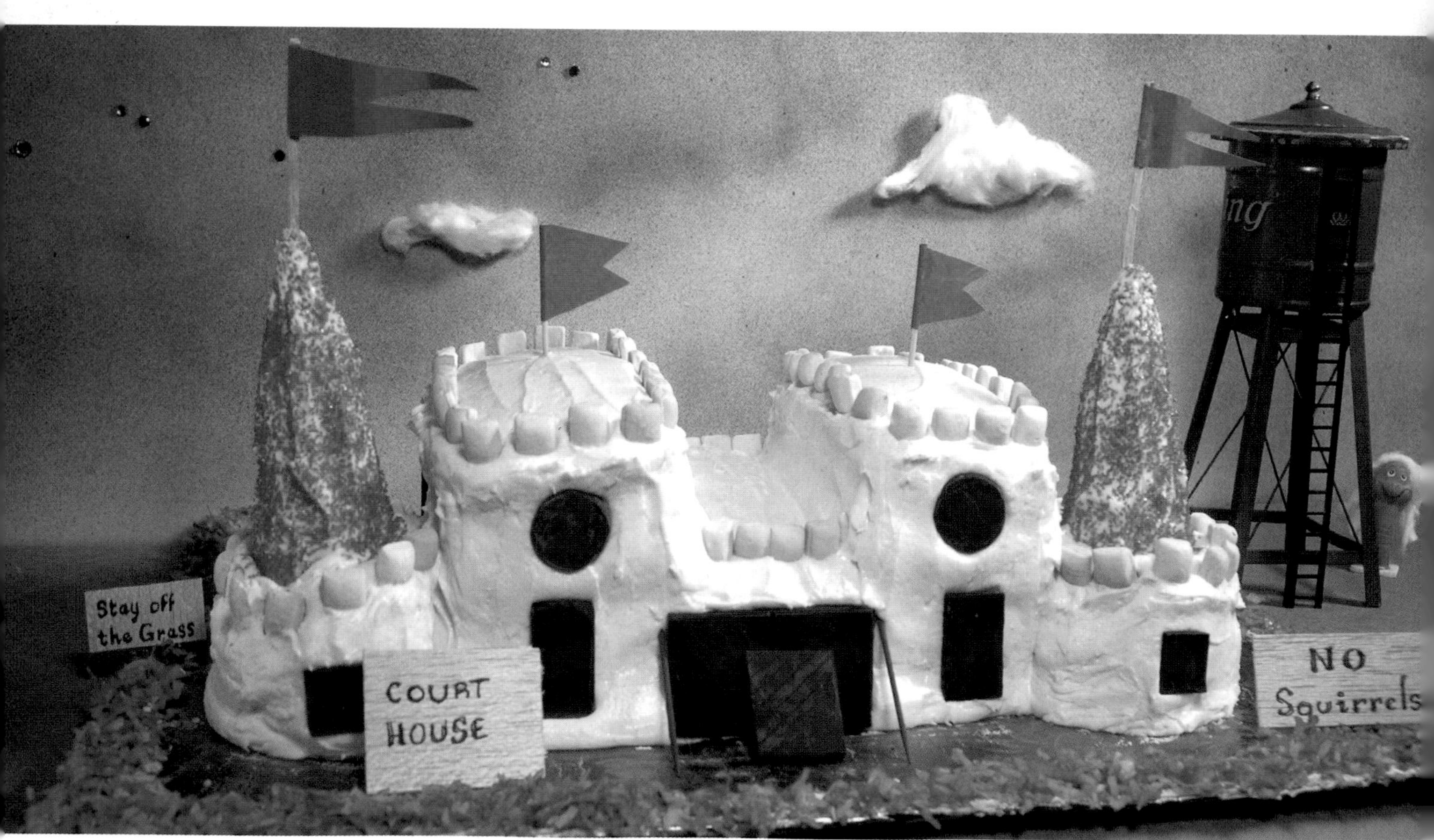

See You in Five to Seven Years

Merci Beaucoup

Be My First Mate

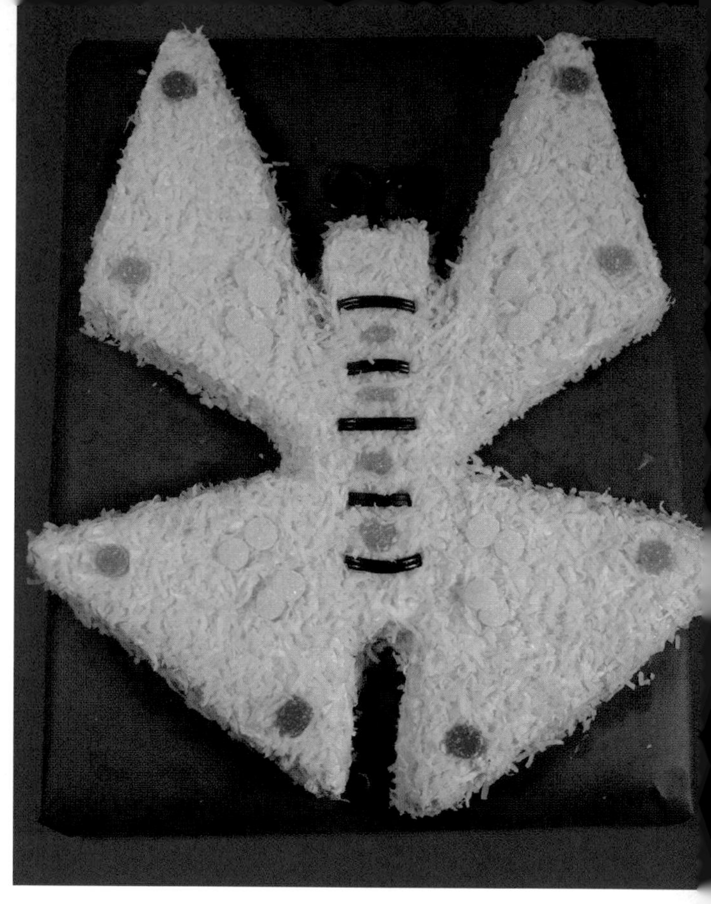

Happy Coming Out

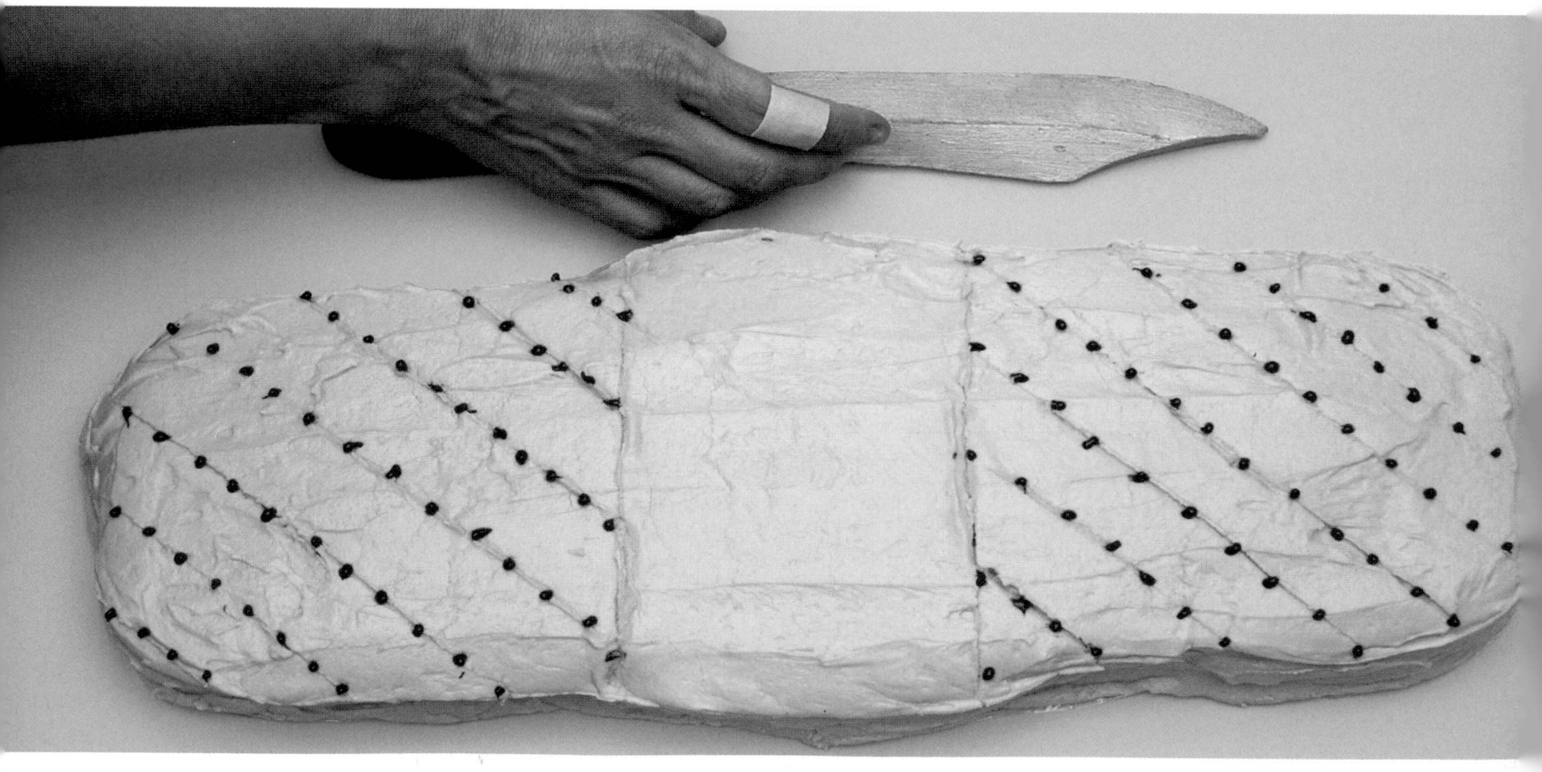

We Can Fix It

STEP
MOTHER

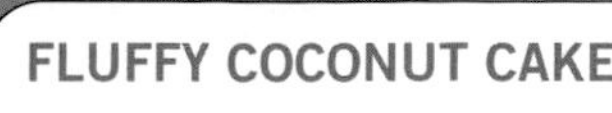

FLUFFY COCONUT CAKE

GENOISE CAKE:

6 large eggs

200 grams sugar

125 grams sifted cake flour (not self-rising)

100 grams unsalted butter, melted

1 teaspoon vanilla extract

Preheat oven to 300 degrees F and lightly grease two 8-inch round pans.

Combine eggs and sugar in a bowl and stir until combined. Set the bowl over a double boiler on low heat, and keep stirring for 5–8 minutes (or until warm to the touch).

When the eggs are lukewarm and look like bright syrup, remove from the heat and beat on high speed for a good 10 minutes. Scrape once in a while and keep on beating until the egg mixture becomes fluffy, cool, and tripled in volume.

Sprinkle in the flour, a little at a time, then gently fold in the melted butter and vanilla. Do not over mix.

Pour the batter into the prepared pans and bake for 20–25 minutes or until cakes pull away from the sides of the pan and basically look golden brown.

Remove from the pans and cool on a rack.

Makes one 8-inch cake, which serves 8–10.

FLUFFY COCONUT CAKE (CONTINUED):

COCONUT PASTRY CREAM:

- 2 cups milk
- 2 cups coconut milk
- 1 cup cream
- 225 grams sugar
- 150 grams cornstarch
- 4 egg yolks
- 4 whole eggs
- 2 teaspoons vanilla extract
- 40 grams butter
- ½ teaspoon coconut extract

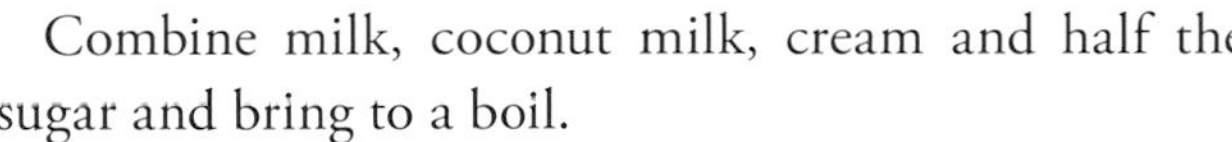

Combine milk, coconut milk, cream and half the sugar and bring to a boil.

Whisk cornstarch, other half of the sugar, yolks, eggs, and vanilla until the mixture whitens and no lumps are left.

Add a small amount of boiled milk mixture to egg mixture to temper the eggs.

Pour tempered egg mixture into pot with the rest of the milk mixture and cook, stirring constantly, until mixture thickens to look like custard.

Strain and transfer the mixture into a mixing bowl, and whisk in the butter and the coconut extract until the pastry cream is smooth.

Transfer to a container and press a plastic wrap onto surface and cool (preferably overnight).

SWISS MERINGUE BUTTERCREAM:

- 240 grams pasteurized egg whites
- 450 grams granulated sugar
- 1½ lbs 83% unsalted butter
- 1 tablespoon coconut extract

Whisk together the egg whites and sugar over simmering water until the egg mixture is warm to the touch or the thermometer reaches 140 degrees F.

Transfer the egg mixture to a mixing bowl and whisk until it triples in volume and the meringue holds stiff peaks.

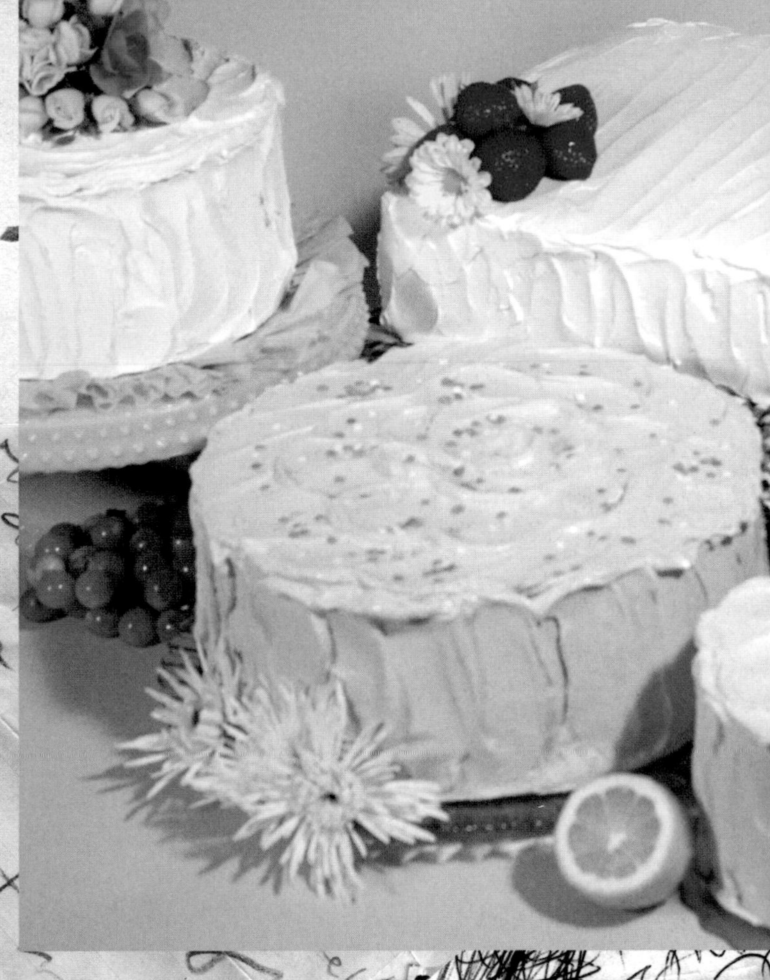

SWISS MERINGUE BUTTERCREAM (CONTINUED):

Let butter come to room temperature and then cut up into small pieces.

Start adding the butter into the meringue mixture and continue to mix until the mixture becomes light and fluffy. Add the coconut extract and keep whisking for another minute or so.

Transfer to a container, refrigerate if not using immediately.

ASSEMBLY:

Take the bottom layer of the Genoise Cake and pipe a buttercream ring around the top edge. Fill inside the ring with coconut-flavored pastry cream. Top with the second layer of Genoise Cake. Frost the sides and the top with coconut-flavored buttercream. Sprinkle the top and the sides with unsweetened coconut flakes. Enjoy. This recipe is from Ayse Dizioglu, Polka Dot Cake Studio in N.Y.C. (the best I've ever had).

HUELLA'S CHOCOLATE CAKE

- 1 stick of butter
- ½ cup of sugar
- 4 eggs, separated
- 1⅓ tablets of good dark chocolate
- 1 small packet of almonds, ground
- 5 T or so of flour

Cream softened butter and sugar. Add yolks one at a time.

Melt chocolate with a few drops of water—you may add some coffee or rum instead. Add chocolate and almonds to batter. Beat egg whites 'til light. Sprinkle in some sugar and beat until peaks form. Stir ¼ of the whites into batter. Sift in some flour. Fold in ⅓ whites, alternating with sifted flour. Finish with the whites.

Bake for 20 minutes or so in 350° oven, until knife comes out with melted chocolate—don't let it get too dry (center should be moist). Cool 15 minutes and unmold onto plate.

AUNT JOYCE'S BROWNIES

- 4 eggs, beaten until fluffy
- 1 C sugar
- 1 C flour, sifted
- 1 tsp. baking powder
- 1/2 tsp. salt
- 1 12-oz. package chocolate chips
- 2/3 C unsalted butter
- 2 tsp. vanilla extract

Melt together chips and butter. Beat eggs and add in everything else.

Bake at 350° for 25 minutes.
Optional: Press pecans on top, down into dough.

Maybe Next Year—Mama's Drinkin'

SWEET CREAM BISCUITS

2 cups flour

2½ tsp. baking powder

¾ tsp. sugar

¼ tsp. salt

1¼ cups heavy cream

Mix dry ingredients in a bowl and add heavy cream. Using wooden spoon or spatula pull together until it tightens and transfer to a well-floured surface. Form into a large ball and press out with the heel of your hand to 1" thickness. Cut into 2"x 2" squares and place on sheet tray. Moisten the tops with some heavy cream and sprinkle with sugar. Bake at 450°F, 10–15 minutes or until golden brown on top.

STRAWBERRY SHORTCAKE

1 quart fresh strawberries

1 cup sugar, adjust to your taste

Sweet Cream Biscuits (see recipe, above)

Optional: split vanilla bean or 2 lemon peels

Summertime: De-stem and -leaf strawberries, and cut in quarters. Pour sugar on top and toss well. Allow to marinate overnight.

Wintertime: Put frozen strawberries in a pan with sugar and just enough water to cover the bottom. Cook mixture until bubbling and starting to thicken. Adding cornstarch is an option.

To assemble, cut the biscuit in half and ladle strawberries on top. Put the hood back on and slather with whipped cream.

LEMON CHESS TARTS

12 small baked tart shells

1¾ cups of sugar

7 tablespoons of fresh lemon

Rind of 2 lemons, grated

1 stick of butter

6 eggs

Mix everything but butter and eggs together.

Melt butter in a double boiler. Add sugar mixture and well-beaten eggs. Cook until very thick. Stir constantly. Cool, cover, refrigerate. Fill each tart shell and top with a dollop of whipped cream.

COCONUT CUSTARD ICE CREAM

This is very rich ice cream. It improves after a day or two in the freezer.

Combine and heat in the top of a double boiler over (not in) boiling water until very hot (about 175 degrees):

2 cups heavy cream (see note 1)

3/4 cups sugar

3/4 cups coconut cream (see note 2)

Beat well:

4 eggs (large)

Add to the egg mixture and whisk until combined:

1/2 cup milk (any kind)

When the cream is very hot, remove it from the boiling water. Leave the bottom pan on the heat and reduce the heat to simmer. While constantly whisking the eggs, add several large spoonfuls of hot cream to the eggs, one spoonful at a time. Slowly add the egg mixture back to the hot cream while constantly whisking the cream.

Add to the custard mix:

3 oz. grated coconut

Return the custard mixture to the double boiler. Stir constantly and slowly while cooking over simmering water. Remove the custard when it reaches 160 degrees. It should be velvety smooth and slightly thickened. Cool the custard and then chill in the refrigerator several hours.

Freeze the custard mixture in an ice cream freezer until very stiff. Place any ice cream that is not eaten immediately in an airtight container and store for one or two days in the freezer to improve the flavor.

NOTES:

1. This recipe makes a super rich ice cream. To reduce the richness, substitute milk or half-and-half for part or all of the heavy cream (perhaps 1/2 to 1 cup). You can also use 3 eggs instead of 4.

2. Coconut cream is found in the grocery store along with cocktail mixes. The brand I am familiar with is Coco Lopez.

PINEAPPLE UPSIDE-DOWN CAKE

I stayed pretty faithful to Fannie Farmer's recipe.

12 T butter

1 C dark brown sugar

1/4 C pineapple juice

5 whole pineapple rings

1/2 C milk

1 egg

1-1/2 C flour

2 t baking powder

1 t salt

1/2 C sugar

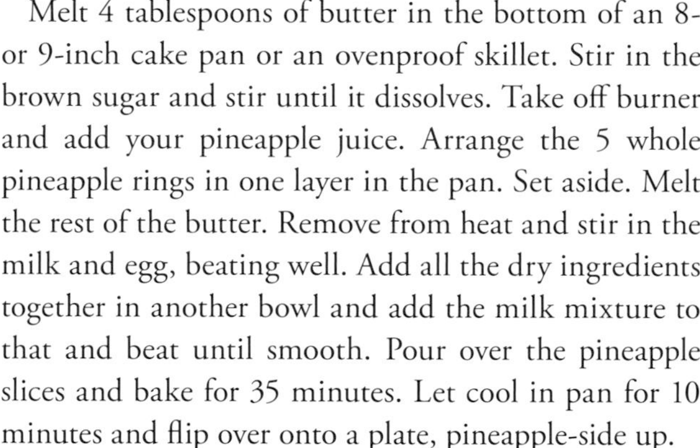

Preheat oven to 400 degrees.

Melt 4 tablespoons of butter in the bottom of an 8- or 9-inch cake pan or an ovenproof skillet. Stir in the brown sugar and stir until it dissolves. Take off burner and add your pineapple juice. Arrange the 5 whole pineapple rings in one layer in the pan. Set aside. Melt the rest of the butter. Remove from heat and stir in the milk and egg, beating well. Add all the dry ingredients together in another bowl and add the milk mixture to that and beat until smooth. Pour over the pineapple slices and bake for 35 minutes. Let cool in pan for 10 minutes and flip over onto a plate, pineapple-side up.

Serve with whipped cream.

COCONUT CUSTARD ICE CREAM VARIATIONS

Add 3/4 cup crushed pineapple to the finished custard before chilling.

Add 3/4 to 1 cup banana puree to the chilled custard before freezing.

Try black cherries with black cherry concentrate (from the health food store).

Courtesy of Bob Evans.

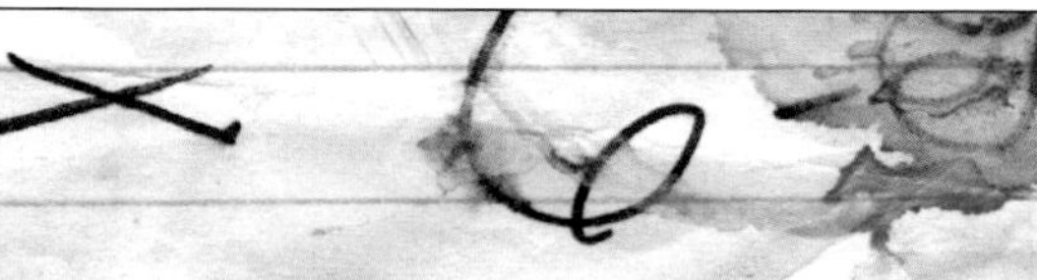

GRAPE ROOT BEER FLOAT

Take 2 scoops of vanilla ice cream and put it in your favorite frosted glass.

Pour as much grape soda as you can on top until the head rises above the rim.

CHOCOLATE MILK SHAKE

Add chocolate ice cream and milk in a blender and blend.

Pour into tall glass.

VANILLA MILK SHAKE

Mix vanilla ice cream and milk in a blender and blend.

Pour into a tall glass.

FRUIT SALAD

This was my favorite food growing up. All I remember is mixing canned fruit cocktail with whipped cream.

I am sure more goes into it but that's how I remember making it.

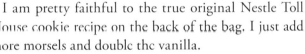

CHOCOLATE CHIP COOKIES

I am pretty faithful to the true original Nestle Toll House cookie recipe on the back of the bag. I just add more morsels and double the vanilla.

- 2 sticks unsalted butter
- ¾ cup of sugar
- ¾ cup brown sugar
- 2 eggs
- 2 t pure vanilla extract
- 1 t baking soda
- 1½ t salt
- 2¼ cups flour
- ¾ cup chopped pecans
- 18 oz. semisweet chocolate chips (1½ bags)

Beat butter and sugars together. Add eggs and vanilla.

Gradually add flour, salt, soda.

Stir in the chocolate chips and nuts.

Chill.

Roll into small balls and flatten in palm of hand so it looks like a flattened crab cake or medicated face pad.

Place on greased cookie sheet. Bake for about 9–11 minutes at 375 degrees.

I like you

I like you

I like you

Carrot Cake

4 Eggs well b[illegible]

2 cups sugar

1½ cups Wesson oil

3 cups sifted flour

2 tsp baking soda

3 tsp baking powder

¼ tsp salt

2 tsp cinnamon

1 cup nuts

5 large carrots grated

Beat eggs - [illegible] add oil

flour baking powder baking soda salt

add carrots - nuts, cinnamon

Can also add some raisins cherries and Choc Chips

Bake 350 for [illegible] hour & 15 minutes in a

large tube [illegible]

add nuts + cherries

Oil

Flour

carrots

cream cheese

soft cream cheese

Brown sugar

Pineapple Upside Down Cake

BOB EVANS'S BOURBON APPLE PIE

5 to 7 apples (use a combination of two or three tart, sweet, juicy, flavorful apples such as Staymen Winesap, Jonagold, Golden Delicious, Pink Lady)

2/3 cup sugar, divided

1 cup bourbon whiskey

2 tsp. cornstarch (more or less)

1/16 tsp. cinnamon

1/16 tsp. ginger

6 gratings fresh nutmeg

1 pie pastry (store-bought, refrigerated)

Milk

Heat 1/3 cup of sugar in a deep heavy pan over medium-high heat until melted. Reduce heat to medium-low and stir continuously until sugar is moderately caramelized, about the color of clover honey or darker if you prefer. Remove from heat and immediately pour the whiskey s-l-o-w-l-y over the sugar to stop the caramelization. Return the pan to the heat and allow the hardened sugar to dissolve. Reduce to a thin syrup and set aside.

Peel, core, and thickly slice the apples. In a small bowl, combine the other 1/3 cup of sugar (use more or less depending on the sweetness of the apples and the desired result), cornstarch, cinnamon, ginger, and nutmeg. Add the sugar mixture to the apples and mix gently to coat. Place half of the apples in a deep 10-inch piecrust, arranging them to fit closely together. Warm the syrup if necessary and pour over the first layer of apples. Spread the dry apples over the first layer of apples. Place the remaining apples on top. Position apples to mound slightly high towards the center.

Preheat oven to 375°. Place the pastry on top of the apples, fold inward any excess pastry and press to the sides of the pie plate to seal. Brush the top of the pastry with milk and rub it in lightly with your fingers. Remove any milk puddles by blotting with a paper towel. Sprinkle sugar liberally and evenly over the top and cut three or four 1-inch steam vents in the crust.

Cover edges of pie with foil. Bake for about 50 minutes until dark golden brown and crusty (remove the foil for the last few minutes to allow the edge to brown well without burning).

SUSAN AND GRACIE'S AMAZING BUTTER COOKIES

1-1/3 cup of unsalted butter

1-1/2 cup of sugar

2 teaspoons of vanilla extract

2 eggs

8 teaspoons of milk

4 cups of flour

3 teaspoons of baking powder

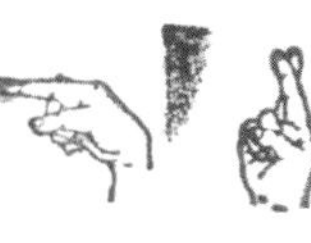

Mix all ingredients together and refrigerate overnight. Roll dough out (I use 2 pieces of wax paper and a rolling pin, floured if needed) and use cookie cutters to make your shapes. Place on a greased cookie sheet and bake for 6–8 minutes at 375 degrees.

Get your cookies to room temperature and refigerate overnight. Frost cookies next day (see frosting recipe, below) and place the cookies back in refrigerator for another night until the frosting hardens on cookie. You cannot eat enough of these.

FROSTING:

1 box confectioners' sugar

¼ cup of half-and-half

1 stick of unsalted butter

2 teaspoons of vanilla extract

Mix longer than usual. It's good to decorate these cookies with a cinnamon Red Hot on top. Also, this is a good dough to dye a different color, like red or green.

PEANUT BUTTER COOKIES

Mix:
1 stick of unsalted butter

½ cup of sugar

½ cup of brown sugar

Beat in: 1 egg.
Add: 1 teaspoon of pure vanilla
Add: ¾ cup of peanut butter (I prefer crunchy)
Combine: ½ teaspoon of salt, ½ teaspoon of soda, 1½ cups of flour

Add dry ingredients to moist ones. Roll into balls. Place on greased cookie sheet and press with a fork.

Bake at 350 degrees for 11 minutes.

LULA'S BROWN SUGAR PIE

(Makes one very large or two small)

- 2 cups brown sugar
- 1 tablespoon flour
- 3 eggs beaten
- 1/3 cup melted butter
- 1/2 cup milk
- Pinch salt
- 1 teaspoon vanilla extract

Mix all ingredients. Pour into uncooked pie shells. Cook at 400 degrees (preheat) about 30 minutes. It's soft in middle when done. (Add pecan meats before cooking for delicious pecan pie.)

"This recipe came from Lula Barksdale, a black woman who worked as a cook for my maternal grandparents in Danville, Virginia, in the early 1920s. My mother, Bebe Dickenson, was a small child at the time, but she learned the recipe and continued using it for the rest of her life. The recipe card is in my mom's handwriting.

"Lula Barksdale always made her Brown Sugar Pie at Christmastime, and she was the one who introduced my family to the concept of Christmas Zar, an obscure Southern Negro holiday observed on December 23rd. We white folks never knew the precise meaning of Christmas Zar, but the Dickenson and Wyatt families embraced it joyfully and and have always considered it a high point of the season.

"In the 1990s my dad wrote: 'Lula has long since passed away, but it would be interesting to know where she learned the name Zar in reference to the day before Christmas Eve. It's possible that the word was passed down to her from the days of slavery.'

"I recently came across some information that may shed light on the significance of Christmas Zar. In the writings of author and folklorist Zora Neale Hurston there's an entry she calls 'Negro Mythological Places.' One of these places is Zar, described as 'the farthest known point of the imagination, way on the other side of far.'

"It's also possible that the word derives from the ancient Zar cult found in Sudan, Egypt, and Ethiopia. This is a women's cult that involves trance dancing, spirit possession, ritualistic drumming, chanting, hair tossing, and animal sacrifice. The idea is to cure an illness caused by a demon. Combine all this with the concept of Christmas, throw in some Brown Sugar Pie, and I'd say you've got one heck of a holiday . . ."
—Marshall Wyatt, N.C.

BAILIWICK GINGERSNAPS

- 4 cups flour
- 4 teaspoon baking soda
- 3 teaspoons cinnamon
- 2 teaspoons ginger
- 1½ teaspoon cloves
- 3 sticks (1½ cups) margarine, melted
- ½ cup molasses
- 2 cups sugar
- 2 eggs
- Sugar to press into cookies

Mix dry ingredients (except sugar) in a bowl. In mixer add margarine, molasses, sugar and mix well. Add eggs and incorporate well. Add dry ingredients and mix. Refrigerate dough for several hours, overnight is best. Roll into balls about one inch in size. Place 13 at a time on a cookie sheet and press out with a flat-bottomed glass (rocks or highball) rubbed with margarine and dipped in sugar. Bake at 350°F for 8–9 minutes. Yields 7 dozen.

Courtesy of Ann McCullen.

LUMBERJACK'S VANISHING OATMEAL RAISIN COOKIES

- 2 unsalted sticks of softened butter
- 1 cup of brown sugar
- ½ cup of sugar
- 2 eggs
- 2 teaspoons of pure vanilla extract
- 1½ cups of flour
- 1 teaspoon of baking soda
- 1 teaspoon of cinnamon
- ½ teaspoon of salt
- 1¼ cup raisins
- 3 cups of oatmeal
- 1½ cup raisins

Cream butter and sugars together. Add vanilla and eggs.

Mix all the dry ingredients and add to batter, then add your raisins.

Chill the dough. Form into balls, flatten (with hand). Bake on a greased cookie sheet, at 375 degrees for about 10–12 minutes.

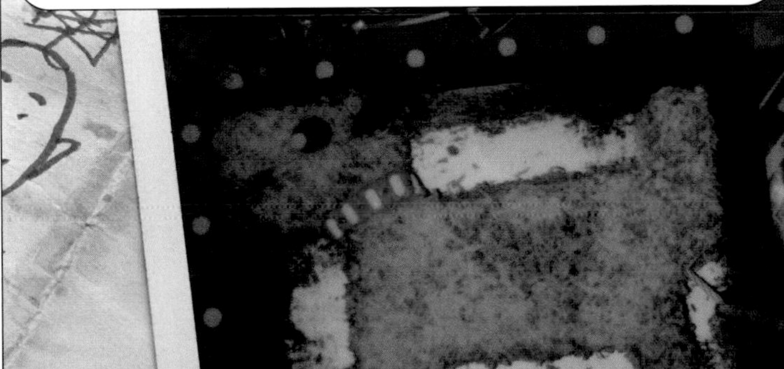

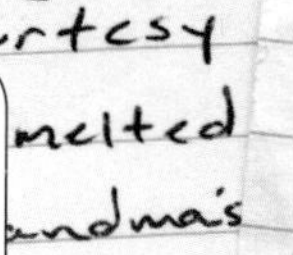

KOURAMBIETHES (POWDERED BUTTER COOKIES)

Makes 4 dozen cookies.

2 sticks of unsalted butter

1 egg yolk

2¼ cups of flour divided

½ teaspoon baking powder

1½ cups of confectioners' sugar, divided

3 tablespoons of brandy

1 teapoon of vanilla extract

½ cups of almonds, finely chopped and toasted

Cream your butter for 10 minutes in a mixing bowl, until fluffy.

Add ½ cup confectioners' sugar. Beat for 5 minutes. Beat in egg yolk, vanilla, and brandy.

Combine baking powder with 1 cup flour, and beat into butter mixture.

Add almonds and enough flour to form a soft dough. The dough should not be sticking to the sides of the bowl.

To shape the cookies, take a walnut-size piece of dough and roll it into a crescent shape. Place cookies on a foil-lined baking sheet, and bake at 350 degrees F for 20 minutes, or until tanned. Remove and place on a cooling rack. Let cookies cool for about 5 minutes.

Sprinkle the confectioners' sugar on a large sheet of wax paper. Transfer the cookies (should still be a little hot) to the paper, placing them close together, and dust with confectioners' sugar.

When cool, place each cookie in a cupcake wrapper and fit them closely to one another in a shirt box.

Some people will suggest that you push a clove down into the cookie before baking.

If you ever have a toothache, you can kill the pain by placing a whole clove right up against that tooth. Cloves are very expensive.

ANTONIA'S KOULOURAKI (GREEK COOKIE TWISTS)

1 pound Land O Lakes butter, softened

2 tablespoons Crisco

1 pound sugar

2 whole eggs and 4 yolks

5 teaspoons baking powder

1 cup Greek yogurt

1 teaspoon vanilla extract

6½ cups flour (enough flour to make the dough soft and kneadable)

FOR TOP OF COOKIES:

1 egg yolk

Preheat the oven to 300 degrees F.

With a mixer, beat butter and Crisco really well until they are well combined. Add sugar slowly, beating thoroughly until mixture is light and fluffy. Add eggs one at a time, beating well after each addition. Beat in the baking powder, yogurt, and vanilla. Add flour, one cup at a time, adding the last of the flour slowly to make sure dough is not too tough. Dough should be soft and kneadable. Pinching off a small amount of dough, roll it into a long strand about a half-inch thick. Strand should look smooth. Fold strand in half and twist. Alternately roll into a circular spiral. Place shapes on baking pan an inch apart. Beat egg yolk in a bowl with 2 tablespoons water and brush over each Koulouraki. Bake in preheated oven for 20–25 minutes until Koulouraki are golden brown. Cool on a baking rack.

COUSIN KATHY'S CHEESECAKE

3/4 cup of graham cracker crumbs

1 tablespoon of sugar

1 tablespoon of melted butter

3 8-oz packages of cream cheese

4 eggs

1 teaspoon vanilla extract

1 cup of sugar

TOPPING:

2 cups of sour cream

1 tablespoon of sugar

1 teaspoon of vanilla extract

Preheat oven to 375 degrees. Combine crumbs, sugar, and butter. Press into the bottom of a spring-form pan and refrigerate it. Then beat eggs until light and fluffy. Add sugar gradually, beating well after each addition. Add softened cream cheese and vanilla, then beat thoroughly. Pour into the crumb shell. Bake 35 minutes. Remove from oven. Spread on topping. Bake 5 minutes longer. Cool and refrigerate. Optional: Top with fruit.

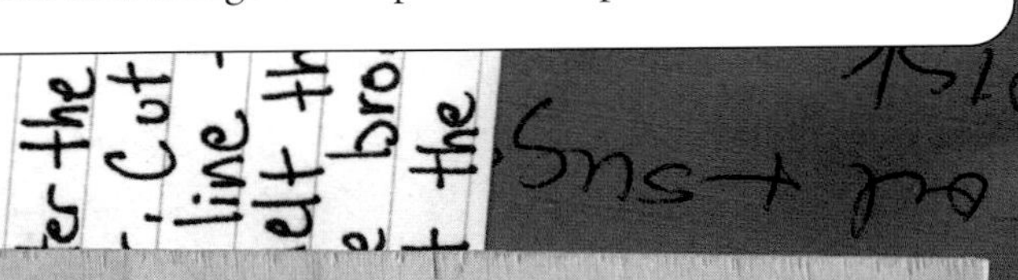

SAUSAGE TWIRLS AND DUPLEX CREAMS

SAUSAGE TWIRLS:

1 lb of sausage

1 can of crescent rolls

Make 4 rectangles using the crescent dough. Separate the sausage into 4 parts (uncooked). Spread the sausages evenly onto the dough. Like a jelly roll, roll each rectangle and slice. Tenderly flatten sausage wheels with hands and place on a baking sheet.

DUPLEX CREAMS:

Make any cookie of your choice. Place ice cream of your choice between 2 cookies and kindly press. Then dip the edges of your ice cream wheel into a plate full of jimmies or shredded coconut or chopped nuts. Wrap in Saran Wrap, label it, and place in freezer.

Art by Tom Bonauro

MISC

THWIMP COCKTAIL

Boil shrimp, remove shells.

Arrange on the rim of a glass or serve on top of a bed of lettuce. Serve with lemon wedge and cocktail sauce.

To make sauce: ketchup, horseradish, and lemon. If desired, a little hot sauce.

EXCELLENT SCAMPI APPETIZER

2 lbs fresh shrimp with shells

4 T butter

4 T olive oil

1/3 cup white wine

1 T chopped parsley

½ fresh basil

½ fresh oregano

Salt and pepper

1 T lemon juice

Heat your butter and oil in a frying pan. Add the wine, parsley, basil, oregano, salt and pepper.

Add the shrimp until they start to turn a different color (2–3 minutes). Sprinkle with lemon.

LEMON FISH

Use any kind of baking fish for this, about 2 pounds. Slash the fish in 3 places on each side. Mix some fresh lemon juice with salt and pepper and rub it all over the fish. Place in an oiled baking dish. Take about 1 pound of sliced potatoes and toss them with a little lemon juice, oregano, and olive oil. Place around the fish and drizzle some oil on top of fish and sprinkle a little oregano. Cover pan with a lid or some foil. Cook for 35–40 minutes. Remove lid or foil and cook for another 15–20 minutes or until the potatoes are done.

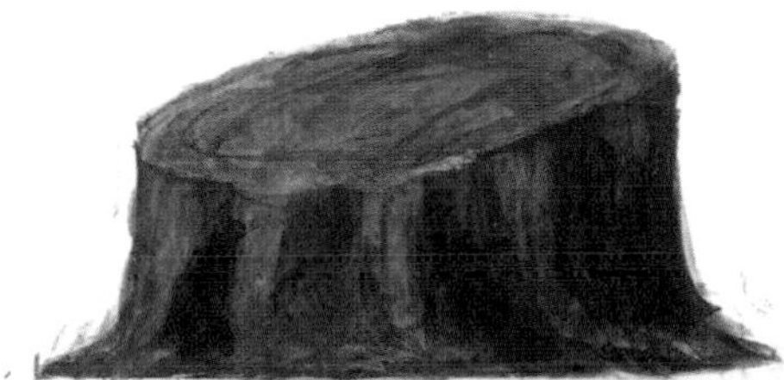

COLBERT'S SHRIMP PASTE

2 lbs. shrimp, boiled and peeled

¼ tsp. lemon juice

¼ lb. cream cheese

3 tbsp. mayonnaise

1 tsp. Worcestershire sauce

Dash Tabasco

Dash mace

Salt and pepper

Break shrimp finely. Soften cream cheese. Mix cream cheese well with shrimp and mayonnaise. Add lemon juice, Worcestershire sauce, Tabasco, mace. Salt and pepper to taste. Serve molded or in dish with mild crackers, like water crackers or Bremner Wafers.

Courtesy of Stephen Colbert.

SHRIMP AND FETA CHEESE SERVED IN SCALLOP SHELLS

I make this as an appetizer only when I want those fancy serving shells on my table. The shrimp amount depends on how many people you are serving.If it's 4, figure 5 large shrimp or prawns per person.

Large shrimp or prawns

4 oz. of feta

½ cup of white wine

2 crushed garlic cloves

1 cup of green onions

Olive oil

Oregano

Sugar, Salt, Pepper

2 cups of crushed tomatoes

Parsley, for garnish

Sauté your onions and garlic in oil until transparent.

Add everything else except shrimp and feta. Cover and cook for about 25 minutes or until the sauce is somewhat thick.

Clean and shell your shrimp, leaving the tail intact, and de-vein them.

If you are serving 4, then spoon ½ of this sauce into the individual scallop shells. Arrange your shrimp on top and then top your shrimp with the remaining sauce and crumble the feta on top. Put in oven at 425 degrees for 15–20 minutes or until the shrimp look pink and the feta has had a chance to melt a little. Top with parsley.

LOX LUMPS

Handful smoked lox lumps

1/2 chopped onion

1 tbsp butter

1/2 quart heavy cream

Pasta

Chopped chives

Salt and pepper to taste

Put hot water on the stove for boiling the pasta. Fry 1/2 chopped onion with butter in a large frying pan until golden.

Add a handful of smoked lox lumps, shredded into smaller pieces. Fry until salmon is milky/pastelly looking. Add heavy cream (approximately half of a quart). Season with salt and pepper (careful because the lox is already salty—you can always add more cream to make it milder).

Have the stuff in the frying pan simmer for a while, while you take care of the pasta—the water should be boiling by now.

When the pasta is done, drain it and put it back in the pot. Add the lox cream mix, stir, and divide on 2–4 plates. Garnish with chopped chives if you like.

Courtesy of Julia Hoffmann.

PATTIE HOGGIE'S CRABBIE CAKIES

1 lb lump crabmeat

1 T mayonnaise

1 t mustard

1 T minced onion

Dash Worcestershire sauce

1 egg

½ t old bay seasoning

¼ cup cracker crumbs

Carefully check crabmeat lumps for shells.

In a bowl, combine mayonnaise, mustard, minced onion, Worcestershire sauce, old bay, and egg.

Fold in cracker crumbs, mixing well. Fold in crabmeat. Make crab cake in desired portions and refrigerate until ready to cook.

Panfry in canola oil until lightly browned.

Serve with sauce made of mayonnaise, sugar, lemon juice, and fresh dill.

Courtesy Patricia Hogg.

DEVILED EGGS

12 hard-boiled eggs

¼ cup mayonnaise

1 T mustard

1 T vinegar

1 T sweet pickle relish

Paprika to sprinkle on top

Halve hard-cooked eggs lengthwise, remove the yolk and roughly mash. Add remaining ingredients and mix well. Refill egg white halves and sprinkle with paprika.

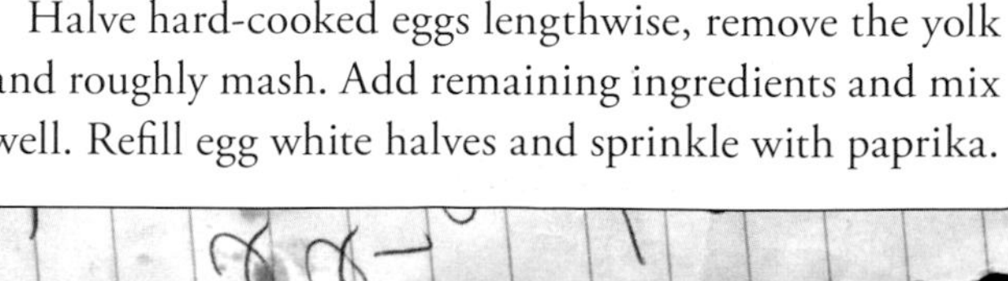

24

MISS SANDY'S
SCALLOPED OYSTERS

OBLONG PYREX PAN OR
MEXICAN CLAY BAKING DISHES
2 PINTS SHUCKED OYSTERS +
liquer FROM OYSTERS
1/2 STICK OF BUTTER
SALTEEN CRACKERS—AS MUCH AS NEED

-USING BUTTER GREASE UP BOTTOM OF PA
THEN SPRINKLE 1½ OF CRACKERS
THEN 1 LAYER OF OYSTERS
THEN little DALLOPS OF BUTTER
EVERY 1" ABOUT.

THEN FOR LAYER TWO SPRINKLE MORE
CRACKERS (LESS than 1st layer)
THEN ANOTHER LAYER OF OYSTERS
SAME AMOUNT, THEN CRACKERS, then
more butter — BEFORE PLACING
IN OVEN POUR A MIXTURE OF
1 cup CREAM MIXED WITH
THE LIQUER FROM THE OYSTERS
THIS WILL NOT LET IT GET TOO DRY

THEN COOK TILL DONE AT
A MEDIUM HEAT UNTIL GOLDEN
BROWN —

DON'T FORGET PEPPER.

CLUSTER HAVEN'S PEPPER MILL CHEESE BALL

1 stick of butter

1 8-oz. package of cream cheese

1½ cups of grated Cheddar cheese

2 T of grated onion

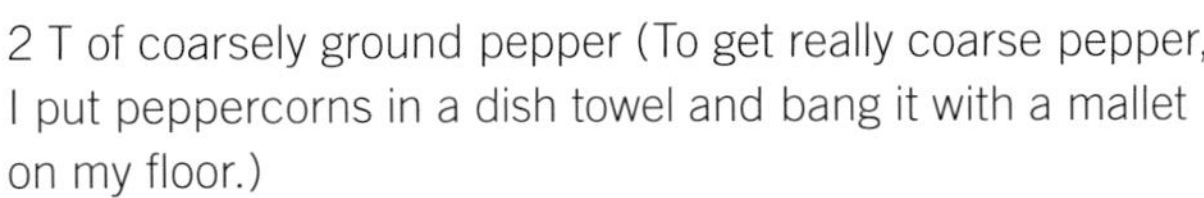

2 T of coarsely ground pepper (To get really coarse pepper, I put peppercorns in a dish towel and bang it with a mallet on my floor.)

Combine your butter and cream cheese. Add in the Cheddar and onion. Mix it really well. Form it into a ball and roll it in the pepper. Refrigerate. Serve at room temperature on a Ritz.

CHEESE PUFFS

1-1/2 cup of butter

1/2 t of salt

Dash of freshly ground pepper

1 cup of flour

4 eggs

3 oz. of shredded Swiss cheese

Combine 1 cup of water and first 3 ingredients in a saucepan and bring to a boil. Add flour all at once, then beat over low heat until mixture leaves sides of pan, about 1 minute. Remove from heat and continue beating for 2 more minutes until cool. Add eggs, beating after each until mixture has a satin sheen. Stir in the cheese, refrigerate mixture. It's easier to spoon out mixture on a greased cookie sheet in mounds from a tablespoon.

Bake in 375-degree oven for 20 minutes.

YORKSHIRE PUDDING

Remove your roast from the oven but leave oven on. Save all the fat and drippings from your roast while it is resting.

Beat until well blended:

2 eggs

1 cup milk

1 cup flour

1 teaspoon salt

Pour a ladle of the piping hot pan drippings into muffin pans (just enough to cover the bottom). Pour batter on top, about up to the halfway mark.

Bake for about 15 to 20 minutes but check in on them at the 10-minute mark to make sure they are rising and popping.

Serve right away with your roast beast.

(This can be made in a 11 x 7-inch pan and cut into squares.)

NEPTUNE'S HUSH PUPPIES

1-2/3 cup (stone ground) cornmeal

1/3 cup all-purpose flour

2 teaspoons baking powder

1 teaspoon baking soda

1 teaspoon salt

1 teaspoon sugar

2 teaspoons black pepper

Mix all ingredients together. Then whisk together and add to dry mixture:

2 eggs

1 cup buttermilk

1/2 cup onion, finely chopped or grated

Optional: 1/8 cup finely chopped jalapeño pepper

Mix well. Gently drop heaping tablespoons of batter into shortening or vegetable oil at 375 degrees F. Fry until golden brown, turning if necessary.

Courtesy of Jennifer McCullen.

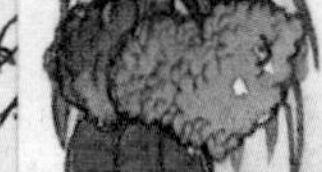
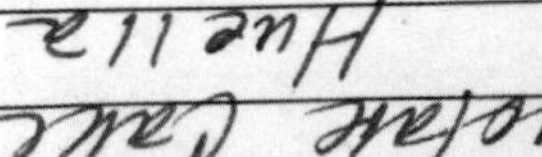

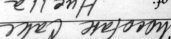

GREEK BEANS

- 1½ pounds of green beans
- 3 tablespoons of olive oil
- 1 bunch green onions, chopped
- 1 small onion chopped
- 2 carrots, peeled and chopped
- 2 crushed or minced garlic cloves
- Oregano, basil (maybe about 1½ teaspoons each)
- 1 28-ounce can of crushed tomatoes
- ½ 6-ounce can of tomato paste
- 1 bouillon cube (optional)
- Salt and pepper

Wash beans. Sauté onions, garlic, and carrots in oil and bouillon (if using). Add can of crushed tomatoes, oregano, basil, and beans. Add ½ cup of water.

Cook covered on low heat for 45 minutes. Take lid off and add tomato paste, then cook for another 15 minutes. Add salt and pepper to taste.

REFRIED BEANS

- 2 medium yellow onions
- 5 cloves garlic
- 5 tablespoons extra-virgin olive oil
- 4 27-ounce cans pinto beans
- 1 11.5-ounce can V8 juice
- 2 teaspoons cumin
- 1 teaspoon celery seed
- 1 teaspoon oregano
- 5 bay leaves
- ½ cup Pasilla/Ancho Paste (see recipe, below)
- 2 7-ounce cans chopped green chilies

Sauté chopped onions and garlic in olive oil. Add rinsed pinto beans, V8 juice, seasonings, Pasilla/Ancho Paste, and green chilies.

Cover and simmer for an hour, stirring frequently to prevent burning at the bottom of the pan. While beans are cooking use a potato masher and mash the beans in the pot.

Serve as main dish topped with chorizo sausage. Or serve as a side dish topped with Cheddar cheese. Very spicy.

PASILLA/ANCHO PASTE:

- 10 dried pasilla and ancho peppers

Cut the dried ends off the dried peppers and remove the seeds and ribs. Rinse and place in a small saucepan. Cover with 1 inch of water. Simmer, covered, on low heat for 30 minutes. Add water as needed. Puree in a blender to make a thick paste.

Courtesy of Lisa Sedaris.

SOUTHERN GREEN BEANS
People go crazy for these. I serve them with barbecued chicken, sweet potatoes, and cornbread.
¼ pound of salt pork and 1 strip of bacon (you can use either or both)
1 pound of green beans, trimmed
1 cup of water
1 onion, chopped
2 T of butter
Brown the salt pork and bacon in a pan. Add the beans and everything else. Cook for 3 hours.

Southern Green Beans

NONNY'S RICE

5 cups of white basmati rice

2 sticks of butter

Saffron

Preheat oven to 350 degrees F.

Boil water with a good amount of salt.

Wash rice in a large bowl with cold water. Swish it around with your hand and pour off cloudy water. Add more cold water, swish around with your hand and pour off cloudy water. Repeat until water is clear. By the time you finish this, the salted water will be boiling. With a slotted spoon, add rice to boiling salted water.

Wait till the water comes to a boil again. Let it boil for 3 minutes, then start testing it. There is a short window of time before the rice becomes overcooked, so be quick.

To test: take one or two grains out, bite it. When the rice is half done (soft on the outside, still hard on the inside), quickly drain it. Don't overcook! Five minutes is too long.

Have your roasting pan with lid ready. You will need a completely sealed cover because you are going to steam the rice and you don't want to loose any steam. After you drain the rice, put it in an airtight roasting pan, adding a 1/3 cup of water. Cover and cook for 1 hour.

Meanwhile, take a large pinch of saffron and put it in a shot glass. Half fill the shot glass with boiling water from the rice. Let it sit while the rice is baking in the oven.

After one hour, remove rice from oven. Add 2 sticks of butter and dump the shot glass of saffron and water in the pan. Cover and shake the pan rigorously to evenly distribute butter and saffron. Fluff with fork if you can't lift the pan to shake it.

Courtesy of Beatrice O'Shana.

SPANISH RICE, POR FAVOR

¼ cup oil

1 onion, chopped

¼ cup celery, chopped

1 garlic clove, minced

1 1-lb. 13-oz. can tomatoes w/liquid

1 t salt

1/4 t dried basil

1/2 t pepper

1 cup rice

Heat oil and cook onion, garlic, celery until softened.

Add tomatoes and seasonings. Bring to a boil, stirring occasionally. Simmer for 5 minutes. Stir in the rice, cover, and simmer about 20 minutes until the rice is tender and all the liquid is absorbed.

Note: Ground beef can be included. Just cook that up first, then do your onions and garlic.

Eat it rapido, rapido!

recipe for an unhappy Kitchen

2 heaping cups Reconstituted Revenge.
1 Broken heartful of Freeze Dried loathing
2 Fists full of Dehydrated guilt-
dash of Spite
1 headful of ground resentment.
Sprinkle generously with granulated Repulsion.
add plenty of chilled Contamination
MixWell
arrange over an eternity
Dish out to anyone who can take it with a Smile.

Courtesy of Conn Brattain

B- Bechemel
E- Esparaghe
T- Tomato
H- Hollandaise (somet
V- Veloute
D- Demi-Glaze

JOHNNY'S CORNBREAD

1 cup Martha White self-rising corn bread mix

1 medium yellow onion, chopped

1 teaspoon salt

1 tablespoon apple cider vinegar

1/4 cup olive oil

1 egg, beaten

1 cup buttermilk

2 tablespoons oil (for pan)

Preheat oven to 500 degrees.

Mix all ingredients in large bowl; batter will be quite thin. On stovetop, heat a 10-inch iron skillet to smoking and water beads up and rolls around. Swirl the pan with the 2 tablespoons oil. It should smoke. Sprinkle the pan lightly with salt. Pour in batter. It will sizzle. Transfer to upper third of preheated oven. Bake 15–20 minutes or until top crust shows cracks. Broil 2–4 minutes until top is brown. Turn onto cutting board, cut into slices like a pizza, and eat immediately.

It's great with a cup of grated extra-sharp Cheddar cheese and chopped jalapeño peppers, for Mexican cornbread. Substitute the vinegar in the recipe for pepper juice.

Any cornbread mix will do, I guess, at least in the South, but I know they change recipes for stuff in the North. The mix is cornmeal, flour, salt, and leavening—some combination of baking powder and baking soda, I suppose. No sugar. Sugar is heresy for the cornbread indigenous to my micro-region in the most remote area of North Carolina, Stanly County.

Courtesy of John Newman.

BAKED SWEET POTATOES OR YAMS

The difference between a yam and a sweet potato is that the yam is sweeter and moister and darker in color but the two are interchangeable.

Scrub sweet potatoes or yams. Lightly grease their skins and put them in an oven at 400 degrees. Bake for about 45 minutes.

To mash them: Boil sweet potatoes, drain, and mash. Add butter, salt, and pepper, and a little nutmeg.

MASHED POTATOES

2 pounds of peeled, quartered potatoes

½ cup of milk

4 T of butter

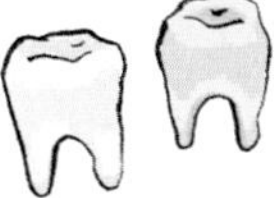

Boil in salted water until tender. Drain your potatoes and mash or press them. Add the milk and butter, salt and pepper.

MASHED TURNIPS

3 pounds of white turnips, peeled and sliced

½ stick of butter

Salt and pepper

Mash the turnips. Add the butter and salt and pepper.

FRENCH FRIES IN OLIVE OIL

Make these fries like you normally would only be extravagant and use olive oil instead of vegetable oil. It will take twice, maybe three times, as long but be really really, good. Top with salt. Treat yourself.

EXCELLENT STUFFED POTATOES

6 large baking potatoes

1 onion, diced

1 medium green pepper, diced

1 stick butter

1 teaspoon salt

1–2 tablespoons cream

1 teaspoon fresh or dried rosemary

1/2 teaspoon pepper

Paprika, for garnish

Serves 4.

Bake your potatoes in an oven for 1 hour.

Meanwhile sauté onion, pepper, and rosemary in your butter, until limp. Then add your salt, pepper, and cream and heat until just before it boils. Take off heat.

Remove potatoes from oven when tender. Cut them in half lengthwise. Scoop out the centers, leaving the shells intact. Mash insides and then add the cream mixture. Mix well. Fill the shells with the mashed potato mixture and dot with butter. Bake at 400 degrees for 20 minutes. Sprinkle with paprika and serve at once.

From *Cooking with Love and Paprika* by Joe Pasternak.

DAD'S OVEN-ROASTED VEGETABLES

3 peppers, 3 different colors, seeds removed cut into ½-inch wide strips

2 red onions, cut into wedges

2 zucchini or yellow squash, cut into ½ -inch slices

1 eggplant, trimmed into 1-inch chunks

¼ cup olive oil

¼ cup Italian flat-leaf parsley

2 t fresh thyme leaves

Salt and pepper to taste

Spread all the vegetables in a roasting pan and top with the oil.

Bake at 400° turning often, for about 40 minutes. Optional: Add fresh spinach in the last minute and mix it in. Also, you can make a pan using all root vegetables, like sweet potato, parsnips, carrots, celery root.

Boil rigatoni in salted water. Drain and toss with vegetables. Top with parsley. Optional: Garnish with roasted pine nuts.

This is good with or without rigatoni.

BAKED BUTTERNUT OR ACORN SQUASH

Preheat oven to 400 degrees F.

Cut your squash in half lengthwise (for butternut—for acorn cut in half), scoop out all the seeds and fibers. Place in a shallow baking pan cut-side down, add ¼ cup of water. I stab the outside of the squash, but I'm not sure why, or even if it's right.

Season with a lot of pepper and salt and bake for about 45 minutes or until tender, checking by inserting a knife. When ready, scoop out the insides and place in a bowl or pot and season with salt and pepper and butter. You can add brown sugar, but I don't. Mash up with a fork and then warm on stove until you need it. This too can be made ahead of time and just reheated.

FRAZZLED LEEKS IN SNAPPING OIL

2 cups of leeks (the white part), julienned

1½ cups of olive oil

1½ cups of flour

Salt

Put the leeks in the flour and shake off the excess. Place the leeks in the hot snapping oil, for about 4 minutes until they look a little frazzled. Take out using a slotted spoon and place on paper towel like you would French fries. Top with salt.

STEAMED CARROTS

Put carrots in a steamer and steam.

CRYING MUSHROOMS IN PHYLLO

About 10 phyllo leaves

1/4 lb. butter

1/2 lb. chopped mushrooms

1/2 t salt

Pepper

1/4 t dill

4 oz. cream cheese

1/4 cup sour cream

1/4 cup plain yogurt

1/2 cup plain breadcrumbs, ground

Some parsley

1 minced scallion

Juice of 1/2 lemon

Sauté the chopped mushrooms in some of the butter. Remove from heat, add cream cheese to hot mushrooms. Toss until the cheese is melted. Add in everything else but the remaining butter.

Melt the remaining butter to use for the phyllo.

On a buttered baking tray, use half of the phyllo sheets and butter between each layer using a pastry brush.

Apply the filling 3 inches wide and roll tight, tucking in the sides, and brushing the top of the roll with butter as well.

Bake at 375 degrees for 25 minutes.

BRUSSELS SPROUTS

They shouldn't be overcooked; they should look bright green. They will brighten up any plate, if you let them.

Wash 1 pound of sprouts and take away any wilted leaves. Trim the stem and cut an "X" in the bottom. Steam them for about 8–10 minutes.

When done, put them in a skillet with 2 tablespoons of butter and salt and pepper. Cover and cook for about 6–8 minutes, shaking them back and forth.

MOUSSAKA

You can use a marinara sauce instead of meat.

MEAT SAUCE:

Sauté in oil:

1 chopped onion, 2 crushed garlic cloves

Add:

1 pound beef

Stir this well, and add:

1 cup canned crushed tomatoes, 1 tablespoon parsley

1/2 small can tomato paste, 1/2 cup white wine

Salt and pepper, 1/4 teaspoon cinnamon (optional)

VEGETABLES:

Mix together:

1/2 pound prepared eggplant (see below)

1/2 pound potatoes

1/2 pound zucchini (shallow-fried in oil)

CREAM SAUCE:

See Pastitsio, pages 79–80.

TO ASSEMBLE:

Grease whatever dish you are using, in my case 13 x 9 x 2 inches. Add a little of the red sauce to the bottom of dish.

Place a layer of eggplant on bottom, top with a little of the sauce, sprinkle with a little cheese, then add a layer of potatoes and or zucchini and top with the rest of the sauce, adding a little more cheese.

For the third layer, add whatever you have left of the zucchini and eggplant.

Arrange evenly and spread the cream sauce and some cheese on top.

I also add some toasted pine nuts.

Bake for 1 hour at 350 degrees.

PREPARED EGGPLANT:

Slice the eggplant, leaving the skins on. Sprinkle with salt and let sit for an hour. Dry with paper towel, place in a baking dish, and brush with olive oil. Lightly brown under a hot broiler, turning once. You can also just shallow-fry in oil.

CREAMED SPINACH

Make a white sauce with 1 tablespoons of butter, 1 tablespoon of flour, ½ cup of milk. Wash, clean, and dry 1½ pounds of spinach. Add the spinach to the white sauce along with 1 tablespoon heavy cream, dash nutmeg, and salt and pepper. Just stir around in the pot until completely mixed together.

ADULT BIRTHDAY DINNER SUGGESTION

Cluster Haven's Pepper Mill Cheese Ball
Lamb Chops with Handles
Hugh's Scalloped Potatoes
Steamed Carrots
Baked Alaska
Coffee

HUGH'S SCALLOPED POTATOES

- 1 tablespoon of minced parsley
- 1 cup of thinly sliced onion
- 2-1/2 cups of thinly sliced potatoes
- 1 teaspoon of salt
- 1-1/2 tablespoons of butter
- 3-1/2 tablespoons of flour
- 1 cup of milk
- Pepper
- Paprika
- 1 cup of shredded Swiss cheese

Boil potatoes and onion for about 5 minutes. For the cream sauce, melt butter. Add flour and milk. Add paprika, salt, and pepper. Stir, then add the Swiss cheese. Oil the bottom of a 9"x 12" baking dish. Place a layer of potatoes and onions, then a layer of sauce, then parsley. Alternate until finished with ingredients. Bake at 400 degrees for 35 minutes.

Adult Birthday Dinner

MENU SUGGESTION
Salad with Italian Dressing
Spaghetti and Meatballs
or
Manicotti with Ricotta, Crêpe Style
Cousin Kathy's Cheesecake
Stinky Stuff

Italian Nights

To make your own Drip Candle, see page 283.

MANICOTTI WITH RICOTTA, CRÊPE STYLE

MARINARA SAUCE:

- 3 cloves garlic, finely chopped
- 2 teaspoons basil
- 2 tablespoons finely chopped parsley
- 4 tablespoons olive oil
- 6 ripe tomatoes, peeled, finely chopped, and seeded or 2 cans crushed tomatoes
- Salt and pepper
- 1 beef bouillon cube
- 2 teaspoons oregano

Sauté boullion cube, garlic, basil, parsley, and oregano in olive oil until brown. Add tomatoes and cook slowly. Add a little hot water and season to taste.

CRÊPES:

- 3 eggs, room temperature
- 1 cup flour
- 1/2 cup milk
- 1 tablespoon olive oil
- Dash salt

Beat eggs. Add flour gradually. Add milk, olive oil, and salt, stirring with a fork. Smooth batter. Don't overbeat. Cook 24 –28 5" crêpes. Cover in wax paper. Store in refrigerator. Don't freeze. Can make several days in advance.

RICOTTA FILLING:

- 1 pound ricotta cheese
- 1/4 cup Parmesan cheese
- 1 egg, beaten
- 1/4 cup parsley, finely chopped
- Dash salt

Beat ricotta. Add parsley, salt, and cheese. Add beaten egg. Blend thoroughly.

TO ASSEMBLE:

Spread thin layer of marinara sauce in baking dish. Fill the middle crêpe with generous tablespoon of filling. Roll like jelly roll. Place seam down in baking dish. Cover with light layer of sauce. Bake 350 degrees for about 20 minutes.

Top with grated Parmesan cheese. Serve with very hot marinara sauce on side.

SPAGHETTI AND MEATBALLS

MEATBALLS:

- 2/3 cup breadcrumbs
- 1/4 cup milk
- 1 onion
- Olive oil
- 1/2 pounds beef
- 1 egg
- 5 tablespoons Parmesan cheese
- 2 tablespoons parsley
- 2 garlic cloves, crushed
- Salt and pepper

Soak breadcrumbs and milk together. Set aside. Sauté onion in the olive oil. In a large bowl combine onion, breadcrumbs, and all the ingredients. Shape into balls. Cover bottom of large skillet with olive oil. Heat until hot. Cook meatballs, turning occasionally till they are brown.

MARINARA SAUCE:

- 1 onion, minced
- 3 garlic cloves, minced
- 1/2 cup olive oil
- 2 cans crushed tomatoes
- Pinch sugar
- Salt and pepper
- Optional: 1/2 cup red wine

Sauté garlic and onion in oil. Stir in tomatoes, sugar, salt and pepper and optional red wine.

Cook 25 minutes.

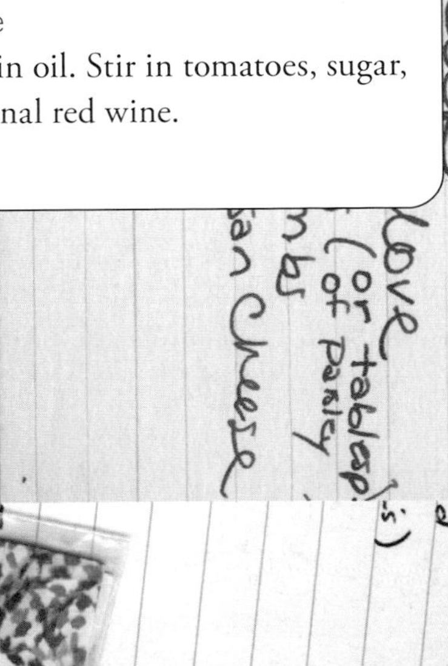

Spring Leg of Lamb

Beef Tenderloin

GREEK SPAGHETTI

Sauté 1 chopped onion, 2 garlic crushed cloves, and 1 chicken bouillon cube (optional).

Add basil, oregano, 2 large cans of crushed tomatoes, salt and pepper, some parsley, and some mint.

Cover and simmer for about 30 minutes. Add ½ cup grated Parmesan cheese. Continue cooking for about 15 minutes or so. After you have boiled your spaghetti and drained it, add it to the sauce.

Brown a stick of butter (be sure not to burn it, so keep your eye on it) and pour the sizzling butter over the sauce and spaghetti, tossing well. Serve with chicken or pork chops on the side. When making Greek meatballs it's pretty much like traditional ones, only you add mint.

DINNER DELUXE "I GOT A RAISE" TENDERLOIN

Serves 6.

Get about 2-1/2 pounds beef tenderloin.

This kind of beef costs a lot of money.

450-degree oven.

You will need an oven-safe skillet pan.

On stove add a little fat (oil or butter) to pan.

Take your trussed beef and aggressively salt and pepper it.

When your pan starts to smoke a little, sear the beef on all 4 sides—you'll want to sear the presentation side first.

Put about 3 pats of butter on top of roast and put right in oven.

For a 2-1/2 pound roast, cook for about 20 minutes if you desire medium-rare temperature.

Another option: Place room-temperature meat in an open shallow pan.

Dot with butter or brush oil on top or ask your butcher to tie salt pork or strips of beef fat on top of your roast. Toss some sprigs of rosemary on top. Cook in 500-degree oven for 10 minutes, then turn oven to 350 degrees and cook for 20 minutes.

KOREAN KORNER

CATHY CAMPER'S ASPARAGUS MACARONI

In 2 tablespoons of olive oil, sauté 3–5 cut-up cloves of garlic and some red pepper flakes. The more pepper flakes you add the hotter it will be. Cut a bunch of asparagus into 1-inch pieces. Add to the hot oil and sauté until tender, about 3–5 minutes. Salt and pepper to taste. Serve over penne. Sprinkle some Parmesan or Asiago cheese over the top.

SPRING SOIREE ROAST LEMON LEG OF LAMB

Lamb

Garlic

Salt and pepper

Olive oil

Butter

Oregano

Lemon juice

Optional: potatoes

Preheat oven to 350 degrees.

Take a 4-pound leg of lamb and cut small slits all over the surface. Insert slivers of garlic cloves. Rub the entire leg with a combination of lemon juice and salt and pepper. Add olive oil and oregano on top and cook for 1 hour. After an hour add some hot water to the pan and top leg of lamb with about 3 tablespoons of butter. Continue cooking for another hour or less.

In the last hour you could add some potatoes to the pan. Just quarter your potatoes and mix with a little lemon juice, oregano, and oil and toss into pan.

MINNIE'S KOREAN STYLE PANCAKES (BIN DA DOG)

Basically put 2 eggs in a bowl with some water and flour so it looks like pancake batter. Get whatever you need to out of your refrigerator, like eggplant, peppers, tomatoes, onion, carrots, whatever.

Put that in a frying pan with a little oil or butter to sauté. Pour batter over vegetables. Flip like a pancake when done on one side. Serve with soy sauce with white vinegar.

BULGOGI (KOREAN FOR "SUNNY THE LION")

5–6 pounds of beef ribs or thinly sliced beef

2 crushed garlic cloves

1 cup of green onions

1½ tsp. of pepper

3 tsp. of sesame oil

2 cups of soy sauce

½ cup of sugar (sugar softens the beef)

Mix garlic, sesame oil, green onions, pepper, soy sauce, sugar in a bowl. Add your beef and coat well, marinate overnight.

Barbecue it somehow.

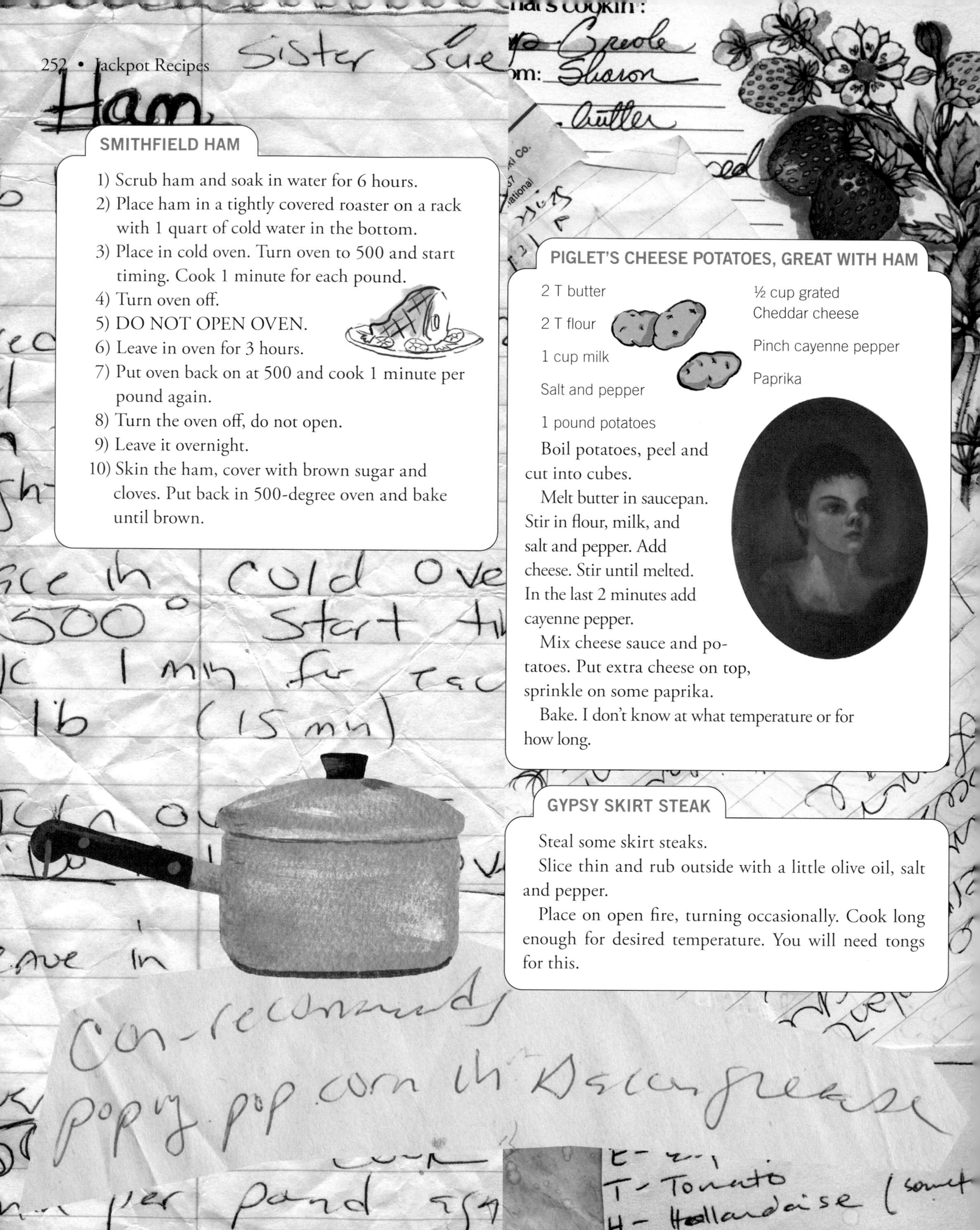

SMITHFIELD HAM

1) Scrub ham and soak in water for 6 hours.
2) Place ham in a tightly covered roaster on a rack with 1 quart of cold water in the bottom.
3) Place in cold oven. Turn oven to 500 and start timing. Cook 1 minute for each pound.
4) Turn oven off.
5) DO NOT OPEN OVEN.
6) Leave in oven for 3 hours.
7) Put oven back on at 500 and cook 1 minute per pound again.
8) Turn the oven off, do not open.
9) Leave it overnight.
10) Skin the ham, cover with brown sugar and cloves. Put back in 500-degree oven and bake until brown.

PIGLET'S CHEESE POTATOES, GREAT WITH HAM

2 T butter

2 T flour

1 cup milk

Salt and pepper

1 pound potatoes

½ cup grated Cheddar cheese

Pinch cayenne pepper

Paprika

Boil potatoes, peel and cut into cubes.

Melt butter in saucepan. Stir in flour, milk, and salt and pepper. Add cheese. Stir until melted. In the last 2 minutes add cayenne pepper.

Mix cheese sauce and potatoes. Put extra cheese on top, sprinkle on some paprika.

Bake. I don't know at what temperature or for how long.

GYPSY SKIRT STEAK

Steal some skirt steaks.

Slice thin and rub outside with a little olive oil, salt and pepper.

Place on open fire, turning occasionally. Cook long enough for desired temperature. You will need tongs for this.

JEAN'S BACK POCKET CHICKEN

Go to your butcher and ask him for 4 chicken breasts. Ask him to design a pocket by putting a 3-inch cut into the thickest side.

In a bowl combine ¾ cup of goat cheese with 1 tablespoon each of chives, parsley, basil, and "king of herbs" French tarragon. Mix this with 1½ tablespoons of olive oil and salt and pepper to taste.

Stuff each chicken breast by putting about a spoon of the cheese mixture in its pocket (use your fingers to work it in) and close each pocket with a toothpick.

Salt and pepper and set aside in refrigerator for at least an hour.

Melt 1½ tablespoons of butter and 1 tablespoon of olive oil in a skillet. Place chicken breasts skin side down in pan and sauté until tanned. Flip over once. Cook each side about 6 to 7 minutes.

Serve with toothpick in or out, depending on who you are serving.

TOOTHPICK CHICKEN ROLLS IN PAN

Take 1 chicken breast, pounded out. Sprinkle on parsley, salt, pepper and some breadcrumbs. Put some cream cheese, Cheddar cheese, and mozzarella cheese, on top of breadcrumbs.

Roll it tight, roll it in flour, then egg and breadcrumbs. Insert a toothpick through it and gently fry in oil or butter in a pan on the stove.

BLT

Bacon

Sliced tomatoes

Arugula

Mayonnaise

Salt and pepper

Toasted bread of choice

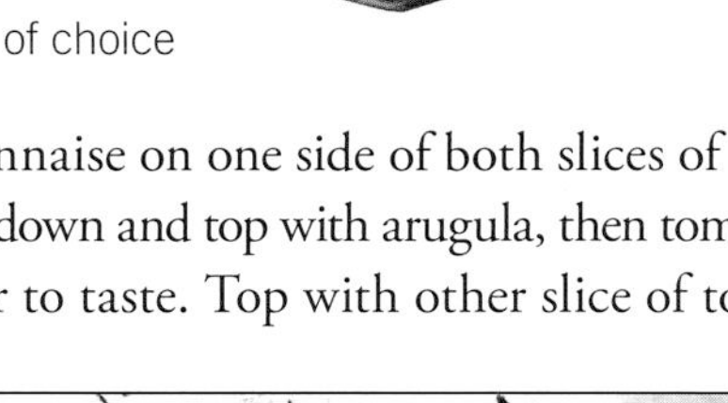

Spread mayonnaise on one side of both slices of toast. Lay your bacon down and top with arugula, then tomato. Salt and pepper to taste. Top with other slice of toast.

LAMB WITH ORZO, TAVERN STYLE (GIOUVETSI)

2 T butter

2 lb. boneless lamb leg cut into 1-1/2 inches (or use shanks)

1 chopped onion

2 minced garlic cloves

Salt and pepper

½ cup dry white wine

1 T tomato paste

3 cups meat stock

12 oz. orzo

Melt butter in large flameproof casserole or roasting pan.

Add meat, onion, and garlic until coated with butter. Season with salt and pepper.

Place in 450° oven and roast for 20 minutes or until meat is browned. Reduce temperature to 325°, add wine, tomato paste, and 1 cup stock. Continue baking for 40 minutes or longer.

Add remaining stock to pan juices. Meanwhile, parboil orzo in a large amount of boiling salted water for 5 minutes. Drain well and add to the sauce in the roasting pan. Stir, and continue baking for 30 minutes, or until orzo is al dente and the meat is tender. Serve meat and orzo. Sprinkle with some cheese.

From *Greek Cooking* by Lou Seibert Pappas.

POT ROAST FOR JACK BLACK

3-1/2 lb. chuck or bottom round beef

1 T vegetable oil

1 large onion, chopped fine

4 cloves garlic, chopped fine

3/4 can chopped tomatoes

1/4 cup red wine

1 T brown sugar

2 bay leaves

2-1/2 cups of water

3 large carrots, cut into chunks

1 lb small potatoes, peeled

1-3/4 T cornstarch

Salt and pepper

Parsley

Sear the meat on all sides in the vegetable oil in a Dutch oven. Transfer meat to a plate. Add the onion and garlic to Dutch oven, cook over moderate heat until onion is translucent. Add tomatoes, red wine, sugar, bay leaves, and water. Bring to boil. Add beef, carrots, and potatoes. Cover and place in a preheated 350-degree oven. Cook for 2-1/2 hours or until done, adding some boiling water if needed. Transfer beef to a cutting board and let rest for 10 minutes. Add some boiling water to cornstarch and add to vegetables and gravy, stirring to a smooth consistency. Discard bay leaf, add salt and pepper to taste. Slice beef and serve with vegetables and gravy spooned over it. Garnish with chopped parsley.

WHAT'S YOUR BEEF, STEW?

1½ cups of flour

Salt and pepper

½ t of paprika

1 lb of chuck, cubed (size of an ice cube)

2 T of oil

1 sliced onion

3 potatoes cut in half

5 carrots

5 onions

Put the flour, salt and pepper, and paprika in a brown lunch bag. Add beef cubes and shake.

Heat the oil in a heavy pan and sauté the sliced onion.

Shake off excess flour from meat and brown on all sides.

Add enough boiling water to cover the meat. Cover the pan and simmer for 1½ hours. Add the vegetables along with some more water, but only if it needs it. Cover and cook for another 45 minutes until everything is tender.

Serve on top of egg noodles or rice.

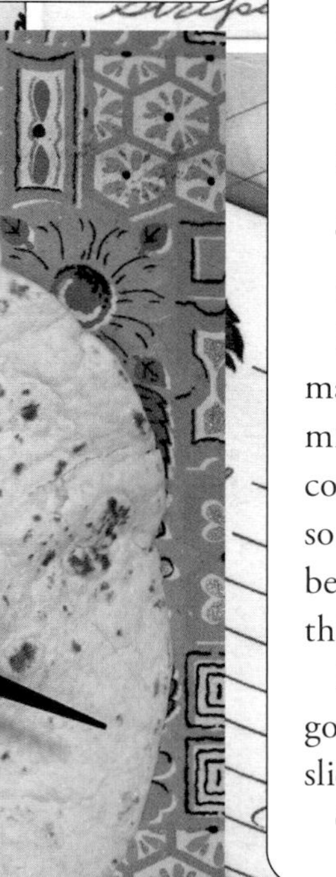

CHIPPED BEEF

1 jar Armour sliced dried beef

2 tablespoons butter

2½ tablespoons Wondra flour or all-purpose flour

2½ cups whole milk

Salt and black pepper to taste

8 slices white bread

Cut ¼ inch strips of the beef. Put aside for later.

In a large sauté pan, melt butter and add in the flour, mashing down with a fork to incorporate. Cook this mixture approximately 2 minutes. Slowly add in milk, continuing to incorporate with the fork or using a wisk, so there are not too many lumps. Sprinkle in sliced beef and season with salt and pepper to taste. Allow to thicken on low heat for 5 minutes.

Place two slices of toasted bread on a plate and ladle a good amount of the creamed chipped beef on top of the slices. You will need a knife and fork. Delicious.

Courtesy of Mary Redding.

TOSINO'S GUACAMOLE

2 avocados (mash with fork)

Chopped fresh coriander
(a couple of pinches)

Minced or chopped hot
green jalapeño chili (seeded)

Juice of 1 lime

Salt and pepper to taste

Chips

Serve with chips. Rapido, una más!!

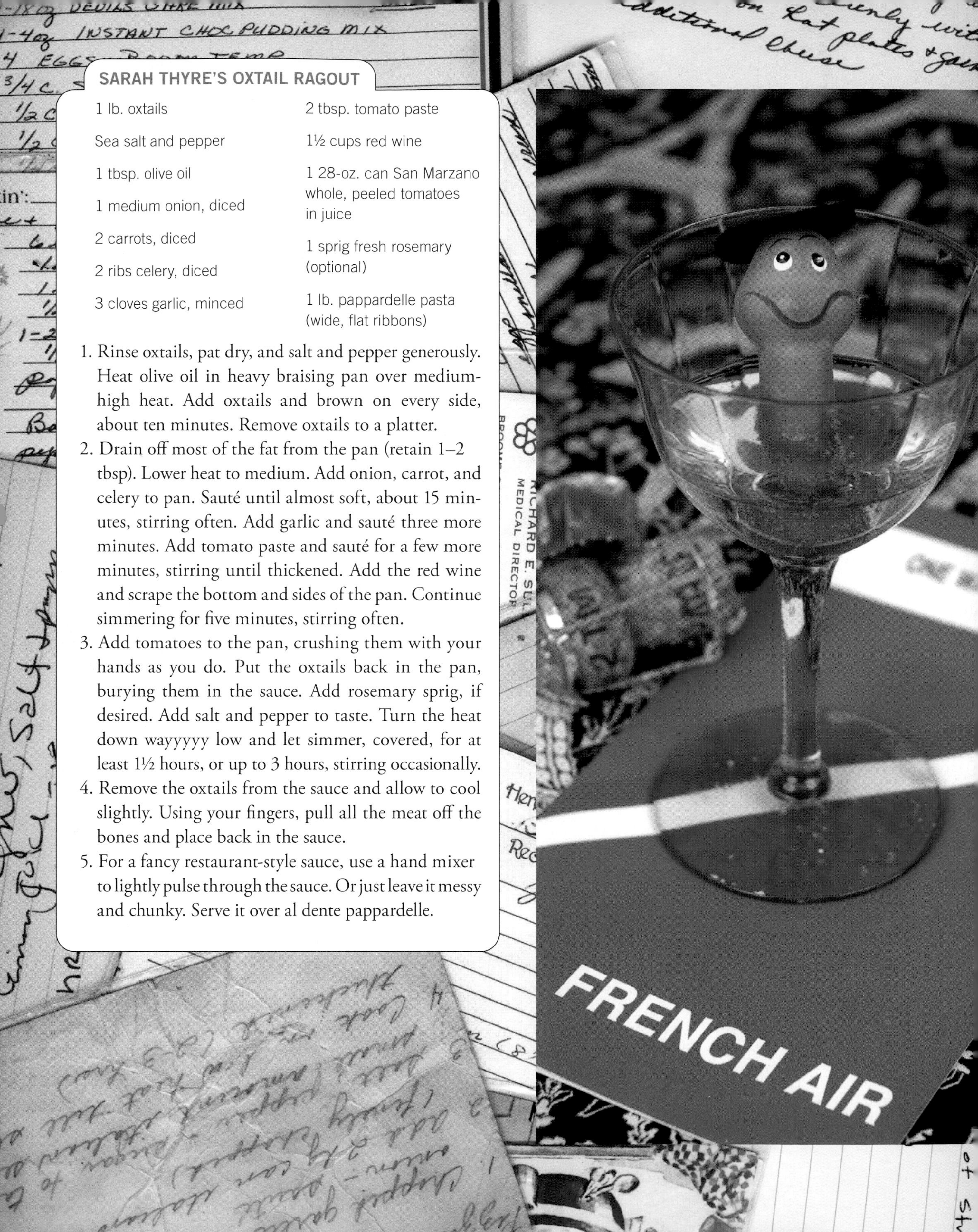

SARAH THYRE'S OXTAIL RAGOUT

1 lb. oxtails

Sea salt and pepper

1 tbsp. olive oil

1 medium onion, diced

2 carrots, diced

2 ribs celery, diced

3 cloves garlic, minced

2 tbsp. tomato paste

1½ cups red wine

1 28-oz. can San Marzano whole, peeled tomatoes in juice

1 sprig fresh rosemary (optional)

1 lb. pappardelle pasta (wide, flat ribbons)

1. Rinse oxtails, pat dry, and salt and pepper generously. Heat olive oil in heavy braising pan over medium-high heat. Add oxtails and brown on every side, about ten minutes. Remove oxtails to a platter.
2. Drain off most of the fat from the pan (retain 1–2 tbsp). Lower heat to medium. Add onion, carrot, and celery to pan. Sauté until almost soft, about 15 minutes, stirring often. Add garlic and sauté three more minutes. Add tomato paste and sauté for a few more minutes, stirring until thickened. Add the red wine and scrape the bottom and sides of the pan. Continue simmering for five minutes, stirring often.
3. Add tomatoes to the pan, crushing them with your hands as you do. Put the oxtails back in the pan, burying them in the sauce. Add rosemary sprig, if desired. Add salt and pepper to taste. Turn the heat down wayyyyy low and let simmer, covered, for at least 1½ hours, or up to 3 hours, stirring occasionally.
4. Remove the oxtails from the sauce and allow to cool slightly. Using your fingers, pull all the meat off the bones and place back in the sauce.
5. For a fancy restaurant-style sauce, use a hand mixer to lightly pulse through the sauce. Or just leave it messy and chunky. Serve it over al dente pappardelle.

FRENCH DRESSING

½ cup oil	Pinch dry mustard
¼ cup sugar	½ teaspoon paprika
⅓ cup ketchup	Juice ½ lemon
¼ cup vinegar	Pinch pepper
½ teaspoon salt	

Beat together, put in jar with ½ onion if desired.

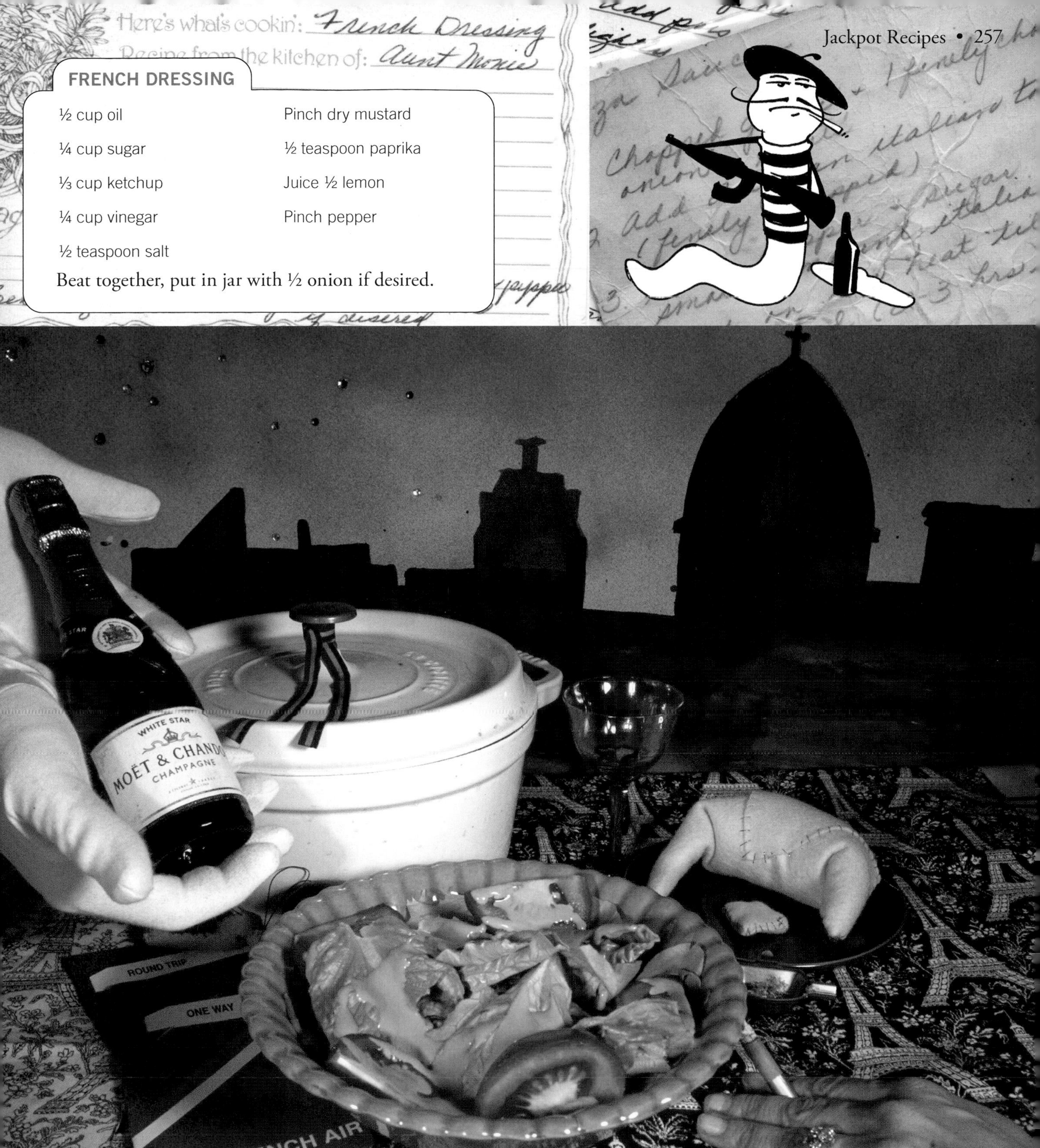

Je M'appèlle French Night

JULIUS CAESAR SALAD

In a blender, crack 2 eggs. Blend with 2½ tablespoons of fresh lemon juice. Add 1 whole crushed garlic clove, 6 minced anchovies (optional), a couple dashes of Worcestershire sauce. Add fresh salt and pepper to taste. While mixing, add ¼ to ½ cup of red wine vinegar. Pour either a very light olive oil or a salad oil in the blender and beat until it all reaches the lid of the blender.

Pour dressing over romaine lettuce (about a head), top with garlic croutons, and ¾ cup of freshly grated Parmesan or pecorino cheese. (It's always classy to rub the inside of the bowl with fresh garlic.)

GARLIC CROUTONS

Melt ½ stick butter with 3 to 4 peeled garlic cloves in a saucepan, until garlic is lightly tanned. Remove the garlic and toss the butter mixture on cubed pieces of country bread. Bake on a cookie sheet in the oven at 400 degrees for 20 minutes. Top with a little salt and pepper. Leave in the bowl and cover until you need it.

LAMB CHOP MARINADE

- 1 tsp. fresh rosemary
- 1 clove garlic
- 2 tbsp. olive oil
- 4 lamb chops
- 1 tbsp. lemon juice
- Salt and pepper

Combine all these ingredients and pour over your chops. Marinate for 3 hours. Then broil.

AWARD-WINNING TUNA FISH FOR PHIL HOFFMAN

Mix together 1 can of award-winning tuna, drained and rung out, 2 teaspoons of finely chopped celery, 1 teaspoon of sweet relish (optional), 1 1/2 teaspoons of thinly chopped red or green onion, a squirt of fresh lemon, 1 1/2 tablespoons of mayonnaise, 1/2 a hard-boiled egg, chopped (optional). Season with salt and fresh pepper. You can eyeball all these ingredients. To me the secret is getting all the water or oil out of the can of tuna.

TANGY BLUE CHEESE DRESSING

- 1 cup mayonnaise
- 1/2 cup sour cream
- 2 T. wine vinegar (or less)
- 2 T. chopped green onions and tops
- 1 T. lemon juice
- 1/4 lb. blue cheese, crumbled
- 1 small crushed garlic clove
- 1/4 cup chopped parsley
- Salt and pepper to taste

Mix well. Dress salad.

ITALIAN DRESSING

- 1/4 C olive oil
- 1/4 C red wine vinegar
- 2 teaspoons of oregano
- Juice of 1 lemon
- Salt and pepper to taste

Combine all ingredients and mix with beater.

BASIC GREEN SALAD

Tear your salad greens into bite-size pieces.

You can toss in any vegetable, such as tomatoes, onions, radishes, cucumbers, green peppers, carrots, celery, scallions, mushrooms, olives, corn, avocodos, small cauliflower or broccoli, or any bean, such as garbanzo or kidney. You can add any crumbled cheese and croutons if desired.

Right before serving and no sooner (to prevent sogginess) toss your salad with any salad dressing.

VINAIGRETTE DRESSING

- ½ tablespoon finely chopped shallots
- ½ tablespoon Dijon mustard
- ½ tablespoon wine vinegar
- ¼ cup olive oil

Combine ingredients and blend.

COLESLAW OF THE DUNES

Mix together:

1 small head green cabbage, shredded

1 small head red cabbage, shredded

1 cup carrots, grated

Whisk together:

1 cup mayonnaise

½ cup white vinegar

1 tablespoon sugar

1 teaspoon celery seed

Salt and pepper to taste

Pour over cabbage mixture and mix well. Allow a short time to marinate.

WHITE BEAN SOUP

2 cups of dried white beans

8 cups of water

1 chopped onion

1 crushed garlic clove

2 diced carrots

½ cup of chopped celery

1 can of chopped peeled tomatoes (like a cup)

½ can of tomato paste (small)

½ tsp. sugar to taste

Salt and pepper to taste

Handful of chopped fresh flat parsley

First wash your white beans really well and cover with 8 cups of hot water for 2 hours.

Sauté your onion, garlic, carrots, and celery in oil.

Add the tomato paste, chopped tomato, sugar, and salt and pepper.

Add all the beans and water that they were soaking in and let simmer for 2 hours, covered. In the last half hour add some of the parsley and then when the soup is to be served add the other half to garnish the top.

LENTIL SOUP

About 2 cups of lentils

1 onion, chopped

Celery, chopped

2 carrots, diced

2 garlic cloves, crushed

3 T of tomato paste

Olive oil

1 bay leaf

About 6 cups of water

¼ cup of vinegar

Salt and pepper

Soak your lentils overnight.

Gently sauté onion, garlic, carrots, and chopped celery in some olive oil.

Add your lentils and bay leaf, water, tomato paste. Reduce heat and simmer for 1 hour or until the lentils are soft.

Stir in the vinegar and salt and pepper to taste.

CUCUMBER, TOMATO, ONION SALAD

Cucumber

Tomato

Red or white onion

Salt and pepper

Olive oil

Eyeball it all.

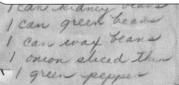

SPLIT PEA SOUP

When I make this soup, I get the ham bone by asking a deli employee if I can have it at the end of the night, because they just toss them.

1½ cup of dried peas

Ham bone from the deli

1 chopped onion

1½ T of butter

1 T of flour

1 cup of milk

½ cup of white wine

Optional: salt pork (about 2 inches)

Soak your dried peas overnight.

Take your deli ham bone and about 2 quarts of water and put them in a large soup pot.

Add the chopped onion and salt pork, if you chose to use it, and bring all to a boil. Let simmer until the peas are soft, about 1½ hours (partially covered). Remove the ham bone and salt pork.

Take ½ of this mixture and put it in a blender. After it is blended add back to pea mixture. Pour in your white wine (note: The only reason I blend ½ the soup mixture is because it always spills out of my blender when I do this and I hate the mess, but it works with only ½ being blended so I stuck with it).

Make your cream sauce by melting the butter, adding the flour and then adding your milk. Stir until thick. Add this sauce to the pea soup and stir. Salt and pepper to taste.

And you can pick the ham off the bone and add it to the soup as well.

Tip: A leaf of lettuce dropped into a pot absorbs the grease from the top of the soup. Remove the lettuce and throw it away before serving.

AVGOLEMONO SOUPA (EGG AND LEMON SOUP)

Chicken, Onion, Celery, Orzo, Eggs, Lemon, White pepper, Salt

Boil a chicken with an onion and some celery and salt and pepper.

When chicken is done move it to another area.

You need about 6 cups of chicken stock so use the broth from the boiled chicken and discard the celery and onion and enhance it the best way you know how to get a good stock.

Bring stock to a boil and add about 1/3 cup of orzo.

Stir until stock returns to a slow boil and cover and cook for 20 minutes until the rice is tender.

Beat 4 whole eggs until really fluffy. I use my blender. Gradually, through the top of the blender add the juice of 2 lemons.

Remove the broth from the burner. When it has cooled off a little, take 2 cups of the broth and add it to the egg and lemon mixture, still beating or blending.

Very slowly and gradually add that mixture to the orzo and broth mixture, stirring vigorously. Add some white pepper and salt. Keep stirring until it looks a little thick and frothy.

You have to serve this soup immediately and you have to be careful that the eggs don't curdle when you add the egg mixture to the broth. You can prevent this by making sure that the broth has cooled off a little before you add the egg mixture back into the broth. Sometimes I have thrown a few ice cubes in. Serve this soup with hot bread and with the chicken you set aside.

You can pick the chicken off the bone and drizzle a little olive oil, oregano, and lemon on it and put it in the oven long enough to get hot and serve that on the side. This soup can be difficult to make. It's inconsistent. It doesn't reheat so it has to be prepared before serving. Only the stock can be prepared beforehand. Some people use flour or cornstarch to thicken it but if you do it right you don't have to.

NEW ZEALAND COCKLES AND RAZOR CLAMS

1/2 pound New Zealand cockles

3 pieces razor clams

2 T garlic, sliced

1 T soybean oil

1/2 C white wine

2 lemon wedges

2 T butter

1/4 C navy beans, cooked

1 T parsley, chiffonade

1/2 t kosher salt

1/8 t black pepper

Whole flat-leaf parsley leaves for garnish

Rinse the cockles and razor clams under cold water to clean.

Sauté the garlic in the soybean oil until light brown. Add all your clams carefully, away from flames. Add white wine (also away from flames) and cover pan. When all clams and razors are steamed open, remove with a slotted spoon and set aside, cover with a towel to keep warm. Using the remaining clam broth, add butter, navy beans, salt, and pepper. Reduce until viscous. At very last minute add parsley chiffonade and the juice from two lemon wedges and taste, once again, for salt and pepper.

Place all clams and razors on a plate. Swirl clam broth, beans and parsley and pour over pile of clams. Garnish with parsley leaves. Serve with sliced baguette.

Courtesy of Mary Redding.

LONG NECK RITA

Large can of limeade

½ can of tequila

¼ can of Cointreau

Bottle of beer

Mix in a pitcher and add beer.

Pour in blender with ice.

Trust me, it's the best margarita, it's very mellow feeling, you'll feel even.

LONG NECK STEW

Take 2 pounds of boneless, cubed stew meat. Coat in seasoned flour. Shake off excess flour and put aside.

In a pot, melt 1 tablespoon of butter and sauté a cup of sliced onions. Remove the onions, add 1 tablespoon of butter and brown the meat. Add 1 bottle of dark beer, 1 pressed garlic clove. Cover and simmer for 2 and half hours.

Spotlight On...

RUM PUNCH DAZZLER

1 12-oz. can lemonade, frozen concentrate

1 12-oz. can limeade, frozen concentrate

1 pint rum

Fill with 7UP to top

Add ring mold for ice before serving. Use a 9" ring mold filled with water or 7UP and maraschino cherries and freeze. Serve with punch bowl and ladle.

GENERAL RULE FOR PUNCHES

It's better to use a ring mold of ice instead of individual ice cubes. It will prevent your punch from getting watered down.

Punches

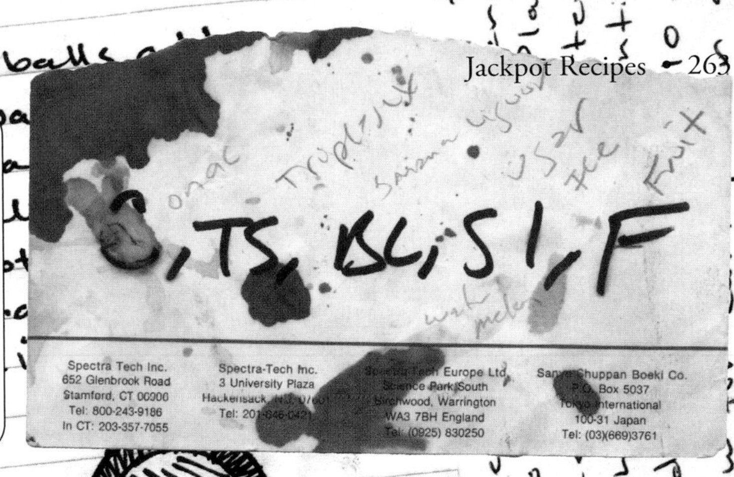

SANGRIA

Chop up whatever fruit you have: apples, melons, oranges, limes, peaches, grapes, strawberries, pineapple, pears.

Eyeball all the ingredients: banana liqueur, brandy, Cointreau, coconut rum if you have, a little sugar, red wine.

Add all into a pitcher and pour over ice. Just keep adding more wine when it gets low.

PATIO PUNCH

- 1-1/4 cups sugar
- 2-1/2 cups banana, mashed
- 2-1/2 cups pineapple with juice, crushed
- 2 cups orange juice
- 2 T lime juice
- 15 maraschino cherries
- Pinch salt
- 4 quarts ginger ale

Mix all ingredients in blender, except for ginger ale, until frothy. Freeze in ice cube trays. Place in punch bowl and pour ginger ale over cubes, or 2 cubes per eight-ounce glass. Add rum and more ginger ale.

Courtesy of Jeanette Pope.

ICED CITRUS TEA

- 8 tea bags steeped in 1 quart boiled water
- 1 6-ounce can limeade, frozen concentrate
- 1 6-ounce can lemonade, frozen concentrate
- 1 6-ounce can orange juice, frozen concentrate
- 1 cup sugar

Add these ingredients to a one-gallon jar. Fill to top with ice cold water and mix well. Garnish with lemon, lime, and orange rings.

Courtesy of Alice Wells.

BLOODY CLAMMY MARY

Add equal parts clam juice and tomato juice and then add vodka. Serve on the rocks (see page 131).

JUAN CARLITO'S MOJITOS

In a mortar and pestle, mix:

- 7–10 mint leaves
- 1 tsp. sugar
- Squeeze of lime

Crush to a pulp.

Fill glass to ¾ with:

- Crushed ice

Add:

- Pulp
- Juice from 3 limes
- 2 shots rum (preferably aged Cuban rum smuggled from DR or elsewhere in the Caribbean)
- 2 tbsp. sugar, or to taste

Stir well until sugar dissolves.

Add a sprig of mint and a splash of seltzer water.

SHAGGY D.A.

- Black rum
- Spicy ginger ale

Mix in a tall glass, on the rocks. Serve with a straw. Garnish with a lemon.

PANTYHOSE,
CRAFTS
AND
GOOD IDEAS

1. Take off any rings or bracelets. Put on cotton or nylon gloves, most snags happen while you are putting the pantyhose on. Get comfortably seated.

2. Start by putting both hands into the hose and giving them a gentle stretch.

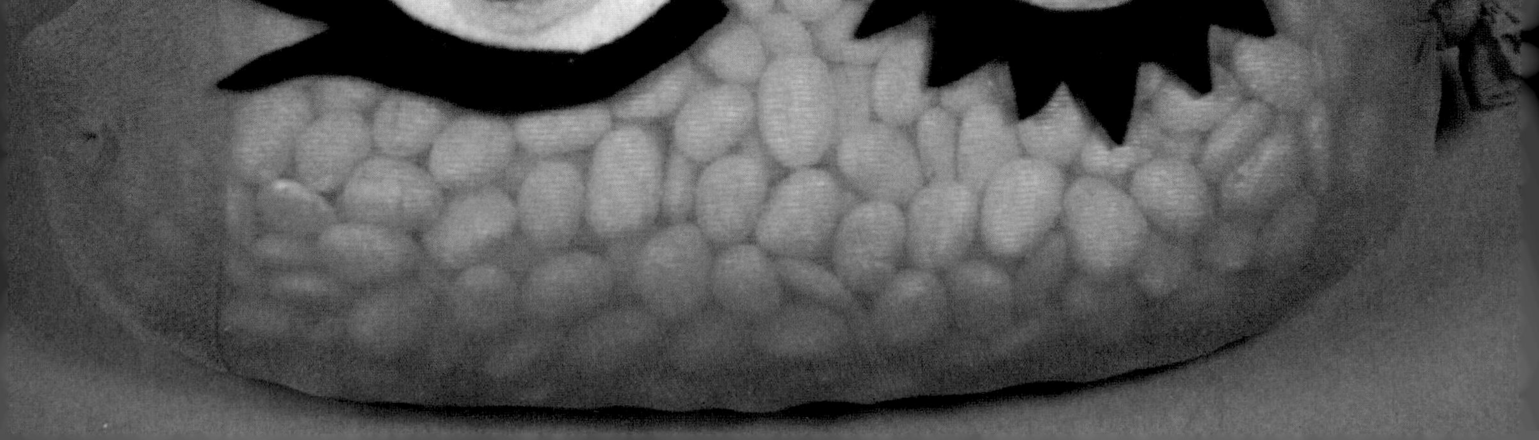

3. Gather the leg up to the toe area by pulling the pantyhose over your hand.

4. Put your toes into the toe pocket and begin gently pulling hose up toward your knee. If you are applying knee-highs, you're done. Put your toes into the toe pocket and begin gently pulling hose up toward your knee.

EYE BURRITO

A soothing eye compress for tired eyes.

Directions:

Fill the foot of an old pair of pantyhose with a bag of lima beans, lentils, or barley. Or popcorn kernels, dimes, or kitty litter. Cut and tie. Double the hose over the whole thing with the other foot and tie a knot.

Decorate the front with felt eye cutouts. You can keep it in the freezer in the summer. Lean back with the eye burrito over your eyes and take a five-minute siesta. The weight of the burrito will rejuvinate your eye sockets.

NOTE: You can extend the shape and make a neck burrito as well. For ching-chong eye burrito, use mung beans.

BATH SACHET

Directions:

Fill the foot of an old pair of pantyhose with fresh herbs like parsley, sage, rosemary, or thyme. Tie securely over your bath spigot and fill the tub with a soothing infusion. Soak (yourself) for 20 minutes.

5. Repeat this on your other leg, being careful to not get the legs of hose twisted.

6. Keep pulling and gently stretching, alternating legs, until you wiggle the hose up to about mid-thigh.

PANTYHOSE PLANT HANGER

2 pairs of pantyhose

potted plant

Directions:

1. Tie the 2 pairs of pantyhose together at the crotch, making a decorative knot. Lay flat on the floor with each leg spread separate.
2. Place potted plant on top of center knot.
3. Lift all 4 legs over the top of the plant, twisting the 2 adjacent legs over each other once.
4. Tie a decorative knot at the toes of each leg.

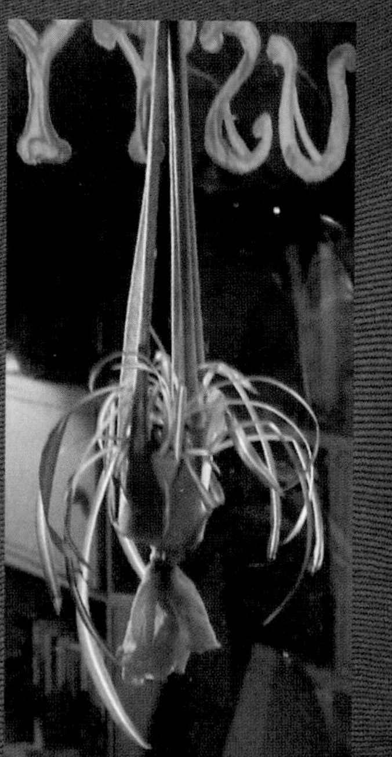

7. Now stand up. Continue alternating legs and pulling the hose until they are all the way up. Don't worry if they seem to be riding low because the next step is going to fix that.

8. Change from cotton gloves to rubber or latex dishwashing type gloves. Starting at your toes you are going to smooth the hose upward to your waist until they are perfectly positioned and as comfortable as they can be.

MINI HOSE PLANT HANGER

5" X 5" scrap of leftover pantyhose

soda cap

pinch of soil

mini plant

I like you

Directions:

1. Plant mini plant in the soda cap using soil. Set aside.
2. Make 4 cuts on the pantyhose from each edge toward the center. Avoid cutting the piece entirely in half.
3. Tie the center of pantyhose into a decorative knot.
4. Place soda cap on the knot and follow directions from step three for the regular-size pantyhose plant hanger.

PANTYHOSE SCREENS

5 to 10 pairs of pantyhose in assorted colors

an assortment of sturdy rings
(we used inexpensive wooden embroidery hoops)

a wooden dowel & pipe cleaners cut into 4" pieces

Directions:

1. Cut pantyhose in half through the crotch, separating the legs.
2. Fill each leg with an assortment of rings.
3. Working from the bottom up, stretch the hose over the rings and secure by wrapping with a piece of pipe cleaner.
4. Attach each leg to the wooden dowel allowing them to overlap slightly.
5. Hang in a window or a doorway and enjoy.

I like you
A
petites
Bark
I like you
A
I like you
A
I like you
A
petites
reinforced panty and toe
Regular
sheer pantyhose
Dung
GUARANTEE

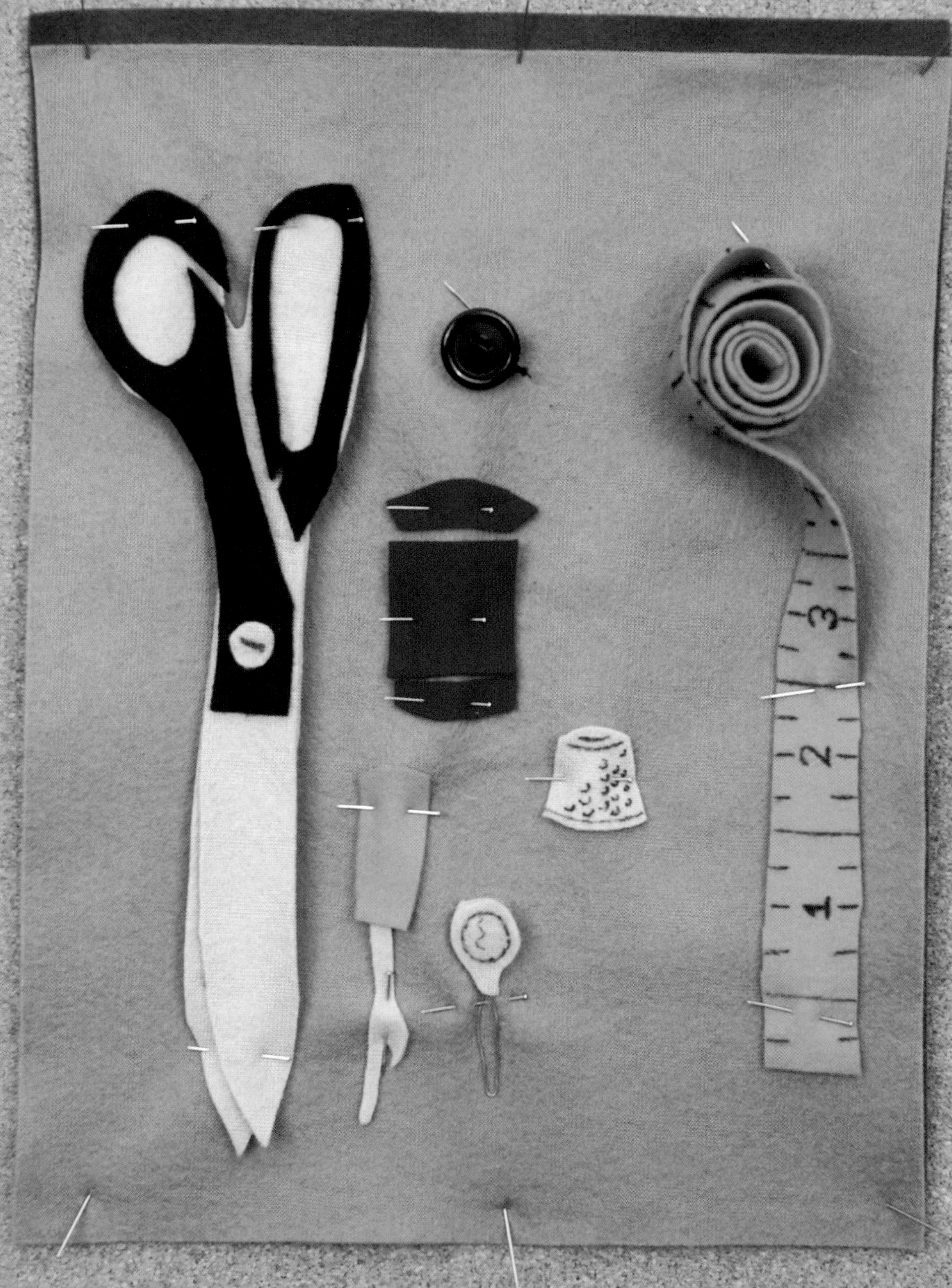
3
2
1

ALWAYS ADD MORE
ONE HOME FROM WORK KEEP FULL MAKEUP ON
THEN ADD
NIGHT TIME GREEK DATE
DARKEN BROWS SOFT BLACK PENCIL
USE APPROPRIATE OLIVE TONE FOUNDATION
TO ACCENTUATE TAN
POWDER LIGHTLY
EYESHADOW - WHITE CREME IRRID.
PUT ALL OVER LID TO BROW. TAUPE CREME I
CREASE, BLEND WITH SOFT BRUSH.
OVER THAT SWEEP VERY METALLIC SILVER
(OR GOLD WORKS) OVER LID FROM LASH LI
TO BROW
ADD LOTS OF BLACK LIQUID LINER
WORK INTO LASH LINE. FOLLOW LASH LINE F
INNER CORNER OUT TO OUTTER CORNER
WING OUT
LOTS OF BLACK LINER ON BOTTOM
ADD LOTS OF LASHES (OVER LAYERS OF
BLACK MASCARA) USE INDIVIDUALS OVER
2 OR 3 PAIR OF FALSE LASHES - MORE MASC
ADD AN IRRIDESCENT PINK BLUSH
OR PEACH.
OVERDRAW LIP LINE SLIGHTLY WITH DAR
NUDE PENCIL
FILL WITH WET PEACH GLOSS

GREEK DRESS DIRECTIONS

Use black fabric of your choice. Choose a sleeveless dress pattern in your size with a bodice that you like. Cut out bodice and neck and sleeve facing. Sew darts and stitch facings to bodice. To make skirt cut out a rectangle of fabric 25" by 3 times your waist size. Fold in half with right sides together and sew 25" sides together using 1/2" seam and leaving 7" opening for zipper. Gather waistline until it matches waist measurement of bodice. Stitch to bodice with 7" opening in center back. Sew zipper into center back of dress. Hem skirt to desired length. Trim waistline with golden Greek trim.

NEEDLE WALLET

Cut out two rectangles of felt with pinking shears. Appliqué a design on one of them. Stitch down the middle and fold.

Make your own bathmat or decorate your own towels using rick rack and pom-poms.

LESLIE SNAKE

Cut out a spiral snake-like shape from paper. Place over a bandana with spiral shape in the center and cut out. Cut another matching snake spiral from calico fabric. Stitch with right-sides together leaving a 3" opening near head and another near tail for turning and stuffing. Turn right-side out and stuff. Blind stitch openings shut. Stitch on eyes and tongue.

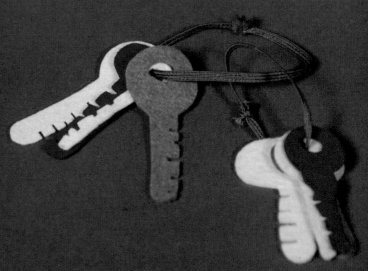

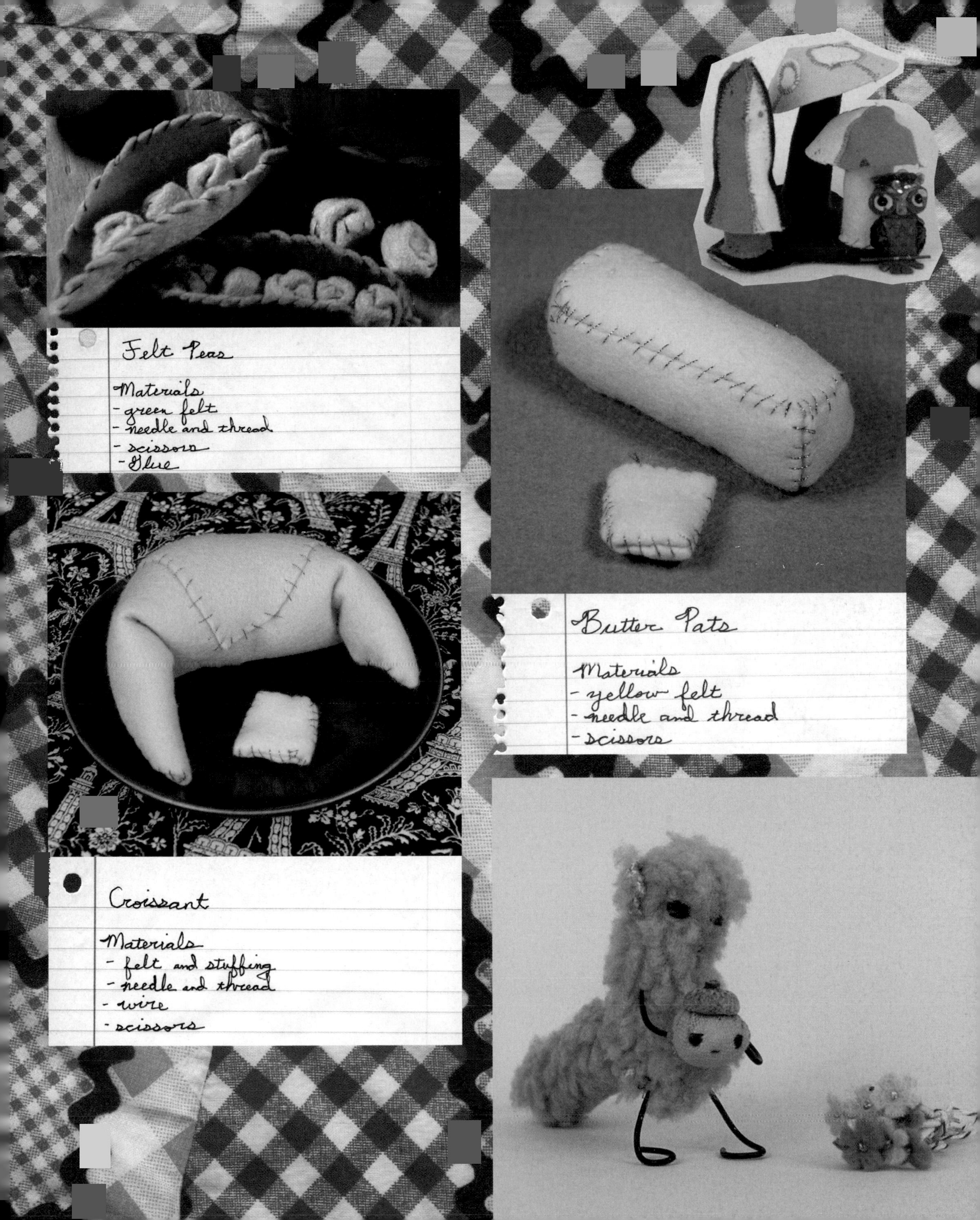
Felt Peas
Materials
- green felt
- needle and thread
- scissors
- Glue
Croissant
Materials
- felt and stuffing
- needle and thread
- wire
- scissors
Butter Pats
Materials
- yellow felt
- needle and thread
- scissors

THE ART OF HOSPITALITY

FELT DISCS

Cut out two identical circles of felt. Crazy stitch them together with a cotton ball between them. “Crazy stitch” is only for people who don’t know how to sew.

BOOKENDS

Take two bricks and cover them with sticky shelf paper. Do it the way you would wrap a present the size of a brick.

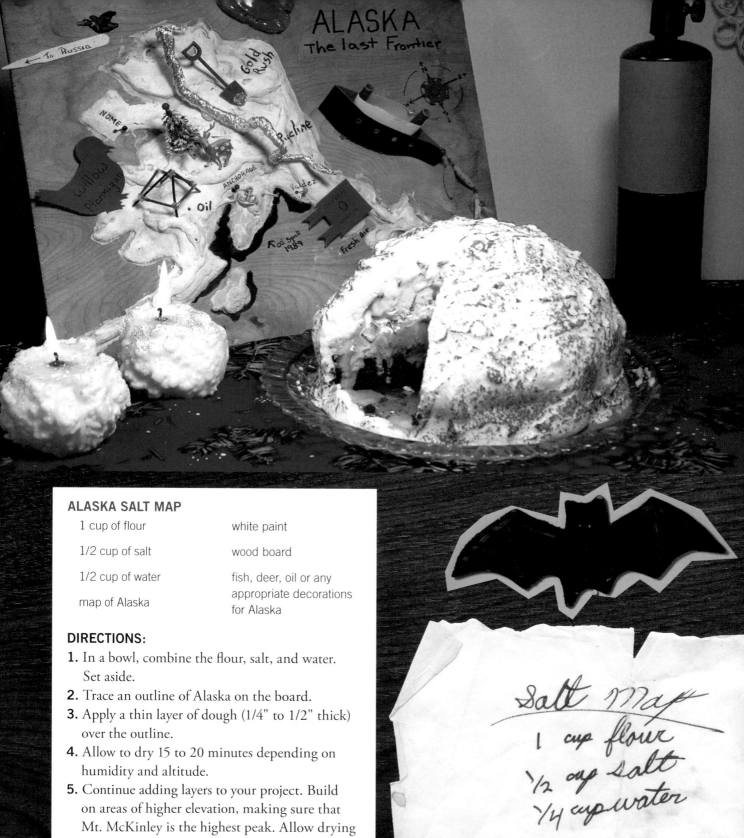

ALASKA SALT MAP

- 1 cup of flour
- 1/2 cup of salt
- 1/2 cup of water
- map of Alaska
- white paint
- wood board
- fish, deer, oil or any appropriate decorations for Alaska

DIRECTIONS:

1. In a bowl, combine the flour, salt, and water. Set aside.
2. Trace an outline of Alaska on the board.
3. Apply a thin layer of dough (1/4" to 1/2" thick) over the outline.
4. Allow to dry 15 to 20 minutes depending on humidity and altitude.
5. Continue adding layers to your project. Build on areas of higher elevation, making sure that Mt. McKinley is the highest peak. Allow drying time between each application.
6. Paint the map white and decorate.

Salt Map
1 cup flour
1/2 cup salt
1/4 cup water

FAKE CAKES

10-inch frosting knife (don't try it without one)

8 to 10-inch by 4-inch round Styrofoam cake form (You can use a hatbox, scraps of Styrofoam, or any kind of cake-shaped cardboard box.)

2 cups ultra-lightweight spackling

1 cup dry plaster of Paris

3 tablespoons water (plus more)

Glossy latex paint

Set your timer for 15 minutes. (The frosting will begin to set in about 15 minutes, so you need to work fast.)

Mix all ingredients but water with the frosting knife in a small bucket or something you can toss afterwards.

Start with 3 tablespoons of water and continue adding more water until you get the right consistency. The frosting should be light and fluffy but not too wet and blobby.

Frost it good and heavy and get as creative as you can in 15 minutes. Do the sides first.

Let your cake dry overnight and paint it with a glossy latex paint.

Here are a few suggestions on color:

Brown is for chocolate.

Yellow is for lemon.

Green is for pistachio.

Cream is for French vanilla.

You can add cut excelsior to the wet paint for toasted coconut. I used a brown magic marker on the marshmallows so they would look toasted and to secure the marshmallows onto the cake I used toupee tape.

This cake is a great gift for anybody—diabetics and dieters alike will eat it up. Put it in a cake box or leave it on a windowsill and fool your friends.

P.S. Hatboxes make great places to hide cakes.

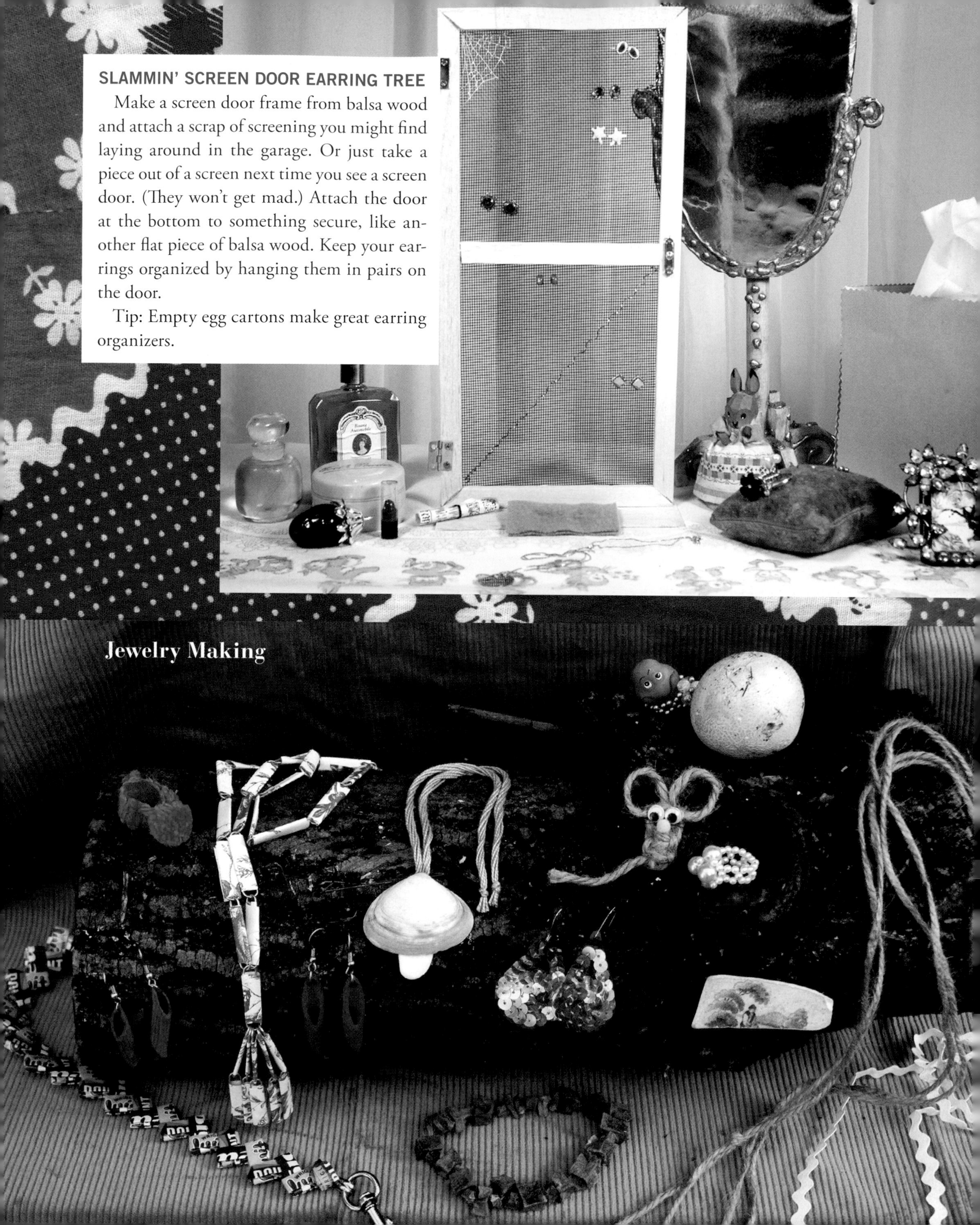

SLAMMIN' SCREEN DOOR EARRING TREE

Make a screen door frame from balsa wood and attach a scrap of screening you might find laying around in the garage. Or just take a piece out of a screen next time you see a screen door. (They won't get mad.) Attach the door at the bottom to something secure, like another flat piece of balsa wood. Keep your earrings organized by hanging them in pairs on the door.

Tip: Empty egg cartons make great earring organizers.

Jewelry Making

CARROT AND POTATO BRACELET

I remember seeing this craft on the *Mike Douglas Show* when I was little. Chop carrot and potato up into small shapes like cubes and coins, put a needle (using thread or dental floss) through the carrot and then potato alternating between the two. Hang your strand in a closet for about 4 to 5 days. When the carrots and potatoes look all dried up and feel hard, tie the two ends together and wear it around your wrist.

NOTE: If you have a mildew problem hang the strand somewhere else—or don't make this bracelet.

NOTE: If you want it shiny use clear nail polish and dab it on.

Rick Rack Choker

Take a piece of Rick Rack, any color, any size. Cut it so it is about 16 inches long - tie it around your neck. Wait for Raves

PAPER CLIP NECKLACE

You'll need:

paper clips & sticky shelf paper

Cut several 1" squares of shelf paper. Link two paper clips together. Peel off and wrap the shelf paper square around the first paper clip to secure the link. Now link another paper clip to make a chain. Keep securing the links and adding paper clips until the desired length is achieved. You can make a tassel from several short chains.

PENNE EARRINGS

Boil penne or other shape of macaroni till done. With large embroidery needle and thread, pierce hole near edge of macaroni and string onto thread. Separate on thread and hang in window overnight to dry. When dry, remove thread and put jump rings through holes. Attach to earring wires. Paint desired color or coat with clear nail polish.

THE NOSEY TISSUE GHOST

You'll need two sheets of nose tissue. Lay one sheet out flat and take the other sheet and ball it up and place it in the center of the flat sheet. Wrap the flat sheet around the ball to make a head. Use dental floss to tie the head off just at the neck. Dot with felt tip pen to make eyes. Hang your nosey ghost anywhere—I suggest a ceiling fan.

TAPE KLEENEX BOX

Go over the tissue box you have now with either different colors of tape or the same one. When the box of tissue is empty you can either throw it away and decorate a new box or cut the bottom out and press your new box up under the old box—it fits snugly.

TISSUE FLOWERS

Start with several sheets of multicolored tissue paper. Fold back and forth accordion style with folds about every 1-1/2". Tightly tie off or secure with a pipe cleaner in the center of the folded strip. Unfurl each individual sheet separately and fluff. You can trim the flower to shape it if you want to. ¡Que linda!

DRIP CANDLE

STEP 1: Drink one bottle of chianti.

STEP 2: Burn lots of cheap candles in the bottle, letting them drip down the sides (a flickering flame will make more drips). You can melt crayons to add more color. You can do this by putting it in front of an open window on a breezy day.

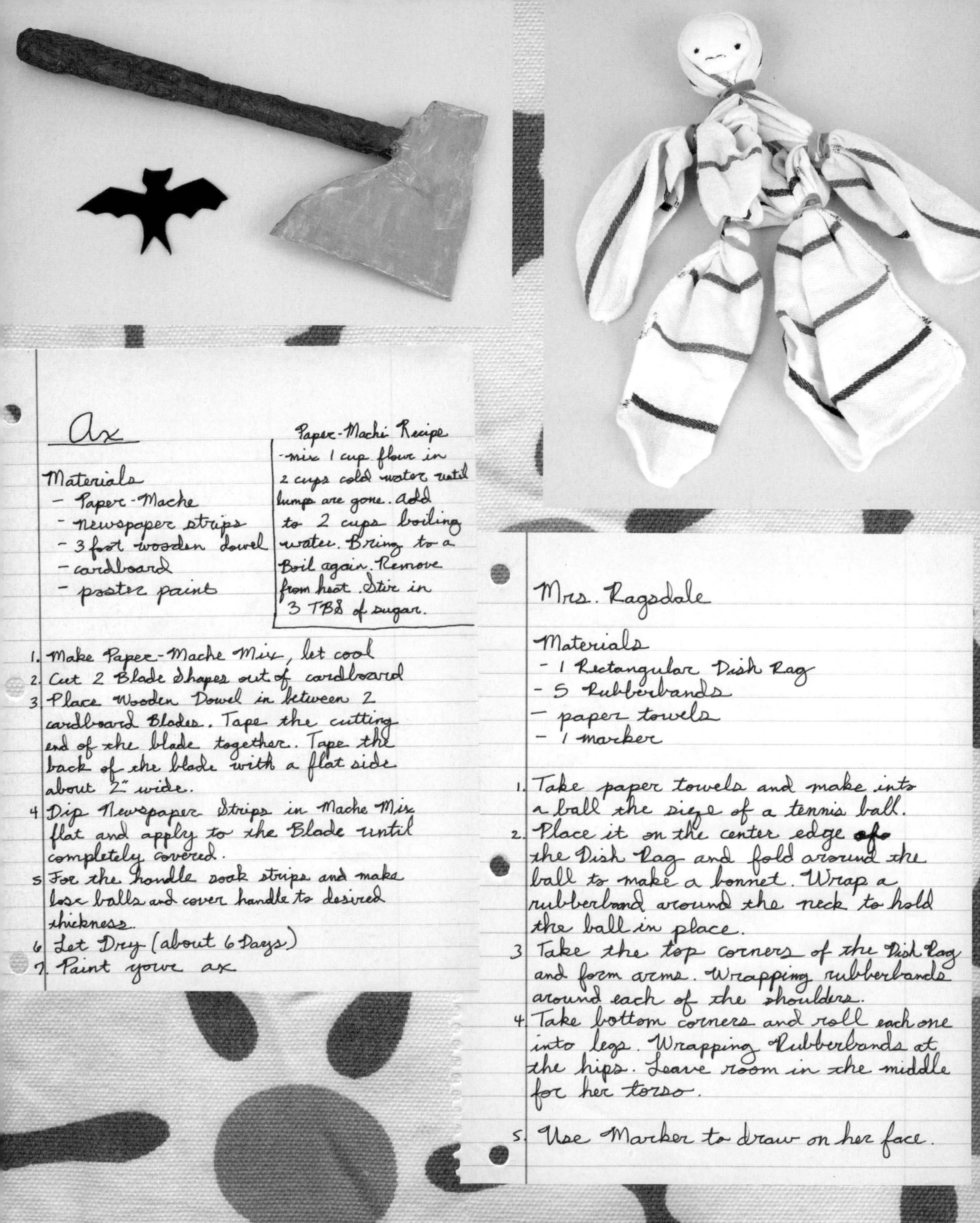

Ax

Paper-Machi Recipe
-mix 1 cup flour in 2 cups cold water until lumps are gone. Add to 2 cups boiling water. Bring to a Boil again. Remove from heat. Stir in 3 TBS of sugar.

Materials
- Paper-Mache
- newspaper strips
- 3 foot wooden dowel
- cardboard
- poster paint

1. Make Paper-Mache Mix, let cool
2. Cut 2 Blade Shapes out of cardboard
3. Place Wooden Dowel in between 2 cardboard Blades. Tape the cutting end of the blade together. Tape the back of the blade with a flat side about 2" wide.
4. Dip Newspaper Strips in Mache Mix flat and apply to the Blade until completely covered.
5. For the handle soak strips and make lose balls and cover handle to desired thickness.
6. Let Dry (about 6 Days)
7. Paint your ax

Mrs. Ragsdale

Materials
- 1 Rectangular Dish Rag
- 5 Rubberbands
- paper towels
- 1 marker

1. Take paper towels and make into a ball the size of a tennis ball.
2. Place it on the center edge of the Dish Rag and fold around the ball to make a bonnet. Wrap a rubberband around the neck to hold the ball in place.
3. Take the top corners of the Dish Rag and form arms. Wrapping rubberbands around each of the shoulders.
4. Take bottom corners and roll each one into legs. Wrapping Rubberbands at the hips. Leave room in the middle for her torso.
5. Use Marker to draw on her face.

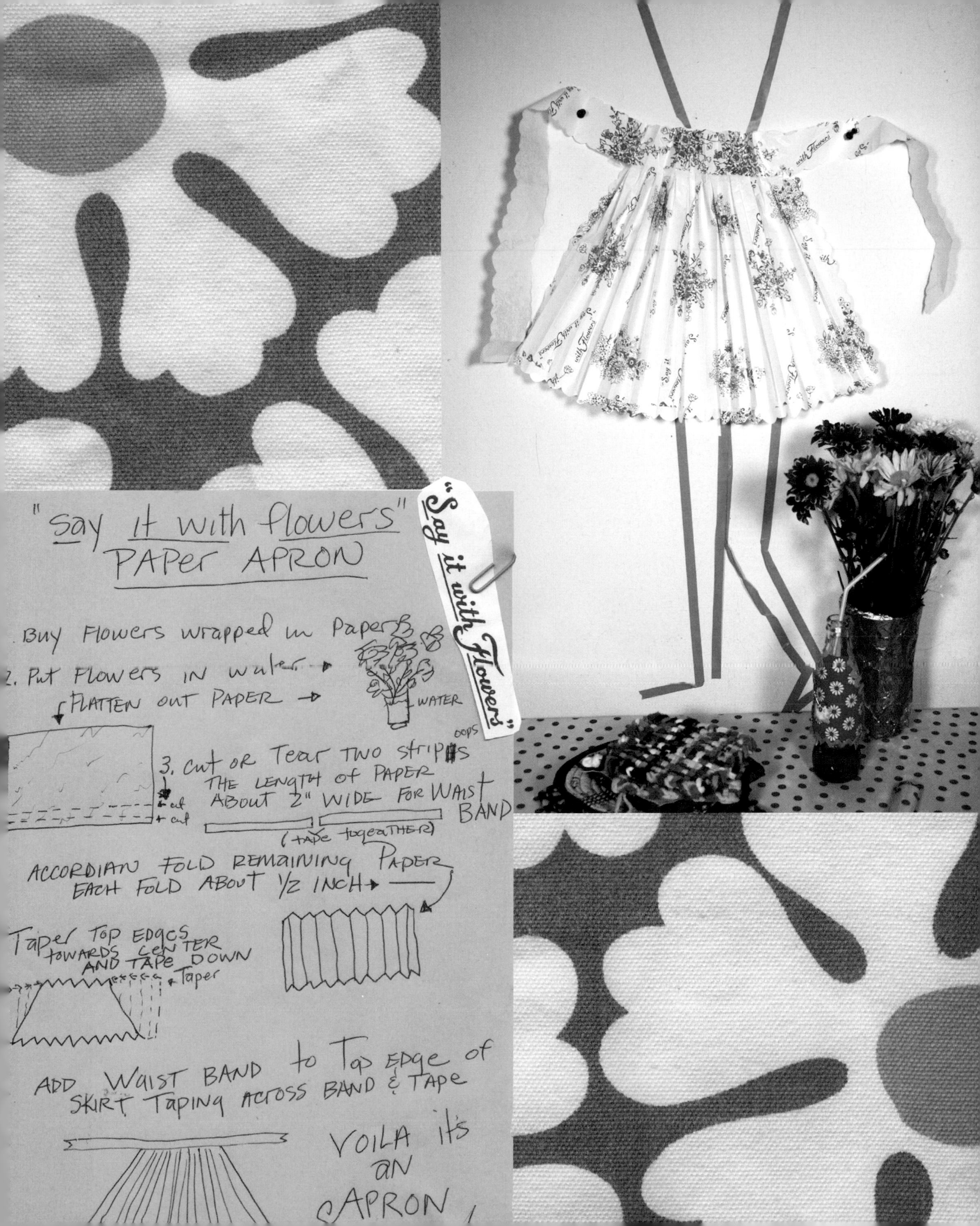
"Say it with flowers"
PAPER APRON
. Buy Flowers wrapped in paper
2. Put Flowers in water
FLATTEN OUT PAPER
WATER
3. Cut or Tear two strips
THE LENGTH OF PAPER
ABOUT 2" WIDE FOR WAIST BAND
cut
cut
oops
(tape together)
ACCORDIAN FOLD REMAINING PAPER
EACH FOLD ABOUT 1/2 INCH
Taper top edges towards center
AND TAPE DOWN
taper
ADD WAIST BAND to Top edge of SKIRT Taping across BAND & TAPE
VOILA it's an APRON!
"Say it with Flowers"

Make your own phone book covers.

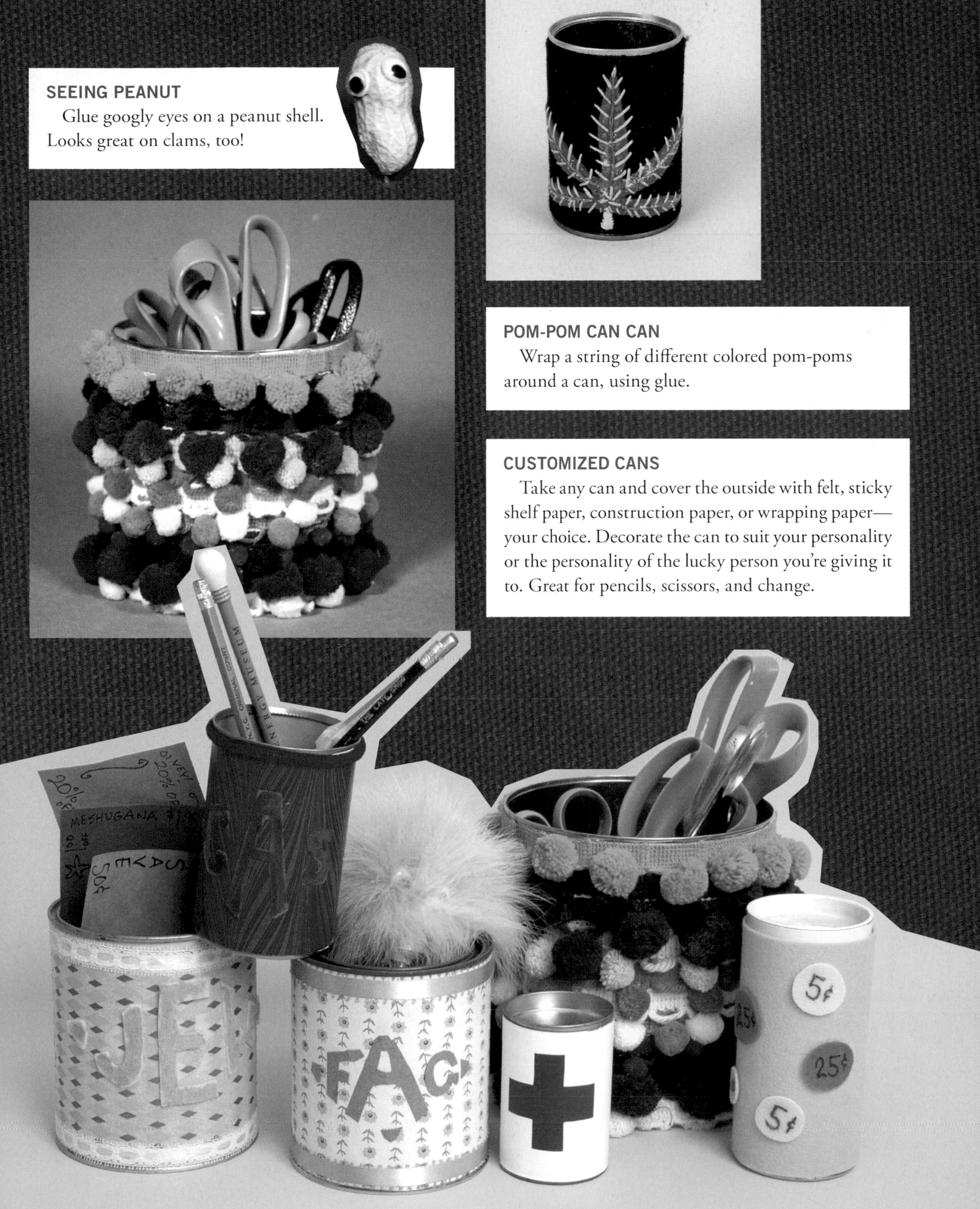

SEEING PEANUT

Glue googly eyes on a peanut shell. Looks great on clams, too!

POM-POM CAN CAN

Wrap a string of different colored pom-poms around a can, using glue.

CUSTOMIZED CANS

Take any can and cover the outside with felt, sticky shelf paper, construction paper, or wrapping paper—your choice. Decorate the can to suit your personality or the personality of the lucky person you're giving it to. Great for pencils, scissors, and change.

PERSONALIZED LIGHTERS

Take a lighter and cut some sticky shelf paper 3 x 2-3/4 inches and cover lighter. Don't use fabric (tends to catch fire). Felt gets dirty fast. Colored tape—great. Vinyl tablecloth material—perfect. Rickrack—a little thick.

UNDER THE INFLUENCE
JIM

Fuck It Bucket

Fuck it Bucket

How To Make A Fucket Bucket

Go Get A 1 Gallon Paint pail

Fill it with Candy, Write

Fuck it Bucket on it

"when shit Gets you Down

Just SAY Fuck it, and

eat some mother fuckin'

CANDY

Paul Sellers

The Rooster

ABCDEFGHIJKLMNOPQRSTUVWX

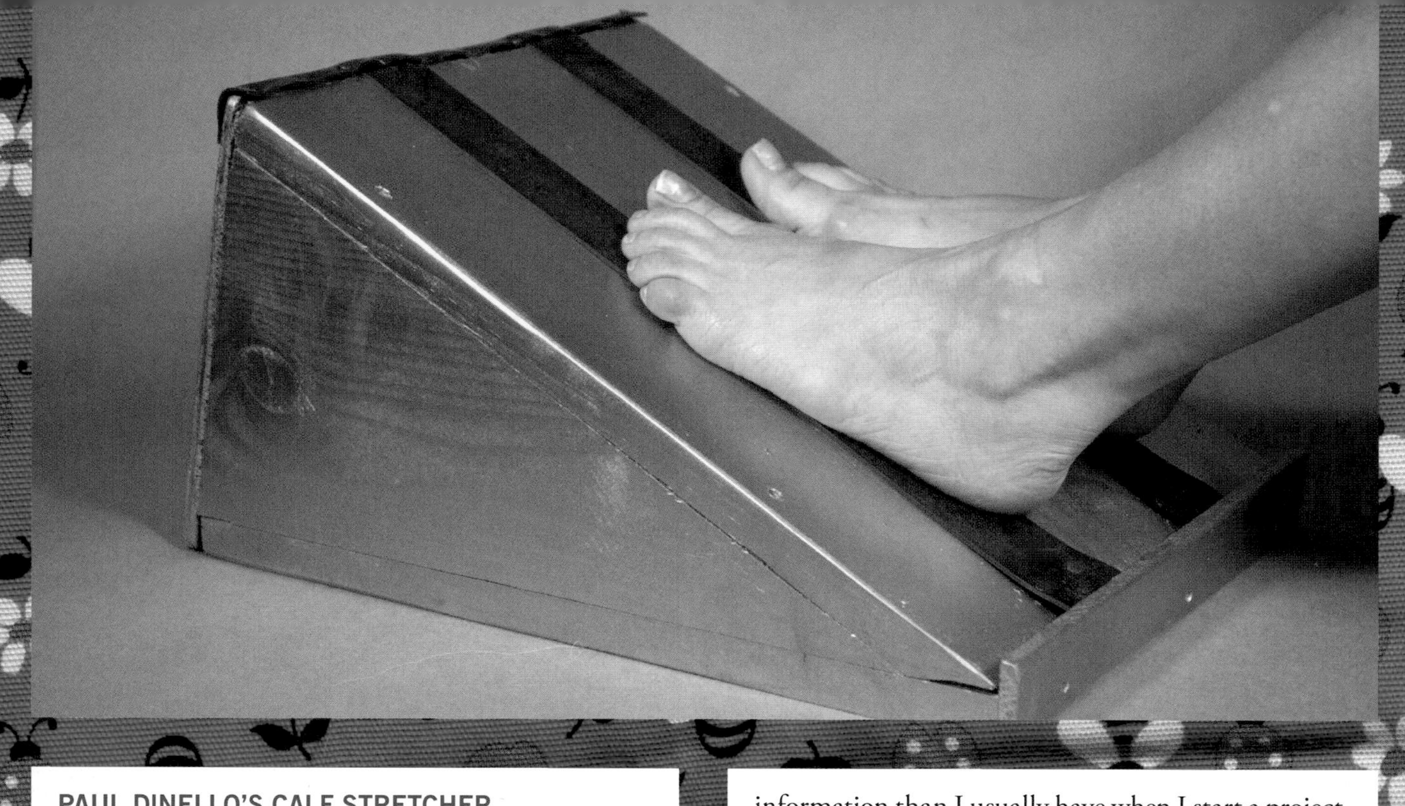

PAUL DINELLO'S CALF STRETCHER

Anyone can build a calf stretcher. It is simple and fun. One only needs a few items to easily accomplish this crafty limbering device:

1) A saw. **2)** Wood. **3)** An insatiable burning desire to have your calves stretched.

FIRST, ACQUIRE WOOD. Anyone can go to a lumber store and purchase wood, but this seems silly because so much wood is lying around just asking to be cut into pieces and then assembled into a nifty flexor wedge. I found my wood on a busy street by my house. It must have belonged to the department of sanitation because they were working in the same area. I figured it must have fallen off a truck or something. Picking it up revealed a massive hole in the street, so I was clearly doing the city a favor by removing it and exposing this menace that needed immediate attention. Imagine what would happen to some unsuspecting driver if he hit that hole driving at a good clip? And it being evening and all, the hole is practically invisible. No, this must be fixed, and who knows how long the hole would have remained untended, hidden by that board and those flashing sawhorses.

SECOND, MEASURE THE BOARD. A tape measure is probably best for measuring. I have to get one. For this project I used a lot of guess work. I knew I wanted to end up with a wedge, which is much more information than I usually have when I start a project. All I can really say about this part of the project is you will need a couple of rectangles, two smaller triangles, and then a single smaller rectangle.

THIRD, CUT THE BOARD INTO DESIRED PIECES. I like saws, especially electric table saws. You would be amazed what an electric table saw can cut through and cut through really fast. A shoe. A tennis racket. As a scientific test I once cut a Pioneer stereo receiver in half. I can't really say what I was testing, but I can say I now know that with the exception of all the sparks, a table saw doesn't have a problem cutting a stereo receiver in half.

FOUR, ASSEMBLE PIECES. I used screws and glue.

FIVE, DECORATE WITH PAINT. I used spray paint for this project. I use spray paint whenever I can because brushing wears me out. Continue painting until the wedge is completely covered or until your headache is so disorienting that you are having trouble pressing the nozzle.

SIX, ADD NONSTICK SUBSTANCE TO TOP OF WEDGE. This additional step was added after my cousin tested the wedge and found out firsthand that gravity and momentum coupled with slippery spray paint can result in a humorous, yet serious, head injury.

FIG

DOGWOOD

Weeping Willow
1812 – 1982

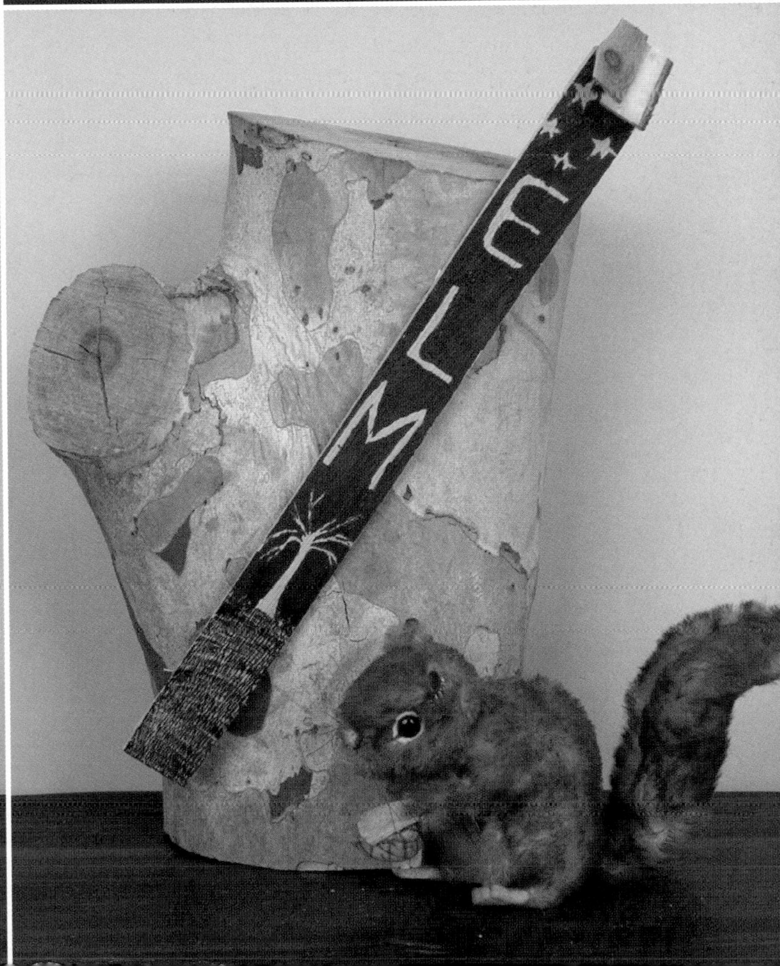
ELM

For the birds
Save the lint from the dryer and toss it in the yard. The birds will use it to make their nest.

Popcorn Cherry Blossoms

Find a nice branch. Pop some corn. Glue the popped kernels on the twig and dot each one with a little bit of pink nail polish.

THE INSECT HOTEL

Make a little lodge for an insect or small animal whose lifestyle you admire. Give each guest some food and furnishings. Maximum stay is ten minutes. Set them free and think about what you have learned.

competitive ribbon making
25
8
3
tie
Last
BEST RODENT
THERE IS ALWAYS NEXT YEAR
2nd
6th Place
12
LAST PLACE
OLDEST
1

TOTEM POLE

CAN BE MADE FROM A PAPER TOWEL TUBE OR SMALL MAILING TUBE AND LEFT OVER WRAPPING PAPER OR ANY CRAFTY SCRAPS

- THE TOTEM POLE IS ASSEMBLED FROM THREE DIFFERENT PARTS, BASE, MIDDLE AND WINGS.
- BASE. USING THE TUBE AS A PATTERN TRACE ONE CIRCLE ONTO ANOTHER PIECE OF CARDBOARD ALREADY DECORATED WITH A COLORED PAPER. CUT OUT CIRCLE THEN CUT 1½" AROUND CUT CIRCLE. (like a donught) THIS SHOULD FIT SNUGGLY AROUND PAPER TUBE.
- TUBE, AFTER COVERING TUBE WITH TOTEM POLE LIKE SCAREY FACES USING YOUR CRAFTY BITS, LIKE PAPER SCRAPS, YARN, GOOGLEY EYES OR WHAT HAVE YOU. (SEE PHOTO) AFTER DECORATING CUT 1½" NOTCHES INTO TOP OF TUBE TO FIT THE WINGSPAN AT BOTTOM OF TUBE CUT TABS EVERY ¼" AT ½" LONG SO YOU CAN GLUE TO BOTTOM OF BASE. (SEE DIAGRAM)
- TO CREATE WINGSPAN FOR THE TOP OF THE TOTEM POLE CUT WINGS OUT OF ALREADY DECORATED CARDBOARD OR DECORATE AFTER - THE WINGS SHOULD BE ABOUT AS WIDE AS TOTEM POLE IS LONG - USE YOUR OWN JUDGEMENT

YOU CAN DECORATE YOUR WINGS WITH ANY MATERIAL I USED A METALIC DOILEY

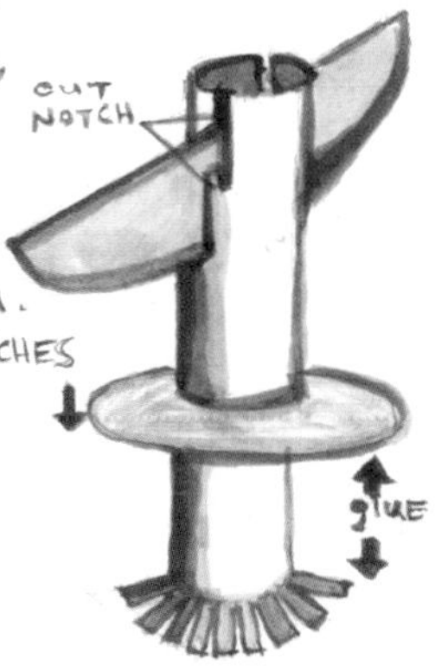

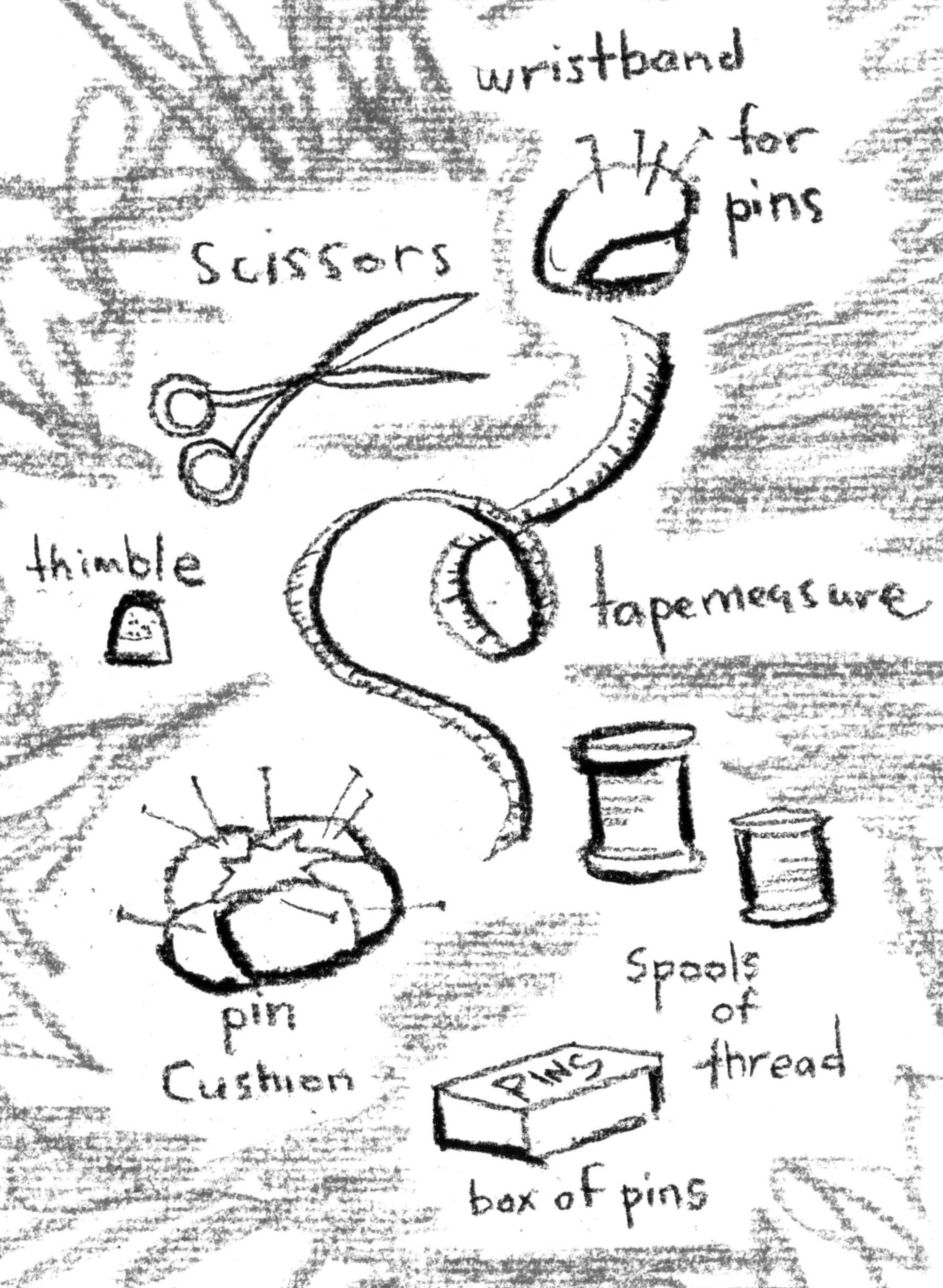
wristband
for
pins
Scissors
thimble
tapemeasure
Spools
of
thread
pin
Cushion
PINS
box of pins

Be Prepared

MEDICINE CHEST

Petroleum jelly
Cotton
Tweezers
Band-Aids
Gauze
Laxatives
Scissors
Thermometer
Aspirin tablets
Rolaids or Tums
Adhesive tape
Hydrogen peroxide
Rubbing alcohol

EMERGENCY NUMBERS TO HAVE ON HAND

Pharmacy
Hospital
Police
Ambulance
Neighbor
Fire department
Liquor store
Suicide hotline
Poison control center
Veterinarian

HOUSEHOLD PHONE NUMBERS*

Hardware store
Plumber
Electrician
Exterminator

*Tip them "right" and they will put you first on their list.

RABBIT KIT

Eyedropper
Nail clippers
Oral feeding syringe
Baby simethicone (for gas)
Frozen bottle of water in the freezer (in case of heat wave you can lay this next to them)

ALWAYS HAVE

Spare keys
Flashlight with extra batteries
Matches
Water
Money jar
Landline phone
Candles
Backup medication
Firearm
A good book to read

ITEMS THAT MAKE MY LIFE EASIER IN THE KITCHEN

Green bean frencher
Carrot peeler
Garlic press
Nut grinder
Corkscrew
Bottle opener
Tongs
Extra ice cube tray
Pastry brush
Poultry shears
Timer
Extra sponges
Lemon press

TOOL KIT**

Safety glasses
Nails
Screws
Tacks
Hammer
Screwdrivers
Pliers
Measuring tape
Sandpaper
Small hand mirror

**Everybody needs a tool kit in his or her home. If you want someone to fix something for you, you can at least have the tools. The same goes for in the kitchen, have a decent pan.

ACKNOWLEDGMENTS

When I started this book I fantasized that I would be able to do it on my own and in my spare time. (How hard can it be? It's recipes . . .) But after a few minutes of actually trying to type, that quaint fantasy quickly turned into desperate phone calls. It turns out to be very hard to steal a recipe. Luckily, I was considered special from a very early age—from my ability to glue two popsicle sticks together to the bus I rode to school. What makes me most special is my uncanny ability to corral other special people and then use them to make me look good. And countless people did just that. And even though my name is on the cover, I couldn't do it without them. I can't put their name on the cover since it is not their book. It is mine. But this is their page—well, what's left of it—and I'd like them to think of it that way.

When I say "written by me," what I mean actually, and possibly legally (if he ever becomes smart enough to hire a lawyer), is by me and Paul Dinello. And for the woman's touch, I also relied upon the Greek expertise of Antonia Xereas.

The book is full of crafts, food, lushly-appointed sets, props, and costumes. To accomplish this, I assembled a group of crackpot craftateers called *The Creative Daze Team* who made it all happen on location in my apartment in the dead of summer (hence the melted food and covered dishes . . . and E. coli). But back to the team and their page. They were: [names on jars]. I am so grateful. And I would like to give an extra thank you to Billy Erb, who went beyond his call of duty. Working with these slaves made me feel like I had magical powers. I'd utter my desire: "make a stuffed snake with pom-pom eyes," "make a portrait of me and my rabbit out of beans," "I want a fake cake. Make that four," and—poof—it would appear, leaving me plenty of time to herbally gear up for my next request.

At Warner, I'd Also Like to Thank:

Amy Einhorn, Jamie Raab, Emily Griffin, Tareth Mitch, Stephen Callahan, Tom Whatley, Bob Castillo, Harvey-Jane Kowal, Justine Gardner, Anne Twomey, Evan Boorstyn, Nicole Kuritsky, Jennifer Romanello, Emi Battaglia, Karen Cera, Anthony Goff, Rebecca Oliver, and David Young.

And at William Morris, I'm Grateful to:

Tracy Fisher, Jon Baker, and Eric Zohn.

Both my agent and editor got pregnant at the same time. Thanks, ladies.

The Underbelly

Finally, countless friends and others contributed and helped in countless ways. They are my seamy underbelly, my galley slaves, without whom this book wouldn't be in your hands today. They are:

Conn Brattain, John Giordani, Joe Oppedisano, HelenAnn Lally, Lily Thorne, David Rakoff, Peter Belsky, Paul Tough, Ken Siman, Andrea Ciannavei, Cathy Camper, Kelly Rakowski, Jennifer Nielsen, Jill Watson. Eric Blume, Danny Murphy, Adam S. Wahler, Mary Adams, Mary Cotter, Rosanne Quezada, Paula Scher at Pentagram, Sarah Thyre, Paul Ruben, Marshall Wyatt, Todd Oldham, and everyone in my family, including Kathy and Madelyn Rose Sedaris (crying child on page 105).

Photography by

Billy Erb and Mark Ibold

Additional photography by: **Michael Ingulli**—cabinets, gouged cheese ball, page 38, butter mint dish, tissue bride and groom, bowl of googly-eyed peanuts, individual miniature foods, art deco cigarette holder, jimmies, ghost cake, squirrel with potatoes, end pages

Amy Sedaris Photography by

Todd Oldham

Hair and make up by: **Pia Guccione**

Additional photographs of Amy by:

Michael Ingulli (cab face)
Andrew Eccles (whipped cream)
Mark Ibold (pumpkin built by Wendy)
Lou Sedaris (Mr. Mushroom)

Charcoal Drawings by

Tobie Giddio

Hand Lettering by

Ellen Berkenblit, courtesy of Anton Kern Gallery.

Additional lettering by:

Tobie Giddio—This Sturdy Book Belonged To, Other Books By Amy Sedaris, Step Right Up, Soap Opera Box, Worth Flying Home For, Spotlight On . . . , Out of This World, Munchies, I Like You (page 190), Competitive Ribbon Making, and

Billy Erb—popcorn cherry blossoms

Hillary Moore—I Like Us, Pound Cake, Coffee Cake, No Squirrels, My Success Story, Poof It's Magic

Drawings by

Hillary Moore

Additional art by:

Ellen Berkenblit—bat, mouse, squirrel (pages 128–129), graveyard, spiders, pink "I Like You," squiggly dingbat, and

Conn Brattain—Chianti bottle, first-aid box, shell, hobo stick, art pallet, cake on stand, needle and thread, leaf (page 182), bacon, cherry pie slice, lobster, large fancy ribbon, peanuts, popcorn, brown rabbit, tall glass, coconuts, envelopes, spider plant, 25 cents, pink mushrooms, strawberry, pineapple, lighter, noose, hatchet, Band-Aid, Revere ware pot, crab

David Rakoff—salt shaker

Billy Erb—thumbprint guys

Gretchen Sedaris—page of leaf drawings, beetle, marching ants, teenage wasp, young Amy portrait

Hugh Hamrick—stump, toadstools, witches pot, oval piglet painting, end pages, airplane, leaf curtain backdrop

Justin Theroux—bucktoothed cucumber, praying lumberjack hands, drug eyes, drugs and paraphernalia, worms, stiletto heel, sad sack society, garlic pot, Korean corner

Tobie Giddio—full release jar, ink drawings of rabbits (page 179), ice cube tray

Design Team

The Dingbats: Jessica Rosenberg and Lenny Naar

I like you

THE CREATIVE DAZE TEAM

PAUL DINELLO

JENNIFER McCULLEN

BILLY ERB

MICHAEL INGULLI

Male hand model:
Mark Ibold

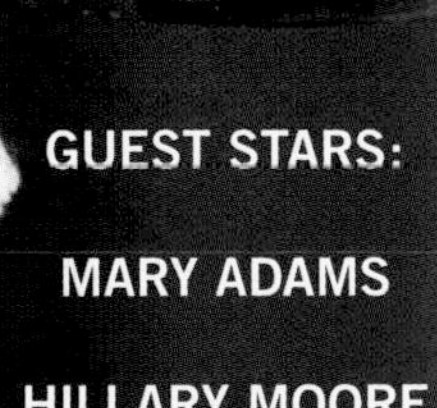

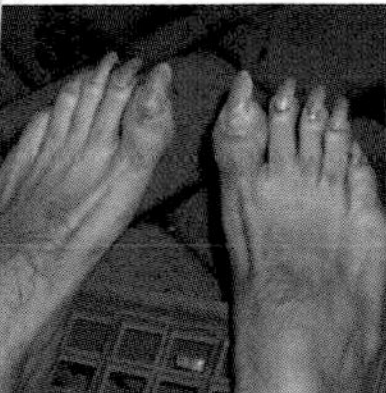

Male foot model:
Tony Longoria

INDEX

A

B

C

D

E

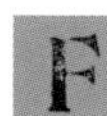
F

My Test Kitchen